MARINER'S REST

MARINER'S REST

DR. RAY SOLLY

Whittles Publishing

Published by
Whittles Publishing Ltd.,
Dunbeath,
Caithness, KW6 6EG,
Scotland, UK

www.whittlespublishing.com

Reprinted 2012

ISBN 978-184995-043-5

Printed and bound in Great Britain by
4edge Ltd, Hockley. www.4edge.co.uk

CONTENTS

OTHER BOOKS BY DR. RAY SOLLY

Supertankers: Anatomy and Operation

Picturesque Harbours

Gravesend: A History of your Town

BP Shipping: A Group Fleet History (Co-author)

Athel Line: A Fleet History

Mariner's Launch

Mariner's Voyage

Nothing Over the Side: Examining Crude Oil Tankers

Manual of Tanker Operations (Co-author)

www.raysollyseabooks.com

Preface

Mariner's Launch and *Mariner's Voyage* chronicled the semi-autobiographical accounts of the author in the guise of narrator Jonathan Caridia, commencing his sea-going career and serving as third and junior-second navigating officer aboard a range of dry cargo ships. A narrator was considered the most useful vehicle to express freely the varied colourful personalities encountered in the Merchant Navy, and to relate incidents all of which occurred (although not necessarily to the author). Such latter incidents however, are based on sources sufficiently reliable for the event to have credibility and justify inclusion.

Mariner's Rest concludes the trilogy and is again based on the author's direct experiences. We see Jonathan as a professional officer, doubtless a little battle-worn and even weary in places, but continuing to perform his duties responsibly (even if neither he, nor the various ships upon which he serves, his colleagues and the incidents that happen to him are taken *too* seriously). He has certainly lost the naivety bedevilling his earlier years – some of which was carried hesitatingly forward to colour his junior officer days. But there is now an additional ingredient visible: something of a steely determination which seems to have been acquired along with the third ring of a chief officer (or Mate as his rank continues to be known) that is painted in frequently humorous style.

In this volume, Jonathan has an eerie jungle encounter whilst travelling through Far Eastern waters on local leave in Malaysia, before being transported to a large mini-bulk carrier with an alcoholic Captain who has been at sea far too long. Subsequently, he leaves much of the running of his vessel to the Mate – his only other deck officer aboard – until they are joined by another alcoholic officer, adding certain *piquancy* to the existing mayhem and confusion aboard the vessel. Jonathan is then appointed to a supertanker – the class of ship for which he has positively yearned since his cadet days and a vessel upon which he is delightfully happy and professionally content. He might undoubtedly have remained aboard for an indefinite period, were he not transferred within the Group to fill an urgent vacancy aboard one of a company's light-air draft coasters. The events related aboard this vessel reflect the attitude existent with some coastal operators in the 1960/70s. They represent a *laissez-faire* approach to seafaring that was already encouraging officialdom ashore to take more than their previously cursory interest in these trades that resulted in a subsequent tightening of regulations.

Virtually all of the seafaring incidents related in this volume occurred to the author and were handled by Jonathan more-or-less as related. Collectively however they made no contribution, in any way whatsoever, affecting decisions to leave the Merchant Navy. This momentous career move was cumulative (as in William Congreve's *The Way of the World*) with origins residing in a number of seemingly unrelated circumstances. Fundamentally, he experienced a growing dissatisfaction with the social and academic limitations of seafaring, coming to believe that there was more to life than transporting cargo around the world. In such a subtle way was a boyhood dream shattered. Admittedly, such *force majeure*, breaking a long-time vow to the Merchant Navy, were topped by a (perhaps?) imagined inadequacy from the blow to Jonathan's confidence emanating from difficulties experienced with the Gyro Compass paper in which he just narrowly scraped a pass in his First Mates' certificate. This subconsciously (for at least it is never admitted) was responsible for a fairly consistent deferring of enrolment for his Master's (Foreign-Going) Certificate of Competency. There was a further dominant contribution. Jonathan, as related in *Mariner's Voyage*, re-kindled his secondary school love of English literature following the influence of a deck cadet during navigating watches in the South China Seas. As a result, he continues in *Mariner's Rest*, taking away in his gear poetry books that were found to be more challenging than appropriately advanced seafaring tomes.

In this final volume to the trilogy, we see developing gradually the love of teaching acquired as a duty upon promotion to Second Officer, directed through necessity then to navigational and seamanship subjects. This is soon to be translated – one could say eagerly – into a desire for studying and teaching literature. The inevitable happens. The death of a Master on board ship projects Jonathan into focussed instead of routine decision-making. English transcends 'matters maritime' in the final analysis, and we leave our irascible navigator as he successfully survives a rigid university undergraduate interview that ironically proved as demanding as the initial interview launching him into his first career.

ACKNOWLEDGEMENTS

My publisher and I are indebted to a number of people who have kindly provided photographs for this publication. Once again, I owe considerable debt to BP Archives for permission to use photographs from their library resources at the University of Warwick, especially to Peter Housego, the Global Archives Manager of Communications and External Affairs, who has proved extremely helpful.

Among others who have allowed me use of their photographs are Captain "Tinker" Taylor, chief officer V. Volden, A. Duncan, Captain Peter Adams, Kelvin-Hughes Marine Limited, Shell International Trading and Shipping Company, Athel Line archives, Victor Pyrate Limited, Jotun Paints (Europe) Limited, Fotoflite, Palphot Limited, Komardoc SA, British India Line archive, P&O Line archive, World Ship Society and Mike Jackson.

As with the earlier volumes of the trilogy, all photographs used serve only as representations to illustrate situations described in the text. They do not portray people, places and ships served with or on, and there is no direct connection between textual statements and attributed copyright owners.

FOREWORD

Autobiographical fiction is a difficult trick to pull off since it combines a truthful account, a sufficiency of disguise to render it free of awkward litigation and a carefully judged degree of self-revelation.

In this account of the adventures of Jon Caridia, the author steers us along an almost hour-by-hour timeline of the third and final part of his alter ego's life as a mariner.

Caridia is a likeable individual, shrewd and detailed in his observations about his seafaring and those with whom he shares it. From cargo-ships by way of a super-tanker, he ends his days aboard a coaster, all of which vessels are owned by the remarkable Ellerton Group whose precise identity is well-concealed.

What Caridia experiences is the variety of life to be found in merchantmen in the last years of the existence of what in any meaningful way could be called the British Merchant Navy. What the reader will experience is an intimate, detailed and personal account of all the multifarious duties that were the lot of an aspiring navigating-cum-deck officer of the era. The human lapses will be recognisable to anyone familiar with seafarers, but so too will the long hours, the pre-eminent importance of the ship, the lack of a home life, the frustrations when trade denies what little was available and the absolute necessity for the career officer to possess inner resources of his own upon which to fall back in his bleaker moments.

While Jon Caridia might have been lost to his shipping company by giving up the sea, his like have been lost to a nation which, almost without noticing, abandoned the commercial arm of its sea-power. Few who read this thorough, amusing and sometimes moving tale of a mariner's life can fail to see the tragedy in all this. In *Mariner's Rest* Jon Caridia is rather more than an alter ego; he becomes a metaphor for a loss the consequences of which have yet to be played out.

Captain Richard Woodman.
FRHistS, FNI, Elder Brother, Trinity House

1

TRAVELS ON A TRAMP

My thoughts were confused during the twenty-minute train ride to London Bridge railway station. I was heading for a pre-voyage interview at 'the Kremlin', as we seafarers respectfully referred to Ellerton Shipping Group's London head office, following my recall from leave, which had arrived two days earlier during breakfast. I saw in my mind's eye the pure-white envelope with its brightly coloured embossed house flag adorning the top left-hand corner, lying on the table next to the marmalade. Although the letter did not affect my appetite too much, it had awoken a dichotomy of recent weeks. Part of me still desperately wanted to be back aboard ship revelling in my duties and lifestyle, but another part felt reluctant to return. I had become firmly established at home during my four months' leave from the *Earl of Nottingham*, thoroughly enjoying sharing the pleasures and unutterable joys of married life. It seemed that each successive recall was increasingly difficult to bear. These reservations had been voiced to my good wife, but uncharacteristically she proved far from helpful. Something in her quiet smile confirmed her desire that she would really like me to remain at home and was willing to discuss this, but the making of any alternative decision remained firmly within my domain. There was also the realistically practical question of what I might follow as an alternative career. This represented one of those paths posted 'reluctant to tread', because I had no fixed idea, merely a line of remote possibilities. Certainly, vague ideas of developing my increasing love of English literature were 'in there somewhere' but, frankly, I had not the slightest notion how or where these might be developed.

There was another problem obstructing my usual clarity of thought as our electric train smoothly approached London Bridge and I glanced with vague interest at nodding cranes and funnels of ships in the Surrey Commercial Docks. My resolve whether to attempt a Master Mariner's certificate wavered like a piece of paper in a gale. Again, I simply could not make up my mind. I wanted the prestige of possessing this ultimate qualification, rightfully regarding it as a logical pinnacle of my seafaring career, but I remained very unsure whether my waning interest in 'academic matters maritime' would sustain the requisite six months in nautical college preparing for the thing. It had never been my intention to sit for the department's highest qualification of Extra Master because I felt the content was too technical and largely irrelevant to practical seafaring. What had urged me finally to shelve indecision, put down the coffee and open the smouldering envelope to respond with as good grace as could be mustered, was the thought of my outstanding eleven-month contractual obligation.

After booking in at reception I was led to Captain Henshaw, the marine super-intendent responsible for senior second and chief officer appointments, by a uni-formed messenger boy in smart black Number 10 uniform with the name of the operating company engraved in gold wire across the high collar. Walking the marble floors and imposing stairs awoke memories of my first visit to the company's head office and of my own few months as a junior clerk with another shipping company while awaiting entry to nautical college. The boy trying to race energetically ahead of me looked very young. This made me ponder if at his age I also had been so obviously and enthusiastically filled with the sheer joy of living all those seemingly 'light years away'. He responded to my questions about whether he intended to go away to sea with an open smile, and I could read the eagerness in his voice. I had guessed correctly; here was another one 'smitten with the sea bug'. Indeed, with interview and medical examination behind him he was now waiting to be called for deck boy training at the reputed 'hell-hole' vessel *Vindicatrix*, moored at Sharpness in Gloucester. Obviously, he knew the work of the Captain to whom he was tak-ing me and enquired if I were an officer with the group; something I was happy to confirm. He announced me to the good Captain's secretary, accepted my heartfelt best wishes for his future over his shoulder, and shot off with alacrity towards his next adventure. The secretary, after thanking him before he disappeared from view, phoned to announce my presence and smilingly confirmed that this messenger boy was the most cheerful of the current batch who worked for a while ashore before setting off to sea. It seemed very few lads remained to make a shore career with the company. Occasionally they went away as deck or catering boys aboard the deep-sea bulk carriers or managed vessels owned by the Empress or Regal shipping compa-nies, but never with Ellerton's, who employed only Asian ratings. As I entered the inner sanctum, she stated how much this youngster's engaging personality would be missed. It seemed to me that if he survived the training he could settle well into his new lifestyle.

It was the first time I had met Captain Henshaw following our brief introduction after signing off *Earl of Nottingham* before my leave. As I entered, he glided from his chair, greeting me warmly and, almost in one breath fired a battery of jumbled questions about our recent holiday (inevitably '*beside* the seaside' for a change with family at Cliftonville, near Margate), leave in general, and future study plans, all of which I batted back with due equanimity. I assumed his was yet another 'of those urgent personalities' which seem to flourish in the merchant navy. After sharing the customary tray of coffee and biscuits and being advised (before I asked) that there were currently no vacancies aboard Ellerton Line's vessels, nor any of the group's tankers, I left armed with joining instructions as senior Second Officer aboard Regal Supreme Shipping Company's motor vessel *King William*. She was the fourth delivery in a line of fast modern motor cargo ships whose planning was consistent with the 'new image' of Ellerton policies, relegating to the knackers' yard (at long last) some of the company's stately steam tubs, which were more than twenty years old. My ship was well equipped with the latest items of navigational and cargo gear, plus other luxuries designed to improve crew comfort. There was a swimming pool on the boat-deck starboard side and television sets in the smoke-room and lounge, with air-conditioning (the greatest of all benefits) that would be a godsend in the extremes of temperatures into which most merchant ships sailed. She would also be the first vessel upon which I had served that had all accommodation aft, but no particular difficulties were foreseen with this arrangement, which was probably just as well seeing as there was little I could do to alter the situation. I had served as second mate on one of the group's 'old timers', the three-islander Empress Shipping's *Lady Vedera* for an extended voyage, before she sent herself for scrapping with almost suicidal instincts a few weeks after I had left. Thinking back to the high jinks aboard that illustrious craft, I concurred wholeheartedly with the good Captain's suggestion that modern shipping trends and markets could no longer support operation of such seagoing liabilities.

I would be the only second mate carried on a ship of this class, with nothing more than extra salary and further experience to benefit my new rank. The significance of company policy in promoting to senior Second Officer was to impress holders that they were being groomed for stardom and quick promotion to chief officer. As variety on this occasion from joining previous ships, there were two differences. Owing to the previous Second Officer being hospitalised with some obscure back injury, I would travel to Montreal and join the ship by sailing as a passenger aboard Cunard Steamship Company's comparatively new 5,586 grt refrigerated cargo liner *Saxonia*. Final details of my joining instructions had to be established beforehand with Cunard's marine superintendent. Additionally I was to take in tow and escort a first-trip deck cadet named Martin Pollard. I trusted the boy would appreciate joining a brand new vessel not only just halfway through her maiden voyage but, as it transpired, already homeward bound. The company must have rated him pretty highly, because normally first-trippers were appointed to some of the remaining older tonnage on lengthy voyages, even if all of these ships were now less than ten years of age.

King William was what the super termed a 'handy size' ship of some 6,750 grt on an equally handy summer draught of 25 feet 1 inch. She was of 462 feet overall length and some 59 feet beam. The ship was fitted with a powerful main diesel engine that gave a nifty cruising speed of 16½ knots. She had a mixture of derricks and slewing cranes to serve her five hatches. Following the group's experience with European crews, ratings aboard this vessel had been replaced with Asian crews from traditional Ellerton countries of India, Goa and Bangladesh. The vessel was berthed at Montreal and had just commenced a forecast slow discharge of a full general cargo from a mixture of Far Eastern and African ports and, after cleaning hatches, was due to commence loading cut timber for Surrey Commercial Docks along with massive rolls of paper for Bowater's Jetty in the River Thames. I had suggested that coming from Canada the latter could be little else than 'superior' newsprint, raising a very direct look and then a weak smile from my good captain. The proposed voyage sounded like a typical tramp-ship cargo and run aboard one of the world's shopping trolleys. This was fine in terms of variety, but once she left the United Kingdom it would mean living with the constant uncertainty of possibly prolonged trips, with officers never knowing from or to where they would be sailing, or for how long they might be away. While this had advantages for those interested in gaining sea-time towards certificates, it was not good news for family life. Our Asian ratings were not affected, for they were on one-year contracts and what happened in between joining and leaving was of little significance. The ship sailed…she docked…she sailed…she anchored…she docked… *ad infinitum* until the end of twelve months. A further oddity was encountered at this interview. Without being drawn into explanations, the super had fixed me with what could be described only as a whimsical smile while advising 'further changes in company policies that might possibly affect your good self,' continuing rather pointedly, 'which will be revealed once you are on board, as there is little point discussing these now.' To say my interest was aroused was putting things mildly. I was all agog, but to no avail – nothing further was forthcoming although his farewell smile as he shook hands was equally whimsically pointed, with an element of mute satisfaction. I had never previously realised that non-verbal communication could be so expressive.

The company had suggested the cadet or his parents phoned me to put their minds at rest but, more importantly, to arrange a suitable meeting point in London as their 'son and heir' was travelling from some remote spot on the Essex coast. I had to confess a feeling that Ellerton's were being perhaps just a little fussy, for after all Liverpool was not exactly Outer Mongolia for young Martin to find his happy little way as a solo effort. However, 'spreading a little happiness' had invariably been one of my maritime mottoes for some years now, so I resigned myself to an amenable if prolonged conversation with them after supper one evening when they conveniently phoned. It seemed their lad was just two days into his seventeenth year and had finished a one-month Outward Bound course at Aberdovey in Wales – so he could not have been too much of a wimp, otherwise he would not have survived the cut-and-thrust of these quite demanding pre-sea training schools. He also was an ex-grammar-school boy so, as I explained to Sue, we had at least something in common. To be honest, flickering around my memory bank were thoughts of gratitude and reassurance when meeting experienced officers travelling to Amsterdam as a very inexperienced cadet to join my first ship, *Earl of Bath*, just after leaving Keddleston Navigation School. I rapidly thrust aside cringing thoughts of mishaps that had occurred during my own very definitely maiden voyage, and quietly wished young Martin well.

I almost missed the boy at King's Cross railway station outside the barrier of platform six, for the youngster I saw accompanied by an inordinate amount of luggage and obviously his parents looked only about fourteen years of age. At first I thought he was one of the 'young admirals' from London Nautical School, as they were known colloquially. It was only his golden uniform lapel gorgets on his doeskin reefer which identified him as a serving navigating officer cadet that caught my eye as he turned towards me. I allowed vague thoughts of merchant naval 'cradle-snatching' to meander through my mind as I approached and sized up both parents and our future cadet. I also felt he should not have joined in uniform because the capacity in which he had been assigned to the *Saxonia* was as passenger. Still, be that as it may... Secretly I felt he ought still to have been in school, let alone zooming quarter-way across the world to join a tramp ship, however modern she might be. But then I thought back again to my own nautical launching... Anyway, having sorted out the platform at the other end of the concourse, and making customary introductions, I enticed 'Pollard-minus', as I privately named him (less parents and, I breathed a sigh of relief, three of the suitcases) and we headed for our own train. It seemed mum and dad were off on holiday and had dropped off their son and heir before going by tube to Victoria and the on-going delights of 'Costa del Thanet', or more specifically, Broadstairs. I wished them well.

Pollard was quite tall, slim and fair-haired without even a wisp of pimple on his innocent, unshaven features. As we settled on opposite seats in the window corner of our compartment and eyed each other cautiously, he answered my ice-breaking questions about his schooling and adventures at pre-sea training intelligently, if initially with some hesitation. It seemed he had fared extremely well in his recent GCE examinations by obtaining near-top marks in eight subjects, including the essentials of maths, physics, chemistry, English and geography. Doing a 'Captain Henshaw,' I gently teased that his A grade in religious knowledge might come in handy, as he could undoubtedly on occasions find himself doing a great deal of praying and, without offering further enlightenment, smiled quietly to myself, enjoying the look of concern which flashed across his features. About his passes in history and art I offered no comment. He relaxed as we chatted, and by the time the grim facade of Liverpool loomed steamily through misty, rain-drenched windows, had drained me dry with his run of pertinent questions about ships, cargoes, life at sea and sundry nautical ephemera. I wondered if I too had given my first officers a similar 'ear-bashing' during the ferry trip to Holland. He also ate an extremely hearty lunch, giving few signs that nervousness had affected his digestive system. His innocently persuasive smile brought endless courses of extra helpings from the steward, much to the amazement of the elderly couple at an adjacent table who clearly thought we were father and son – and even more to me. I wondered where the hell he packed it all away. I was even more staggered when the bill came to find he (or more accurately, we) had not been charged for these additional goodies. I could only assume that the steward fancied the boy or something...

As we left the train, my impressions strengthened that Martin would be all right once settled on board our own ship, equipped with a few days' sea-time (and the contents of doubtless lavish menus under his belt) as the good ship *Saxonia* ploughed through North Atlantic waters. Neither of us realised, I fear, just how wrong I was doomed to be.

Arriving at Huskisson Dock to join the Cunard cargo ship presented the first interesting interlude, doubtless of many, to greet young Martin's entry into seafaring. The dock police constable had no record of the ship in port and could not suggest her whereabouts. He kindly allowed me to phone the ship's local head office who informed me that the vessel had been delayed by atrociously severe weather while 'crossing the pond', as we mariners referred to that lovely stretch of water. She had subsequently missed both pilot and berth and was not now expected to come along-side until late next day, and then in Canada Dock next door. I immediately instructed the taxi driver to take us to the local Missions to Seamen, and checked before pay-ing him off that they had available two cabins. Passing on the office information to Pollard-minus as we travelled Liverpool's grimy streets, I noticed his pale face go even paler in glorious anticipation. There was little I could do to reassure him, other than to mumble something about praying that perhaps the weather would have blown itself out and would not be too bad for our crossing. I do not think either of us was convinced.

I instructed him to change out of uniform into civvies and, following an exciting evening meal in a newly established local Chinese restaurant and then watching a so-called comedy 'on the box' in the mission, we both phoned our respective families and retired to our cabins. Contacting the office later next morning confirmed that the ship had indeed not docked but was expected on the afternoon tide when, it was suggested, we joined her immediately. I was all for this move for, although our expenses would be reimbursed in full, living ashore was costly. As it was, we spent the day meandering around the good city, especially the second-hand and nautical bookshops. I purchased what looked like an interesting volume of poetry by Matthew Arnold and a cathedral novel by Hugh Walpole, both of whom were Victorian authors who had attracted my interest. To yet another cadet, my suggestion of the Warsash navigation guide was eagerly accepted by Martin even though, to my chagrin he experienced what was becoming known universally as a cashflow problem, meaning that I had to advance him money to pay for the thing. Such is life.

The dock office had kindly left a message with the Missions porter confirming that *Saxonia* would be docking at 2000 that day so, following lunch and an evening meal ashore, we set out once again for the docks only to find the good vessel had berthed after all in Huskisson Dock. Repairing on board with the customs, immigration and office staff – nothing like showing enthusiasm – I walked into a conversation between the purser and Catering Department superintendent and offered their first news that they were to be blessed with two passengers until Montreal. It seemed that it was not only Ellerton's that suffered occasional communicational breakdowns. The purser was not a happy bunny. He was ready to go on leave but suddenly had to work out accommodation and bunk changing for two extra officers. There was no problem regarding my temporary stay, for the owner's suite was made available. An initial difficulty arose concerning where to berth young Martin in the absence of a suitable spare cabin into which he could be shunted. I refused point-blank to share the suite with him and my suggestion that perhaps a bunk could be made up in one of the lifeboats was met with limited enthusiasm, especially by Martin. All manner of suggestions were thrown around without resolve until, in an effort to break the impasse, I suggested a word with the Mate might possibly bring forth a berth in the cadet's accommodation if there happened to be a spare bunk. A quick phone call to the newly arrived chief officer confirmed that only one cadet was due for the trip (so far as they knew) which would leave available three berths across two cabins. This was an ideal arrangement for it meant that each boy could have his own quarters. It looked as if peace was established, until the steward told Martin to collect his bedding from the stores. With a quick 'hold on a minute, please' I suggested that as he was not signing articles aboard this vessel as cadet but as supernumerary, he should be treated rightfully as a passenger regardless of where he might be billeted, and that he should not have to grab his own bedding and do the job himself, as would also rightfully be expected of him once a cadet aboard his own ship. A very direct look came in my direction from the purser, but I fixed him with that steely glance developed since my promotion to officer that usually froze difficult crew members. In this instance my beady eye hinted strongly my resolve to stand firm.

There followed a meaningful battle of wills, until the purser picked up the phone and called the Master, advising him of the situation and asking what should happen about berthing arrangements for the passenger-cadet. I guessed the outcome, so was not surprised to overhear the Old Man's irritable tones vibrating the line as he ordered the boy to the spare cadet cabin. This left the purser little option other than instructing his second steward to report to the office. There he was advised of the situation and told to make up both Martin's and my bunks and to look after these for the duration of the trip. With honour satisfied, the cadet and I then adjoined to the smoke-room, where we chatted with Cunard's officers and idly watched television until we felt like turning in.

We ate in the dining saloon with me sharing a spare place at top table with the senior officers and Martin relegated to the cadet's table – an admirable arrangement all round. Lacking any duties at all, we drew a cash advance from the Ellerton agent and spent the next few days sightseeing and shopping once more in Liverpool. I was delighted to be invited with Martin by this jovial crowd to Cunard's version of a SODS opera, so introducing him to this traditional ship's officers' dramatic society element of song, spirits and singing that passed away a couple of very happy evenings. On both occasions we were accompanied by guitars which the engineers had on board until, that is, they became too overcome with the fumes of Bacchus to be able to play them. We had both been granted 'bar-chit-signing facilities' on board, to settle upon arrival in Canada, so were able to reciprocate hospitality. Pouring Martin into his bunk that second night, I reflected that his launch into seafaring was well and truly accomplished although, for some reason, he did not appear for breakfast the following day. In fact, I did not see him until lunch time.

The happy state of affairs lasted until we had run yet again out of funds and had to resort to the shipboard delights of chess, cards, snooker (using pucks instead of balls, for obvious reasons) and highly competitive table tennis and football. We were also invited by the cheerful bunch of petty officers to an evening in their bar, which turned out a hilarious occasion where the ale flowed freely. Eventually, the ship completed discharge and shifted along the canal to Manchester to load a deck cargo of tractors and assorted general cargo for New York and a range of Canadian ports. It was good to run along this waterway once again, and permit memories of a snow-laden passage while on my first trip as senior cadet to waft cosily through my mind. Martin was full of excitement and bounded around the ship like a spring lamb. I established a strong rapport with the Old Man, who allowed us both to spend some of our abundance of spare time in the wheelhouse, providing some interesting experience for the cadet, and whiling away pleasant hours for me, especially watching someone else do the work. This was indeed something quite novel. I sensed Martin's only disappointment was not being allowed by me to wear his brand-new uniform until he signed on our own ship. Naturally enough, I supposed, this young man had a lot to learn.

Normally the ship would have called at an array of St Lawrence riverside ports, beginning with St Johns and then Quebec for her first discharge ports, but an unexpected excess of cargo inducements for New York called for a rearrangement of *Saxonia*'s schedule so she would for this voyage call first at the American port. A message from Ellerton's local office arrived at the ship stating we would disembark there and join arranged flights to Montreal. The change in orders created intense excitement for Martin, but was accepted with typical aplomb by me.

The mv Saxonia, *owned by Cunard Line, served the St Lawrence Seaway and Great Lakes and, according to cargo inducements, New York and various American ports. The ship was scrapped in 1983 following nineteen years service with various owners (Courtesy World Ship Society).*

We ran into a full south-westerly gale gusting Storm Force 10–11 one day after clearing Fastnet. It had been pretty lively since dropping the pilot off Lynas Point, as it was too rough to use the Bar light-vessel service, with shipping forecasts predicting the full blow once out of the lee of the land. All Martin's hopes of a peaceful crossing acclimatising his sea legs disappeared along with every meal he attempted to keep down. Notwithstanding prayer, he was violently and irrevocably seasick as the good ship *Saxonia* rolled almost out of existence in steep beam seas and heavy swell. I popped in to see him occasionally, ascertaining he was still at least superficially in the 'land of the living', but my visits aroused little interest. His wan and almost green

Cargo was loaded variously from slings, strops, chains, pallets, sets and nets, and here a net is lowered carefully into the hold under the direction of the stevedore to the crane driver (Courtesy British India).

face contrasted beautifully with his fair hair and waxy blue eyes as he croaked an anxious appeal asking for how long this agony might continue. When I suggested two or three days, he was far from reassured, and faced the next five days of the crossing with his head bent largely inside the 'gash', or waste-paper bin, in his cabin. The chief steward, to give credit where this is due, did all he reasonably could for the boy, but frankly there was little anyone could do.

The waves encountered were typically spectacular. Angry high swell, with the tops wafted along the crests, created lengthy runnels of salt lines. *Saxonia* certainly made heavy weather of things, taking seas green over the port side with heavy spraying reaching the bridge wing. The ship shook in protest at every crashing wave hitting her plating that smashed over the foredeck. As her propeller occasionally cut out of the water, the race created its own contribution towards her shuddering motion, leaving the vessel rolling to extremes of the inclinometer in her wheelhouse. It was almost metronomic listening to the firm thud as the arm swung hard aport to hard astarboard. At one time the Old Man discussed with the Mate the possibility of altering course a little to ease the stress on her hull, moves that eventually proved unnecessary as the ship rode well to the storm – even if some of the crew certainly did not. After a few months ashore, my own stomach was raising some awkward questions, but having lost my fear of being seasick – which is generally a contributory factor creating the trouble – personal honour enabled me to appear for all meals, and to keep these down. Having no duties to do was part of the problem, for there was nothing except reading sitting in a lashed armchair in the smoke-

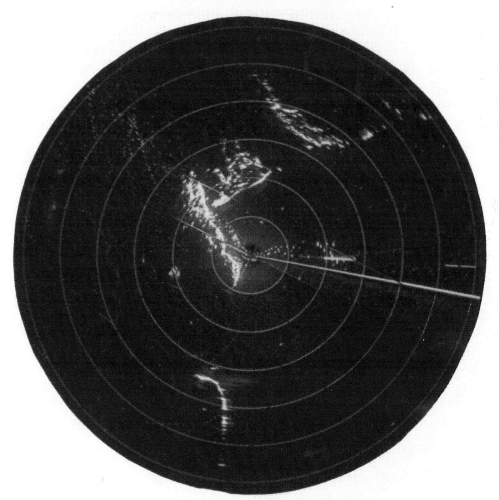

A radar plan position indicator (PPI) of the Port of Liverpool showing the Racon strobe that indicates the Bar light-vessel and the approaches to this busy port (Courtesy Kelvin-Hughes).

room, and chatting with available ship's officers to keep my otherwise imaginative mind occupied. I made good progress with the Arnold poems, especially his *Dover Beach*, *Thyrsis* and *Scholar Gypsy*, but the Walpole cathedral novel I forced myself to leave, anticipating this once aboard my own ship. Relating so well to the deck officers meant I could spend a fair time on the bridge discussing 'matters maritime' and comparing conditions of service. This left me feeling I was quite well off with Ellerton's and it was even possible to sow a few seeds of potential discontent with the third mate. This was all part of that wider psychological warfare usually emanating between deck officers at nautical college, so the novel surroundings added extra piquancy. The Mate and second were far too fly to fall for my patter extolling the carefully exaggerated virtues of Asian-crewed ships with exquisitely superior accommodation, luxurious feeding with company supplied wine at every lunch and dinner, and exotic runs, swimming pools with lido facilities, and stewards bursting themselves to answer every whim. They immediately latched on to what I was doing and added their own questioning contributions as part of that wider subtle solidarity operational between senior officers. Teasing was a maritime activity always guaranteed to help pass moments of potential boredom. It never seemed to occur to the third mate to question if conditions were so great with Ellerton's, why his own colleagues were not sailing with the group.

Mind you, the third officer had his own problems that effectively took his mind for the latter part of this voyage from the virtues of sailing with any shipping company – including Cunard. While he was on morning watch during the third day out a resounding wave hit the ship like a thunderclap. Even I, ensconced in my armchair in the smoke-room, expressed sudden alarm as the ship rolled excessively and found myself holding my breath for a moment. My breathing resumed normal operations as she suddenly, very slowly, almost ponderously, righted herself. Such was the impact that I had not realised that momentarily I had stopped breathing. I really wondered if we were to be one of the fourteen or so ocean-going ships that disappeared world-wide every year while on passage. They sailed and were never heard of again, presumably due to cargo shifting, which upset the meta-centric balance of forces, or were merely overwhelmed by excessively heavy seas, which was much about the same thing. On the bridge, the resulting unexpected roll caught the third mate off-balance and threw him across the wheelhouse like a drunken man until his progress was arrested by the engine-room telegraph. The equally resounding snap as his forearm hit was sufficient evidence of a clean break. His duty cadet raced down to the Master's day cabin informing the Old Man of what had happened. The second mate was placed on watch, while the Captain and chief steward made the poor old third as comfortable as possible in a bunk in the ship's hospital, after fixing the arm temporarily, and filling him with morphine. I knew what was coming even as I responded to the Mate's request as he filled me in on events: 'Jonathan, the Old Man would like to have a word with you. Would you mind popping along to his cabin, please?' It was inevitable. I was asked with a show of measured politeness if I would mind 'kindly helping out, please' by looking after the third's 0800–1200 watch, while the other two mates covered the evening duty by each adding two hours extra to their own watches. I noticed, however, that he took the legal precaution of asking to see my discharge book and First Mate's certificate, even if I did not sign articles to cover the couple of days' watches. I was bored to distraction with nothing to do so, after of course showing considerable reluctance allowed myself to be talked into the morning watch of the unfortunate third officer.

And so it transpired that, towards the end of the crossing, a few hours before we reached the pilot off Ambrose light-vessel, Martin at last made his guest-star appearance in the wheelhouse looking a little more like a member of the human race. His astonishment at seeing me alone on the bridge was total. Understandably, utterly absorbed with his own misfortunes, he was unaware of the third mate's mishap and

Rough seas hit the starboard side of the tanker Anco Sovereign *to sweep over the main-deck as she made a typical crossing of the North Atlantic (Courtesy Mike Jackson).*

The New York skyline in the 1960s offered visitors a spectacular welcome to this American capital city (Courtesy Shell International Trading and Shipping).

my elevation to voluntary sainthood, so just stood there looking remarkably vacant until I appraised him of events to date. I do not think for one moment he had envisaged anything like these last six days as part of seafaring, especially following the 'jolly' of the Manchester Ship Canal passages. His suddenly alert and intelligent blue eyes had been opened enormously by this dramatic introduction. In the saloon he managed to take and keep down a couple of dried toast slices with some mixed boiled vegetables and a cup of tea for lunch, and started to show more of an interest in the world around him. He fared far better than a junior engineering officer also aboard for his first trip. We had caught momentary glimpses of him prior to sailing, but did not see him again before we left the ship. He had succumbed to seasickness even prior to leaving the Bar light-vessel and remained below for the entire passage. I am certain that, with marine vindictiveness not far below his Anglo-Saxon surface, Martin found a measure of comfort in the junior's misfortune compared to his own resurrection.

Shortly after we docked, with the third officer away to the local hospital, the Old Man thanked me profusely for my assistance and in the absence of a watch-keeping certificate, offered me an equally acceptable bottle of quality malt whisky. He did hint that there might be the possibility of a berth with Cunard if I wished to apply to their marine superintendents upon expiry of my contract with Ellerton's. He enthusiastically outlined the virtues of exotic watch-keeping and unparalleled menus and wild social life aboard the company's larger liners, but I kept a straight face while thanking him, even though I felt a certain sense of *déjà vu*. For, after all, had I not attempted the same ploy with his third mate only a few days previously? It seemed that little in subtlety in the deck department at sea had been lost during my short leave.

The Ellerton local agent arrived the next day and arranged for our clearance through customs, immigration and other sundry port officials, as well as a taxi to the airport for the flight to Montreal. We had the usual fair wait after checking in, which was spent eating, drinking, I doing crossword puzzles of the acrostic type and the inevitable reading, before boarding the comfortable local plane for a comparatively short haul and uneventful trip. The agent was at the airport to meet us and within a couple of hours landing in Canadian territory we were safely alongside the good ship *King William*.

My first impressions were not particularly favourable – in fact, they were decidedly the opposite. There was no problem in ascending the gangway, for this was dragging along the quayside to the motion of the vessel, with the safety net caught up in the lower parts. Clearly, as the ship had settled in the water while loading her cargo, the gangway had not been raised correspondingly to compensate. The moorings also looked as if they could do with some attention. Both features were slovenly, to put things mildly, and were outside my experience of the standard normally expected of Ellerton Group vessels, whether managed or directly owned. As we mounted the gangway the Indian duty quartermaster (QM) made his guest-star appearance from the ship's office and met us as we rose to the main-deck level. I asked him about the gangway, but he just shrugged and mentioned something about 'Officer-Sahib not yet on deck'. Catching sight of the deck serang working his crew on the forecastle head and, glancing around the open foredeck, I could see the dockers busily engaged on loading, but there was no sign of the duty officer. I told the secunny who I was and again asked where the officer-of-the-watch might be. He told me he was 'with Captain-Sahib, Sir' in the latter's cabin. Giving him my holdalls so he could at least do something useful, and tagging the boy behind me, I walked swiftly into the accommodation making for the chief officer's cabin to report us on board. Passing the saloon on the way to the companionway, I had a quick distant view of the purser/chief steward talking to his Asian butler, while his lads were busily engaged in preparing the dining saloon, and in the galley engaged in cooking the evening meal. I deposited young Martin – or Pollard, as now I automatically thought of and referred to him – outside the cadets' quarters and made my way forward towards the Mate's cabin. I told the secunny to leave my cases outside my locked cabin and return to the gangway, where he could see the serang for assistance, and then stay there to keep his duty – not in the ship's office. I took his pained expression in my stride. There was no answer to my knock on the chief officer's jalousie and trying the door very tentatively found this to be locked. Attracted by the muffled sound of voices, I crossed to the starboard side of our accommodation deck and knocked on the Old Man's jalousie. Responding to his gentle request to enter, to my astonishment I was confronted by Captain Richard Smart. Seeing him was like turning back the proverbial clock and memories raced through my mind of my early deep-sea voyages as third officer aboard the *Countess Elizabeth* some years previously when he had served as Mate. I suddenly found out where the chief officer was, for there was a three-ringed arm stretched out along the back of the settee with the other hand nursing a large glass of something decidedly alcoholic. Meeting Captain Smart proved a unique experience. He had always appeared to me as an officer of poised confidence with a somewhat austere, but dry-humoured approach to seafaring. This seemed to have changed. His eyes were tired-looking and his faced appeared haggard and drawn. I assumed immediately this might be from alcohol, for before him also was a similarly ambitious tot of something spiritual, as it were. I made myself known to them both, reintroducing myself to the Master and giving my other immediate superior a pointedly direct glance. The Mate stood up and introduced himself as Tom Wilson, telling me he was 'an Ellerton man since cadet days'. I took this on the chin, but inevitably wondered what on earth was happening aboard this hooker. He and I had not met previously, but this was not unusual in such a large shipping company employing around five hundred Masters, deck officers and cadets. In a brief pause, I told them about his new first-tripper cadet who was waiting outside the apprentice's cabin for the key, and advised I had glanced around the main-deck but had not seen the third mate.

Tom finished off his drink and suggested to the Master that we both went below. The Captain agreed so we adjourned to the port side, where he unlocked his cabin, rang the officers' steward for a tray of tea, and invited me to be seated. I sat quietly, determined that he should take the initiative. The pause was not too long for he came over to my chair and apologised for what he described as 'the hiatus'. It appeared he was the duty officer as the third mate had been allowed ashore that morning and was not due back until the next. It seemed they had been working twelve-hour cargo duty watches and Bill Hargreaves, a Regal Supreme officer, had done a double stretch so was making up for lost leave by going ashore with Sparks and the third engineer. I could tell from her marks on leaving the taxi that the ship was well advanced with loading, so it was no surprise when Tom told me we had completed taking massive rolls of newsprint in the lower holds from another berth, and were well advanced with completing sets of cut timber in all 'tween decks. The ship was bound for Surrey Commercial Docks in London and then to Bowater's Jetty in Northfleet Hope. This confirmed my information from the Kremlin and was reassuring that there had been no subsequent change in orders – not an unknown occurrence. I reminded Tom about the cadet and was delighted to see that this had a considerable sobering effect on him. He asked if I would mind taking the cabin key to the boy and tell him to unpack his gear and then change into working rig and report to the Mate's cabin. I went to the cadets' suite on the port side of our deck and passed on the Mate's instructions. Pollard visibly brightened at my news, having been given something constructive to do, and entered his domain. He had clearly detected from my demeanour as we boarded that something was amiss, but lacked the experience to determine what that 'something' might have been.

Over tea I told Tom about the lax gangway and moorings. He batted off an immediate answer by informing me Captain Smart was not drunk, as I 'might have been expected to assume,' but had been suffering recently from severe stomach pains and cramp. He had not wished to report sick, for knowing the vessel was due to return to the UK had decided to remain in command on board and 'sort things out when back in London'. He then admitted they had both been drinking heavily with the chief and second engineers since before lunch-time; advised that the cargo was comparatively easy on loading supervision, and consequently 'things had been allowed to slip a bit for a couple of hours'. The serang was not the liveliest of wires and needed much encouragement. My thoughts were my own, especially in the light of the latter statement. I found my palms itching to get out on deck and do some sorting out of the crew on my own account, but felt it expedient to remember I was only the second mate aboard this hooker, so exercised patience. The thought crossed my mind of the time when as senior cadet keeping my journal had become a really tedious task, so comforted myself supposing my feelings reflected a readiness to 'fly from the second mate's nest and flex my own wings as chief officer'.

At this point Pollard arrived. I made the necessary introductions and relaxed a little when Tom told the boy to follow him and meet the Master, after which he should work cleaning up the wheelhouse, including polishing the brass – when he had been shown where everything could be found in the after locker on the bridge deck. He should keep himself occupied for a couple of hours, but as it was already after 1500 the tasks would not be too lengthy or arduous. The Mate would call him later, giving him time to clean up and change into his best doeskin uniform for supper. Before Tom and Pollard departed, he stood me down to unpack my gear and change, while he would afterwards 'go and sort out the crew.' I must confess to feeling a little happier about things, but was still not entirely convinced. It would clearly be a case of waiting to see how things might develop over the next day or so. I wondered what the third mate was like as an officer.

After stowing away my gear I changed into uniform and went on deck to see what was happening, specifically if the gangway and moorings had been correctly adjusted. Geronimo! All was well, and the secunny shot me a quick salute, while the serang and his happy band were busily engaged squaring off the main deck. Tom had indeed 'sorted out the crew' and my reassurance grew that my welcome on board was a 'one-off'. I meandered over to this important chief petty officer (CPO) to make my number with him. He had a slight cast in one eye (reminding me of the cassab on my first ship) and was undoubtedly obsequious. I told him in no uncertain terms my opinion regarding his efficiency and inability to work unsupervised 'while his officers were clearly busy elsewhere,' and left him under no illusions regarding where he stood with me. After delivering this little homily it was time for supper, following which I volunteered to act as duty officer until 0600 next day when the dockers would return to continue loading.

When I turned to next morning after seeing the working cargo hatches safely opened and the gangs happily started, I noticed the time was 0800, but there was no sign of life on deck including, needless to say, relieving of the overnight quartermaster. The Mate's cabin was locked and I had no idea where the chief or third officers might be. I asked the QM if he had turned to the crew and received a firmly positive reply. Just as I was about to pop down below and have a further word with the serang, I noticed he and his crew ambling out on deck to start work. I shot him a look of daggers as he told me he had looked for the chief officer but there was no one in the ship's office and the bridge was deserted. I told him to arrange a relief for the gangway quartermaster immediately, and then he could start battening down numbers two and four hatches, which had completed loading, and prepare these in all respects ready for sailing. I then turned to Pollard, telling him to come to the saloon in his best uniform, and went to my own breakfast.

The third mate joined me around 0830 and we introduced ourselves casually over toast, marmalade and plenty of strong coffee. It was clear he was still 'well under the weather' having enjoyed a 'terrific time ashore' and was not going to be much use to anyone until after lunch. I suggested that in the absence of the Mate he stood down until 1200, by which time he should have had a seven-bell lunch and then relieved me wherever I was to be found on deck. Top table was deserted apart from the second engineer completing his meal. He and the chief had met me and we had made our number the previous evening in the lounge along with the cadet and some junior engineers. While we chatted idly, Pollard came in looking a little lost once more, so I directed him again to his cadets' table and told him to report to my cabin after he had finished eating. Looking through the saloon windows, I could see the crew working hard (if not very enthusiastically), and decided all they had really needed was some gentle supervision and 'a nudge in the right working direction'.

I was on deck again by 0915, and found cargo proceeding without problems, my duty quartermaster and the lads happily and usefully engaged. My arrival near the ill-fated gangway coincided with the agent coming on board, armed with a briefcase and heading determinedly for the Old Man's cabin. I wished him well. The dockers were slowly but progressively loading the timber. Pollard popped out shortly afterwards. I was pleased to see he had the sense to change from doeskin uniform to working gear, and in the absence of the wheelhouse keys, which were locked in the Mate's cabin, took him over to the serang, introduced them and left them to each others' devices. Then I suddenly recalled that the cadet would not know where to go for his stand-easy – or even what that meant – so it was back again, showing him the duty mess and returning him afterwards ensuring that he knew for whom he was now working and what his routines would be until we met in the saloon for luncheon. Our deck CPO was clearly happy now an officer was on deck, so took the boy under his wing and returned to supervising his lads. The duty secunny looked spruce, alert and keen, in fact just like a typically reliable quartermaster should look. I felt some sense of achievement so went to look for Tom, my own working boss.

His cabin door was still locked but fortuitously the agent chose that moment to appear reporting he had seen the Captain; that the latter still looked very ill but had again refused to see the port doctor. He now wished to discuss cargo completion with the Mate. It proved an ideal opportunity to encourage the agent to bash on the jalousie while I stood by wondering what would result. It was as expected. Tom answered the door looking like death warmed up and clearly still under the influence. I filled him in with suggestions that the cargo could probably be completed sometime next day, or the one after at the latest, and informed him of events regarding *his* deck crew and cadet. Once again I stressed the personal pronoun, but without any appreciable recognition. A tray of coffee did us both wonders, after which he thanked me for my efforts and stood me down to prepare my passage plan and charts, advising he would be all right now to look after future events. Tom was not too far 'shot', however, as he stated the cadet could stay with the serang for the morning, but he would turn him round to complete his wheelhouse tasks that afternoon.

At 1200 hours Bill Hargreaves relieved the Mate, looking a little more responsible and clearly back into action. Over supper that evening he revelled in relating his adventures of the previous twenty-four hours. He and his friends had certainly enjoyed a riotous time ashore even if the finer details were largely unprintable. From a professional point of view, I could see officer potential. He was just out of his cadetship and was on his first voyage as an officer, having only recently qualified with Second Mate's. I thought he would be good, once he became more stabilised.

Pollard settled down remarkably well, but it would have been useful for a senior cadet to have been engaged on his immediate supervision. He was completely green and, not surprisingly, did not have a clue for most things. Luckily, Bill proved completely reliable and worked well, showing a delightfully refreshing sense of humour. He took the boy under his wing according to the chief officer's instructions, confirming correctly my forecast regarding his professionalism. Tom confirmed again that there was definitely something amiss with Captain Smart. When I went to the latter's cabin later that day with my discharge book and certificate, as I signed Articles he was wracked with a spasm of seemingly intense pain and commented that he was 'gripped with something that felt like an iron bar in his tummy and was occasionally violently sick'. I was not sure whether alcoholic spirits were quite the appropriate medicine but did not voice this little aphorism. Certainly, in the absence of his decision not to have his stomach investigated ashore before we sailed, there was little anyone could do to help. Tom was reliable enough, but he 'certainly has something of a drink problem, bud,' as the Canadian dockers astutely observed. I loved this delightfully English euphemism. His difficulty was not 'a problem with drinking' – it was more a case of leaving it alone.

Two days later we sailed, so it was just as well that I had planned the initial stages of our passage along the St Lawrence and outward legs of a Great Circle course from Cape Race towards Fastnet 'just round the corner' to the southern tip of Eire – almost completing a 'kind of square circle' from our outward trip. There was a little time for us to share shore leave amidst cargo watches, so I went with Martin and Sparks ashore for a few hours in the afternoon. I thought allowing the cadet to have shore leave an expansive and surprising gesture from our chief officer, but remained concerned regarding the extent of the Mate's far too many drinking bouts. These seemed beyond the accepted norm (even for the merchant navy) both in frequency and enthusiasm.

The cargo was pretty straightforward with such easy slings to load and not much for unconverted shore gangs to pilfer. I had mentioned the latter to Tom that second day after lunch-time coffee in his cabin. He looked at me swiftly, burst out laughing and acquainted me with the new facts of storing life occurring during my period on leave, assuring me also that there would be no little envelope of cash coming my way this voyage, or probably ever again in the future. With the words of Captain Henshaw resounding in my ears, the Mate told me of new directives from the Kremlin governing the supplies of ship stores across all departments. I listened with intense interest, earnestly seeking this missing link in my knowledge.

It appeared that the purser/chief steward on the old *Earl of Roxborough* had become over-ambitious in Tilbury and unwisely flogged nearly a quarter of his meat- and fish-rooms while the ship was still alongside. With customary subtlety born of long experience, this had not been done with the stores trundled up one gangway and ten minutes later trundled down again into the ever-waiting lorry, for the stores never arrived in the first place. They had been ordered by the purser and an agreement reached with the supplier to the considerable financial benefit of each, leading to the delivery of reduced quantities only. It was there that subtlety expired, for what the purser momentarily overlooked was the risk of an occasional superintendent's pre-sailing inspection. Admittedly there were some grounds for him to be complacent because normally stores inspections across all departments occurred only upon arrival from deep-sea, but the possibility always existed of further visits at any time. On this occasion, one of these had become a certainty, for the local victualling superintendent acting on some capricious whim decided to inspect both dry and wet stores one day prior to departure. To his amazement, whether planned or impulsive, considerable gaps were found in what should have been full store-rooms. A quick tally led to a more exhaustive count that spread the net into the dry stores, leaving the poor old purser with less than half a sea-boot to stand in. To say the viscous substance hit the fan before descending in all directions is more than a mere understatement. A posse of supers visited the ship and, delaying sailing for half a day, checked most deck and engine-room stores as well as what remained in the Victualling Department. All was found in order elsewhere, probably because most of this nefarious bargaining took place abroad where rewards for such trading were considerably higher than in the UK. The purser, who should have taken this into consideration, was arrested by the police and his open and shut case came up in court four months later. A range of interesting ramifications reverberated within Ellerton's head office long before poor old Percy was sentenced to nine months' imprisonment, with subsequent loss of job, career and pension. Telephone lines hummed across the UK and cables were frantically despatched to shore superintendents world-wide, and to the Captains of every vessel belonging to the group. Such cavalier attitudes towards selling surplus stores had always been known in head office. After all, every super there had sailed as Master, chief engineer or purser and was fully aware of existing shipboard dishonesties. A typically 'Nelsonian blind eye' had previously been turned, but the blatancy of this little incident brought it forcibly to the directors' attention, leaving them little choice but to instruct the next lower tier of management to stamp out the rot. A sense of delicate discretion remained for, very wisely, while safeguarding the future, they 'left the past to look after the past'. It was said that many shore-side superintendents and serving senior officers each breathed more than a mere sigh of relief at the decision, while resolving to take a more Biblical approach to future stores management. Mind you, the resolve of crews was strengthened by the introduction from head office of new supervising routines, leading to much closer checks of all stores purchased abroad.

Hilarity knew no bounds once the story was released around the fleet and to other companies via the exuberant medium of countless ship's-radio operators. Amidst the glee, however, a more serious note was struck with officers across all three departments aboard many ships in the entire merchant navy. Each took careful note that what had happened to Percy might just conceivably happen also to them.

A whole raft of suddenly converted Mates, engineers and stewards appeared on the shipping scene. What had been taken very much for granted from 'days gone by' generally became a thing of the past and company head offices soon reported a mass reduction in sea-going stores consumption, amazingly without crew turning into skeletons or ships falling to pieces. The poor old Sparks probably came out of things best, or worst – depending upon the point of view. Other than the immense satisfaction gained from spreading glad tidings throughout the maritime world there was little scope for dishonesty in the radio department. Realistically this had to be, for apart from flogging a few metres of spare copper wire, and the occasional carboy of battery acid to the local distillery in some foreign port, 'Sparks' had otherwise limited scope.

The officer-of-the-watch often took the steering off automatic to round headlands or alter course for other ships retaining a familiarity with the 'feel' of handling directly the ship (Courtesy Mike Jackson).

We sailed for the River Thames at 0330 next day. The passage down the St Lawrence was interesting and Martin spent much of his time between working with the crew on deck and doing the movement book, flags and telegraphs under the supervision of the duty mate. He proved, as I had assumed, intelligent and very quick on the uptake,

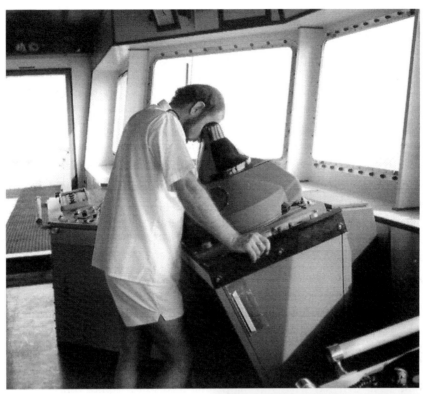

Above: Radar remains an essential device for navigation and collision avoidance and here the duty officer watches intently an interesting target (Courtesy BP plc).

Right: Placing a new cadet on the telegraph during standby for coming alongside or leaving port offered him an excellent opportunity of learning by observing senior officers, yet made him feel part of the Bridge team (Courtesy Athel Line).

which soon endeared him to all deck officers, while he related well to the engineers and Sparks. 'A thoroughly pleasant young man' seemed to be the universal verdict.

On two occasions, separated by only a couple of days, Tom was drunk when he came to relieve me on watch in the wheelhouse. His movements were sluggish, speech slurred, and his breath and clothing stank like a brewery. With years of experience behind him, he was certainly not incapable, and fortunately was supported by a very reliable quartermaster who conferred with my duty man and, in this indirect way, expressed his concern to me seeking information regarding what should be done. I was left in something of a quandary and could only recommend that the quartermaster aroused the Master if his officer collapsed on the bridge. On a couple of occasions Bill mentioned that he had to remove a number of lager cans and the occasional whisky bottle from the bridge when he relieved Tom at 0800 hours. He and I discussed the situation but came to no positive conclusions. The only action I could reasonably take would have been to inform the Captain, but the more I thought about things the stronger became my conviction that the present situation was insufficiently serious. I kept a close eye on Tom and felt sufficiently resolved to have taken the ultimate step if the Mate had been totally and unequivocally incapable on any occasion. After all, for eight hours a day the safety of our lives, and the ship with her cargo, was dependent upon his competency. The Master was far from well and, to all intents and purposes, was out of the game otherwise I am sure he would have 'twigged' what was happening to his next senior officer. It was clear to all officers that there was something quite seriously wrong with his stomach but, again, this was a situation that unless he collapsed completely there was little that could be done. For the entire crossing I felt as if I were walking on eggshells; both situations were outside my experience and could be taken only as each presented itself. If the Master had collapsed, and simultaneously Tom was sufficiently *non compos alcoholic mentis* (as I termed it with typically dry humour) to have coped, or if he had been rambling, I would have had to contact the Kremlin. The issues were common talking points amongst the officers in our smoke-room, and I discussed things with the chief and second engineers, including in the privacy of the chief's cabin my proposed course of 'last-ditch stand action' of contacting the Kremlin, should both collapse simultaneously. With typically merchant naval humour we three compared the situation with the last siege of the Alamo.

Weather-wise, our passage 'across the pond' was a complete contrast to that experienced when coming the other way until, that is, we approached Ireland with a stiff north-westerly blowing down our stern. Apart from causing moderate pitching and rolling it added a knot or so to our speed. Martin – apart from the senior officers, we all referred to him by that name contrary to merchant service conventions – coped well with this and, over a glass of ale bought for him by the engineers, celebrated finding his sea legs. By the time we took the pilot off Dungeness, he was fine and settling well into his new career.

The poor old Master was not quite so healthy for his stomach was causing him considerably debilitating pain and he could not keep down solid food. Living on a mixture of brandy and ginger ale – the traditional Royal naval officer's 'horse's neck' – had not done much to improve the situation. He managed to be on the bridge for berthing, but both the river and dock pilots (as people seeing him anew) were clearly horrified at his ashen face and aged manner of moving. As soon as we had negotiated Greenland Dock and were moored safely alongside Berth 25 in (appropriately enough) Canada Dock, an ambulance took Captain Smart to Guy's Hospital, where he was detained for examination and observation. It was a sad ending to the trip, especially for me – I retained such fond memories of him aboard the good ship *Countess Elizabeth*.

Shortly after our arrival, a new Master and set of officers joined the ship, leaving only Martin and me remaining on board from the old crew. These officers had been away for a comparatively short trip of ten months. Just a couple of years ago there would have been no question of them being relieved until they had served at least half again of this period. It was indeed 'a sign of the times', reflecting modern thought in the light of difficulties experienced attracting officers across all ranks to the profession and, equally important, retaining their services once they were 'in the bag'. Tom greeted his relief with a generous tot of neat whisky and then suitably relieved (as it were) left the vessel. Captain William Cordwell joined as an elderly very senior Master, along with Pete Birchall as chief officer, and Brian Perkiss as third. I had not even heard of the latter, but in later conversation worked out that the Mate and I had just missed meeting each other shortly after I had left the *Nottingham* some months previously. A new senior cadet joined Martin. He was Roger Gifford, who had two years' sea-time and originated from King Edward VII nautical college – or 'King Ted's', as it was known colloquially.

Martin and I were allowed a few days' local leave and lost no time in shooting off for our respective homes. For the cadet particularly this was very welcome, giving him opportunity to meet again with his family and regale his mum and dad with a reassuring update of the way he had settled into his new life. It also gave him the opportunity of offering clear evidence concerning how much he was enjoying himself, now that he had seemingly ambushed his old enemy *mal de mer*.

It was interesting on board in Surrey Commercial, or 'Surrey Com', as we referred colloquially to the dock, during the quiet of evening when cargo was not being worked and I was duty officer. I often lounged on the boat-deck looking across to the varied electric and diesel trains bound to and from London Bridge station – reminding me of a journey so recently made. The silence of the ship was always enjoyable and these evenings of comparative peace were as much part of sea life as sailing. Other ships lay quietly at their berths, or were departing and arriving to and from distant parts of the globe. Amongst timber ships from Baltic ports I recognised a sister-ship to the *Saxonia* a couple of berths away, separated by a Prince Line general cargo ship – the *Lancastrian Prince*, as I recall – and a regularly trading United Baltic Corporation (UBC) vessel. Invariably the sound of tugs broke the silence as they eased their charges to and fro, using varied-sounding whistles to respond to the pilot's instructions from the wheelhouse, or manoeuvring in the Thames adjacent to the docks with their endless strings of dumb barges. Their mournful sounds mixed with deeper sirens of freighters from up river, and sundry coastal traffic. This valued shipboard silence of evening contrasted drastically with day-time competitions of train whistles, the clanging of wagon couplings and buffers, different-toned car and lorry engines, plus, of course, the endless bustle of dockers and officeworkers and the continual stream of visitors to our own and nearby ships.

One evening after returning from local leave, I was joined by Gifford, my duty cadet, and we spent a few moments initially listening to the sounds around us, and then chatting quietly about his career to date and his hopes and fears. Such conversations brought home to me his extreme youth. Invariably this moment, as on previous occasions, ended with us joining other officers in the smoke-room or lounge for a drink, board games, or simply 'watching something on the box'. The evening, equally predictably, concluded with my popping around the main deck seeing all was in order, prior to the sheer joy of reading for a while in my bunk while listening to the creaks of the ship at her moorings, and feeling the rumbling vibration along the bulkhead from machinery below. I continued dipping into my Arnold which, along with Kipling and Browning from previous voyages – plus of course Wavell's *Other Men's Flowers* – proved essential travelling companions. Walpole's *The Cathedral* had lived up to expectations; I had read it while crossing the Atlantic, and then taken it home during a local leave to join my rapidly growing collection of 'old favourites who were occasionally revisited'.

It was uncanny really that, in all my years at sea as duty officer, it had to be that same evening which proved the only occasion I was ever given a rude awakening between turning in and the call from the officer's steward with a welcome tray of tea. I was delightfully pleased that we had not indulged earlier in a SODS opera. The time must have been about 0300 hours when I was aroused from deep sleep by a frantic stomping of feet along the alleyway and a frenetic banging on my door, accompanied by a sharp Asian voice urging me to 'come aquickly, Sahib, there is plenty atrouble'. I almost fell out of my bunk and grabbing my deck-working boiler suit, the clothing immediately on hand, yanked this on and opened the door. The duty secunny was there and, highly agitated, explained urgently and in breathless tones, that 'one of the ag wallahs Sahib, has made adead – him ahanging in the crew washrooms'. Apparently, one of the engine-room wipers had responded to a nightly call of nature and, to his shock and horror, had discovered his colleague swinging gently with the slight motion of the ship from one of the shower heads. The ensuing commotion had, not surprisingly, roused the entire deck and engine-room crews and attracted the attention of the duty secunny from the gangway. He had raced to my cabin. Needless to say, all deck officers with cabins adjoining my own – including, of course, the Old Man – had also been awakened. By the time I had put on shoes and socks, the Master was outside my door and suggested only we two went below to see what had happened. He told the Mate to call the chief engineer, one deck below us, and instruct him to join us in the crew ablutions.

The sight that met our eyes has remained with me for the remainder of my life and will doubtless still be with when I also make that same journey, but hopefully under more peaceful circumstances. The strangely lifeless body hanging limply and forlornly had to be seen and treated in an almost detached way. It was the first time I had seen a man hanging and it was necessary as an act of will to submerge my instantly curious compassion, and force my emotions into control of my intellect by forcing myself to look dispassionately at the gruesome sight confronting me. I noticed the smell first. He had clearly messed himself and urinated at some stage in the proceedings, and I immediately felt repulsion superseding my previous thoughts. We had to act, so Captain Cordwell, clearly shaken but very much in control of his thoughts and feelings – and indeed of the situation – told me to take the weight of the body while he would cut him down with the pen-knife all deck officers invariably carry in our pockets somewhere. It was with considerable will power that I forced myself to place my arms around the trunk of that still-warm and stinking corpse in an act of almost disturbed and disgusted love, while the Master used my jack-knife to saw through the cord supporting him. As we laid the man gently in the scuppers, I could not help noticing his contorted features, with the tongue protruding from swollen purple lips, and slight runnels of blood from ears and nostrils.

By this time, the chief and second engineers had arrived and I was told by the Captain to go to the ship's office and notify the local police, explaining what had happened and asking them to call a doctor and ambulance. I was not sorry to leave the scene of this appalling tragedy and, while waiting for the troops to arrive, reflected quietly on the horror of what I had just done and the sadness in the situation that had led the wiper to commit this terribly tragic act. I could still smell and feel the body, replaying in my mind the repulsive actions I had been forced to take, and the equally sickening scenes I had then been forced to witness. I found that compassion had indeed been driven into a secret recess of my mind by the circumstances of what had been done. I could find no answers, but was left with plenty of questions. My secunny asked me with a doleful expression the inevitable, 'Why this man ado this thing, Sahib? For what reason he acts this way?' There was little I could say or do to reassure him, except gently explain that I quite simply did not know, and could not answer his questions. The same train of thought had clearly affected us both. Rank and race had dissolved, ceasing to be dividing characteristics.

My reverie was broken by the silent arrival of the police, whom I instructed my quartermaster to take below, while I awaited the ambulance and police doctor's car. I was then joined by the chief officer, and we chatted quietly while waiting. Again, the same questions were asked, but Pete enquired also how I was feeling and reacting to things. While his concern was welcome, there was little we could share. I still felt ill, with physical sickness decidedly close to the surface. Momentarily I could not drink anything and even a glass of water seemed repugnant. As soon as the doctor arrived, Pete took him below, by which time my secunny had returned and together we waited for the ambulance. This must have taken at least an hour before it turned up as apparently that night 'had been a particularly busy time'.

Once they had gone below, the covered body was brought up on a stretcher for examination at the mortuary in Guy's hospital. I reflected that our ship had certainly provided medical students there with a mixed bag of investigations. After the doctor returned home and the police sergeant and his constable adjourned to the Old Man's cabin, I was invited to join them along with the chief and second engineers and Mate, while we all signed the official log-book entry which the Master made out on the spot. A generously quick tot of brandy all round did wonders for settling queasy stomachs and served as the nearest we could manage to an immediate wake for the poor wiper. Following this, we each took off to our respective tasks. Mine was quite simple, for I joined the rest of the officers and cadets in the smoke-room, where inevitably, the entire situation was again discussed. All officers and hands remained in a state of shock and for most of us sleep was something immediately unattainable. As I nursed myself with more settled stomach around another equally necessary brandy, most of the assembly gradually wandered off, but I suspect like many others, especially our impressionable young cadets, further sleep that disastrous night was quite out of the question. I threw my boiler suit onto the deck of my shower – it stunk still and was covered in stains that would not bear too close an examination. I resolved to throw it into a bucket later that morning and wash it myself, as I could not expect my steward to deal with this repulsive bundle of rag.

Next day we all turned to as usual and tried to follow the ordinary events of cargo or engine-room watches, or plodding through the routines of galley and menu-making, or simple turning to on deck following the ordinary routines, while each came to terms with the tragedy of the night in his own unique way. Inevitably, the cadets wanted to discuss things, especially Pollard, who suddenly found a further new reality to seafaring that had previously been totally outside of his boyhood dreams and expectations. His deep-blue eyes were being well and truly opened!

When I returned to my cabin after breakfast before venturing out on deck as duty officer, I found my steward had already taken away the boiler suit for cleaning. I called him from where he was working in the third mate's cabin and told him I thought it best for me to do this job myself. As a Goanese his English was perfect, and making direct eye contact told me that this was what he wanted to do for me. It was an act he could not describe, but one that would somehow show he knew what I had been forced to do in the dark hours of the night, and that he appreciated something of what I was feeling and thinking, and indeed what had been done for a fellow rating. I backed off, glad in one respect, for I dreaded having to pick up that ghastly thing again even to put it into the promised bucket. Even while showering that morning I had pushed it with the steward's broom into a corner of my shower and toilet cubicle, unable even to touch it at that time. The officers' steward and I reached a new completely different level of understanding that I had never before experienced with an Asian, and one that would possibly prove unattainable in the future.

Gradually normality returned, broken by the group Indian welfare officer visiting the ship next day and finding himself with something more substantial than petty and often imaginary grievances to occupy his time. I make this remark without cynicism or rancour, for Asian crews aboard the ships generally worked extremely well with their officers. This enabled problems or even minor irritations to be aired and discussed between both serangs and butler with senior officers, before these could develop into major concerns that required the intervention of any outside agency, including the port Chaplain or company Asian welfare officer. The engineers particularly were distressed to discover what had caused the man to commit this tragic act, and even the most hardened junior was clearly shaken by what had occurred. But no one, it appeared amongst his colleagues could offer any constructive light regarding motives.

Gifford was slightly older than most cadets having served for a while in an accountants' office ashore. He described his two years' there as 'boring beyond words or endurance' and finally talked his mother into signing forms for a late entrant into nautical college at the maximum age of almost eighteen years. His twenty-first birthday was celebrated on board in grand style extending over two days and, accompanied by Pollard and two other cadets (one of whom he knew from his pre-sea training days) who were serving on a Bank Line ship in the next berth, they enjoyed magnificent celebrations in their quarters and the next evening, more salubriously attired in mess kit, at a quality restaurant in London – the bill for which was picked up by his parents. Pollard was turned to with the crew the following morning, but Gifford was duty cadet with me (more physically than mentally), which gave him once more but under totally different circumstances an opportunity to unfold his continued thoughts and feelings about the suicide with a therapeutic (I hoped) baring of the soul.

It was good to meet up with the various superintendents who arrived on board in Surrey Com and to exchange views with my old mentor, Captain Atherton, who remained ensconced as the cadet training officer. After inevitably discussing the suicide, he asked me informally my views on Martin's progress and we found ourselves agreeing that he appeared to have settled very well into his new career, and hoped this trend would continue. He also joked about my own cadetship and reminded me of some incidents which frankly I would have preferred to have left forgotten. I was blissfully unaware at the time how tales of the fortunes and misfortunes besetting cadets (and officers, for that matter) reverberated around both the fleet and London office (and apparently still continue to do so) lightening the tedium of ordinary and often mundane routines. What was of greater importance than reminiscences was our desire for orders and we waited, almost with bated breath like the Ancient Mariner, to see what kind of cargo we would carry, and to where, and even for most of us (except the cadets and ratings) for news of how long we might be away. For the moment though nothing but silence emanated from nether regions in the Kremlin.

Captain Cordwell, the chief engineer, engine-room serang and I were called two days later to attend a preliminary hearing of a coroner's court locally to give evidence of what had occurred that fateful night regarding our wiper's death. It was a formal hearing advanced in the light of the ship's imminent departure, and was certainly 'something different' for which to be relieved from a duty watch. The police sergeant gave evidence of finding the body after being called to the ship and stated that he and his constable had found no evidence of foul play, not that I had been aware that he was particularly looking for any. It suddenly dawned on me how different were our lifestyles and professional interests, while I listened ruefully as a little more of my own inherent naivety disappeared down the plug-hole of life's experiences. A preliminary verdict was returned of 'suicide while the balance of the mind was disturbed', which I supposed was as factually accurate as anything else, and served as an additional entry in the Old Mans' official log-book. It did not answer the question why.

A few days later we took on board our river pilot and, with tugs fore and aft until we cleared the dock sill, headed down river for Bowater's Jetty in Northfleet Reach directly opposite Tilbury dock entrance. No one aboard was particularly sorry to leave that berth, but hearing the Master and Mate amicably – and with some humour – discussing mundane shipboard affairs over luncheon just before we sailed,

I found it reassuring to have on board two sober, healthy senior deck officers. It was also pleasing that the 'passing of time' began submerging the suicide from ordinary conversation, even if I was aware that many (particularly I) still held vivid memories of that particular night.

Captain Henshaw visited the ship a few days after our berthing alongside Bowater's Jetty. He was in a particularly sombre mood as he advised me that Captain Smart had been diagnosed with advanced stomach cancer and that the hospital considered it something of a miracle that he had managed to bring his ship across the Atlantic. I was truly saddened by this news. The prognosis was not hopeful, leaving me difficulty in relating the officer I knew aboard the *Elizabeth* with the wreck that finally left our ship. The super asked me about the deep-sea chief officer, who had apparently celebrated his homecoming by knocking his wife around the kitchen in the early hours of his first morning ashore while in a drunken bout, leaving her senseless on the floor. It seemed neighbours had called the police and he had been arrested on charges of Grievous Bodily Harm, or GBH, as it was apparently known in the trade. I related events since I had joined the ship in as neutral a tone of voice as possible, together with my fears and – very tentatively – the action I had planned if things had developed 'along the negative path', as I termed this. It was pleasing that he agreed with my thoughts and particularly rejoiced that I had discussed things with the chief and second engineers. He gave no indication of what might happen to Tom and I did not ask.

The Captain also brought a new very high frequency (VHF) 'walkie-talkie' radio system to the ship. This arrived complete with battery charger and detailed instructions regarding the use of all of this equipment, both operationally and for servicing purposes. We deck officers spent a hilarious time practising its use from various parts of the ship, testing where it was most and least effective. It was an excellent opportunity to practise the 'correct procedures', such as naming the ship and our position relative to that being called, and sending bizarre messages to each other like a set of gleeful schoolboys. Even the Master joined in with unrestrained joy. We could each see the potential advantages with this equipment, obviating the need to rely on the forward and aft telephones, which always rang at the most inconvenient moment when wires and ropes were either under tension or whisking around the main deck, and frequently required a cadet to answer the thing. The phones soon became redundant and were used only on rare occasions when all sets were being recharged during ocean passages.

Returning on board after a further few days leave while alongside Bowater's, I asked the Master if sailing orders had been received. He looked me directly in the eye with some obvious trepidation and advised we had indeed received voyage instructions. The ship was to proceed to, and be fitted with appropriate magazines

Above: The sharing of jokes and humour cemented friendships and made major contributions towards the relaxed ethos that was a hallmark of happy (but not slap-happy) ships (Courtesy Captain 'Tinker' Taylor).

Left: The use of VHF 'walkie-talkies' made a significant contribution towards the fluency and convenience of communications when these sets first appeared in the 1960s....

...superseding the labour intensive telephones which usually required a cadet to deal with them (Courtesy BP plc).

then load from, the Higham Bight powder buoys in Lower Hope Reach, a full cargo of seismic explosives in the form of dynamite and geophex, along with fifty cases of detonators and primers stowed separately in number three 'tween deck. This cargo was apparently used to produce explosions in areas regarded as potentially suitable for oil drilling by creating artificial vibrations that could be scientifically measured and determined. We were also to take from the same anchorage other assorted explosives including nitro-glycerine, along with 'toe puff' in numbers one and Five 'tween decks. The latter was boxed toe board that was used in making shoes and consisted of several layers of fabric impregnated with cellulose nitrate and a solvent, with resin and dye – a cargo we were informed that could be liable to spontaneous combustion. As if that were not enough to satisfy the most ardent maritime romantic, we were to complete by loading numbers two and four 'tween decks with ammunition for the British armed forces who were still actively engaged fighting rebels in Aden province. My own concern in the light of that little lot was to see we did not produce a few bangs ourselves. Bunkers were to be taken while we were in Aden, and after discharging the ammunition we were to proceed to a range of ports in the Persian or, as it was rapidly becoming known for political reasons, Arabian Gulf. Still blanching a little, but latching onto Captain Cordwell's obvious concern, I recounted my adventures as a cadet aboard the brand new *Earl of Guildford* when in dense fog, 'at these selfsame buoys, sir' the ship had been hit by an incoming Red Star cargo liner from South America whose bows had penetrated almost into our number one hold. I watched his emotions fighting the need for self-respect for his rank and the apparent fears evoked by carrying this particular cargo. His complexion blanched and he became increasingly agitated, so I enhanced the immediacy of the situation we had then faced, exaggerating this into a full-blown saga about our transporting ammunition aboard the *Earl of Gloucester*, but careful not to overdo the histrionics and so lose credibility. By the time I had finished, with straight and solemn face, he cast me that even more direct look of a decidedly unhappy mariner. Before leaving his cabin, I suggested, 'On the positive side of course sir, remains the thought that all the time we have on board even one case of the stuff we earn a 25-per-cent danger bonus.' This attracted a barely whimsical look, so I added, 'This might prove sufficient incentive, sir, for *any* of the hands not to be over-perturbed.' I then left the cabin, feeling completely satisfied with the start of a good morning's work of winding up our esteemed Captain. He had clearly lost the eternal optimism of youth.

We finally discharged the last rolls of newsprint and went to stand-by with river pilot happily in the wheelhouse and a tug each fore and aft to see us off the jetty. This stand-by was a good opportunity to practise using the VHF sets 'for real' as we headed down stream for Lower Hope Reach, and their convenience was fully appreciated. It was so useful to have constant communication by simply pressing an ever-ready button. The passage proved completely uneventful, apart from the fact that we departed at 0500 hours in order to be moored between the buoys ready to be inspected at 0800 hours and then commence preparation of the magazines prior to loading.

We brought up to the explosive buoys without incident and, soon afterwards, were passed by the Port of London Authority harbourmaster's staff as competent to receive this dangerously volatile cargo. The inspector just happened to be my Uncle Wag, who specialised in Category A ships amongst his other service duties, and we enjoyed more than a good measure of after breakfast ale while ostensibly 'checking paperwork' and generally keeping an eye on things. It was good indeed to touch base with him again, for much water had passed under the metaphoric bridge since I used to go out on the harbour launches in these self-same waters as an eager-eyed fifteen-year-old awaiting entry to nautical college. He admitted now to having reservations in those distant days that the merchant navy and I might not prove compatible but now readily agreed, as he supped yet another generous waft of ale and glanced at the two-and-a-half gold rings adorning my sleeves, that he had been proved wrong. This, of course, still did not stop him from popping into the galley on his way back to the launch to ask our bemused cook if he 'happened to have a spare ham bone with about ten pounds of meat attached to it'. Luckily his quest proved unsuccessful, otherwise we might have ended up merely with bread, cheese and fresh salad for our suppers.

Precautions extended to a rigidly enforced policy of no smoking on deck and various other safety measures intended to allay concern and of course prevent the ship blowing up. I had related my good work on the Captain to Pete, who promised to keep that particular pot gently bubbling. He did explain that this Master had served throughout the Second World War aboard cargo ships and had been for much of the time engaged on ammunition replenishment to Royal naval warships, during which he had witnessed the results of explosions caused by direct hits from bombs and torpedoes to many of his fellow mariners in that trade. He also explained that the Master had been due to join the ill-fated motor vessel Seistan, owned by Strick Line of London as Captain before she sailed on her run to the Gulf, but had left the company and joined Ellerton's before confirmation of his appointment. This ship had been carrying a similar cargo to ours and had blown up in Bahrain in February 1958 with the loss of fifty-seven men plus four from the tug's crew alongside. Merchant naval humour, however, as Pete readily acknowledged, became decidedly warped 'as officers wormed their weary way up the promotion ladder, seemingly dying to achieve command'. I quietly questioned, without response, how he fitted into this particular category.

I watched the slings coming aboard as they were lifted from dumb barges towed by a motor tug fitted with spark arresters to its funnel, and analysed my own feelings. The barges loaded dynamite and geophex from up river and then chugged down to us at the Mucking explosives anchorage buoys. The live ammunition in the form of assorted bullets, shells and mortar bombs was already being unloaded from a convoy of army lorries onto Cliffe Jetty, momentarily displacing the regular run of innocuous sand dredgers that normally used this berth. Contrary to the delight I derived from winding up our esteemed Master, I certainly held my own concerns regarding this particular cargo. I was not 'nail-bitingly worried', but was well aware of the potential dangers in carrying such a mixed bag of explosives. The cases winched on board by ship's cranes and derricks entering all lower holds seemed so innocuous. It was hard to realise that just one of them could have blown the ship sky-high along with the crew and, by 'sympathetic detonation', as I learnt it was called, half of the storage butts on the adjacent marshes. I doubted if any explosive effects would have reached the oil refinery at Shellhaven a couple of miles across the river, but they would certainly have been aware of events 'on our side', as it were. The marshes with their sound of waders and assorted gulls delving in the mud flats lost a little of their innocence as I watched dockers loading the barges, and saw these trundling delicately towards our own anchorage on the next tide.

We put our cadets handling the cranes and winches servicing the hatches. It was encouraging to see how they related so well together, with Martin learning much and soon beginning to fill many blank pages in his cadet's journal. Watching the boys concentrating intensely on their tasks I was reminded of my own first efforts at winch handling and admitted my dexterity then had fallen a little short of the quickness with which Pollard in particular performed this task.

Our concerns for the Old Man were reflected in a totally unexpected area, for one of the junior engineers announced his intention of not sailing with this cargo. As he had already signed articles, the incident led to an interesting contretemps between the junior, chief engineer and Captain Cordwell. Inevitably, the Kremlin became involved in the intractability of the junior to refuse to sail, and a deputy engineering superintendent visited the ship to see what could be sorted out. We mates were not party to the discussions, but waited with parochially bated breath for developments, especially as the engineering department was concerned. The general opinion (even amongst the engineers) was that as he had already signed it was too late to change his mind. Set against that, of course, was his already packed gear and strongly avowed intent to anyone who would listen – even if we did not want to – that he would not sail. As it happened, we saw him leaving the ship with all gear accompanied by the superintendent. It seemed that he had been allowed to sign off articles and had been offered another ship within the group: so ended yet another 'storm in a proverbial nautical teacup'.

Left: Snooker could still be played at sea but instead of balls with their obvious limitations, coloured pucks were used…

Above: …while table tennis remained a favourite form of relaxation, with often intensively fought tournaments resulting that helped cement friendly deck-engine relationships (Courtesy BP plc).

Right: The fitting of swimming pools to many deep-sea cargo ships and tankers was a welcome addition to crew comfort, particularly in tropical waters (Courtesy BP plc).

Our voyage to Aden followed the by-now familiar pattern for most of us set for numerous ocean passages, taking in our stride the usual mixture of weather conditions including a range of fog banks in varying degrees of intensity; brilliantly warm sunshine once we had cleared Gibraltar, and the inevitable storm virtually anywhere. The novelty was unique for Martin and he also followed the traditional pattern for first-trip cadets, by dropping his own unique selection of clangers, aided and abetted in a few by his side-kick, Gifford. Both boys were keen, unaffected by seasickness and clearly enjoying themselves. They worked directly for the chief officer, spending much of their time with the crew. Ellerton as a group remained an excellent company for cadet training. Both boys were turned to by Pete Birchall with me for one-hour teaching sessions each per week, during which academic and professional areas were covered. These 'tutorials', as I termed the periods, occurred after smoko on Wednesday for Roger and on Friday for Martin (work permitting) in my cabin. The sessions were additional to the very generous full-afternoon study periods twice per week on Tuesdays and Thursdays allowed by the company when the cadets were not required by the Mate for cargo- or deck-work. To make sure these periods were not wasted in idle chat or snoozing, it was my remit either to supervise their own correspondence-course work or set them exercises devised by myself in mathematics or physics after identifying potential areas of weakness.

Owing to their different levels of expertise, I taught them individually, putting the time to more effective use than if they were seen together. With Pollard, it was largely to keep an eye on his varied correspondence-course work, while I often set Gifford a number of chart work or other navigational exercises emphasising celestial navigation theory, and discussing his efforts afterwards. It was strange and rather disturbing to see Martin's efforts at constructing a scale diagram of the ship for one of his course seamanship exercises. His beautifully exercised drawing reminded me of my first efforts at doing this same work for the old *Earl of Bath* light years before. In my mind's eye I could still see myself in the cadets' study, tongue sticking out of the corner of my mouth in concentration and the ship rolling and pitching quietly in a moderate sea, measuring carefully accommodation and deck blocks with derricks and hull structure, trying not to make the ship look too much like a bath tub with sticks and lumps attached. It seemed his 'O' level pass in art was being more than justified and I trusted, in the light of our cargo, that his RE would be equally effective! Pete supervised a half-hour or more as necessary, individual Saturday morning session for each cadet, when he examined their journals, tested them on the collision regulation they had learnt that week, and instructed them in more practical aspects of their training.

Occasionally they were trusted with solo jobs such as looking after the lifeboats under the supervision of the third officer. It was on one of these occasions that the first clanger of the trip was dropped. Gifford as senior cadet became confused between the uses of raw and boiled linseed oil, so enthusiastically instructed his little friend in applying oil to the boat oars after they had both sanded them down. Inevitably he used the wrong one and wondered why the oars would not dry with a delightfully agreeable sheen, but remained sticky and tacky to the touch. I heard the third mate blistering them both while I was on watch and smiled ruefully to myself, as they turned to cleaning off the mess and then applying the correct substance. That particular clanger had not been dropped by me, but a few others I had enthusiastically managed, of equable or even better status, came to mind! After all, neither of these lads almost asphyxiated their officers as I had nearly done while a first-tripper on the old *Earl of Bath*. Both boys worked cleaning the wheelhouse and bridge wings once or so per week, usually before the Old Man's inspection, while Gifford was encouraged to visit the bridge as often as he wished when off duty and learn the practical applications of celestial theory by trying his hand at using the ship's sextant. Occasionally I liquidated a cabin session by allowing him to attempt reductions of sun, but left stars and lunar sights for later into his time when he had gained deeper theoretical knowledge. Both boys were encouraged to visit the bridge in their spare time merely to gain lookout and collision-avoidance experience. I occasionally took Gifford aft with me on stand-by and, under strict supervision, allowed him to work the crew during mooring and tug operations. Like most Ellerton cadets, these youngsters had training coming out of their ears. They seemed to thrive on it!

Our discharge of the Aden ammunition was slickly handled by Royal Army Ordnance Corps officers and other ranks, and we moved without mishap to the bunkering mooring buoys. There were no exchanges on this occasion of mutual visits between officers' messes, as had happened during my previous call loading tanks and ammunition aboard the *Earl of Gloucester* some years previously.

Discharge of the explosives around the Gulf ports was certainly not so slick. In fact, with the monsoon season and no working on Fridays, discharging our explosives proved a long, tedious job, using ship's gear at many of the ports to offload the stuff either into barges alongside, onto a stone jetty, or even directly into lorries or open rail wagons. We became bored to distraction when off-duty in such places as Bandar Shahpour, Bahrain, Sharjah, and Bandar Abbas, to where we were diverted in order to relieve congestion at Korramshahr. Our limited loaded draught of 25 feet 1 inch lightened as we offloaded, enabling us to slide easily alongside within the maximum of around 27 feet permitted in each place. Shore leave was fine and quite safe, but there was little to do and the novelty, even to the cadets, soon wore thin.

Wandering around the main deck in shorts, floppy hat with wide peak of the type recently introduced from the States, and loosely flapping shirt, I watched idly as the last of our explosives was removed. The wooden crates still seemed innocuous, and familiarity had long since bred not exactly contempt, but certainly a gentle acceptance of this lethal cargo. This was particularly true while we were alongside in Bahrain with memories of the 'stricken Strick Line ship', as I referred to it, which became a muted talking point for all on board. Even the deck serang mentioned the incident in suitably serious tones, so it was interesting to see that our crew also were not entirely unaffected by the potential danger residing in this cargo.

Far more interesting was our visit to Basrah, and then only because we received orders to load a general cargo that included bales of cotton, carefully rolled and padded valuable carpets, and bagged wild almonds, with the ship bound for Bombay to complete loading with more general cargo that included the inevitable tonnage of tea, assorted textiles, spices and jute.

The weather in the whole of the Gulf did not help matters. It remained unbelievably hot and humid. As the Mate remarked, 'It is not for nothing that the Gulf is called the "rectum of the world" amongst seafaring folk, and we're right up the end of it – literally, as well as, perhaps, metaphorically.' We could only agree as we sweated and sweated and then sweated again, each taking in excess of four showers a day and lying for rest at night stark naked under a sheet on our bunks. The much-vaunted and prophesied air-conditioning had broken down off Ras al Had – as we had 'turned the corner' and approached entry to the Gulf – at the time it would have been most useful, and we had to resort to the conventional forced-air system that only circulated warm air. Having tasted the fruits of air conditioning, we yearned once more for its repair. The problem seemed to be with the motor powering the contraption, and a broken circulating fan, both of which defied the ingenuity of our engineers to fiddle with and fix. The only consolation we deck officers had was that they also suffered valiantly alongside us, especially in the engine-room. We lamented on missing out on what our imaginations perceived as true luxury, which was compared (as merchant seamen referred to seafaring in an imagined mode of idle comfort) to being aboard the mythological 'daddy's yacht'. The engineers downed numerous cases of beer per man per day, merely to replace the fluids lost in temperatures *exceeding* 120 degrees F near the main engine and generators. At least we on deck could benefit from whatever warm breeze was available, while the swimming pool had received constant use from all officers since we had cleared Suez.

The weather was not much better in Bombay – if anything, it was worse, being compounded by indescribable stenches and the continuous hawking of dock workers spitting out their inevitable streams of betel juice onto our sparkling decks. The Mate, with ever the ready word, referred to this practice as 'the call of the East', as he glanced ruefully on the beautifully holystoned planks of his boat-deck, which was used by the workforce to rest from their labours – at every opportunity. The cadets also regarded the practice ruefully, even more so seeing that their job once we were homeward bound would be to clean and holystone it over once more. In the midst of the sound effects, I noticed as particularly impressive the speed at which new container berths were being constructed in this port of old and new contrasts.

Eventually we left India, bound towards Falmouth awaiting orders for our mixed and varied cargo. These were received as we cleared Gibraltar after topping up bunkers again in Aden. We were to head for complete discharge at King George Dock in Glasgow, which delighted our engineers, as many of them came from this area.

As we closed the Isle of Arran entering the Clyde, the 'mother and father of all fogbanks', as Captain Cordwell described the situation, descended and the vessel was shrouded with such intensity that it was not possible to see the forecastle head from the wheelhouse. Both cadets were called to the bridge to act as lookout; a secunny was placed on the helm, while the Master, pilot, duty officer and radars each worked overtime. I had just taken over the watch and spent my time plotting with a chinagraph pencil on the main radar screen; reading out nearest course and speeds to Captain Cordwell and the pilot. I advised the target's possible intentions assuming all parties held their course and speed. It was impossible visually to identify any of

Dense fog surrounds a large tanker as she proceeds on passage in North Atlantic waters. Fog banks could be experienced virtually anywhere in the world, during which times the Master was informed and the duty officer conformed to strict safety regulations (Courtesy V. Volden).

the passing ships or even to see them. Visibility was down virtually to zero and the damp air penetrated into the wheelhouse, wafting around all areas and adding its own coolly dank contribution towards the atmosphere. The faces of the boys on the furthest part of each bridge wing were white and strained under their tans as they looked for small vessels mad enough to be caught out in this 'pea-souper', or for other small objects which the radars might have missed. The pilot advised we might have to anchor unless things improved because the docking Master would not allow us to berth in such appalling visibility. As it happened, the visibility did increase sufficiently for us to take our tugs and come alongside. We all breathed a sigh of relief and, down aft with my newly working VHF set, I acknowledged with equal relief the order from the bridge that we were now in position, to let go the tug and then 'make fast everything'.

The agent advised that there were to be no officer changes, while the Asian crew still had a few months remaining on their one-year articles. The Master, however, was advised by the Kremlin that this next trip would be his last voyage, following which he would be retired after many years' company service and a total of forty years at sea. Limited shore leave was arranged between us, but there was really no time available for extended leave, much to the chagrin of those of us who lived south of the border. We just went ashore locally, 'watched the box', listened to a range of music, organised a few SODS operas, and awaited orders anticipating where 'the powers that be', might direct us for our next trip. We were also delighted by the appearance of fitters from the air-conditioning-plant manufacturers, who came aboard and not only replaced the much-maligned motor and fan, but offered the engineers numerous spare parts – and additional maintenance manuals that should have been provided initially.

There was not a lot of time to ponder, for a few days into discharging we received orders to load general cargo from Glasgow, Liverpool, Manchester and Avonmouth for Red Sea ports, the Seychelles, and Male and Gan in the Maldives islands, whence onto Colombo and a range of Indian and Pakistani ports – with a possible loading there for Australia and New Zealand. Certainly, the Seychelles and Maldives were rarely visited by British merchant ships other than Brocklebank Line, which ran a direct service to these countries. Clearly, something had gone amiss with these traditional arrangements, not that we were bothered too much either way. On the contrary, a chance to see these normally out-of-the-way places held a certain appeal for us all. The cargo included a number of buses and vans for India, which were loaded in Manchester as deck cargo on the port and starboard sides of numbers two and three hatches forward. It was strange being 'up north' again and, during a teaching session with Pollard catching up on his returned correspondence course lessons, we ruminated on the last occasion we had visited there, and how much he had since gained in advancement of his profession. He had also filled out and with a deep tan on his smiling face, expressed delight with the promising marks on his returned work. I found this quite satisfying and quietly rejoiced with the boy that he was so contented with life and, more importantly, his chosen career.

The remainder of that trip was for me somewhat fateful. Following a series of sharp stomach pains while outward bound, and the inability of our medical 'experts' on board to work out what might be the problem, I was despatched by the Captain to be a member of my own sick parade. Of course, with memories of our late Captain in mind, I was convinced I had stomach cancer and remained inconsolable. The outcome was totally unexpected for all concerned, let alone my poor self, for I was diagnosed with a suspected peptic ulcer which led to my being, very unexpectedly, signed off the vessel at Mahe in the Seychelles islands. I spent one month in hospital on this delightful island with its warm, friendly people, and was then evacuated as a first-class passenger on British-India Line's *Santhia* to Mombasa, from where I flew home on a British Airways VC10 jet. Following successful treatment and further diagnosis at home, it was decided that the 'ulcer' was probably something of a false alarm and that perhaps my signing off the ship had been premature. A fat lot of good was that information to me, but great relief that the cause of my pain had been nothing more serious. Inevitably, within a few weeks of additional leave, I found myself back at the Kremlin requesting appointment to my next ship.

2

ENGAGEMENTS IN THE EAST

I had not visited Millwall Docks for some years, in fact not since serving on *Countess Elisabeth*, but my journey there hardly filled me with enthusiasm. Standing by the gangway holding my sextant in its strong wooden case, waiting for the taxi driver to sort out my gear and assist me carrying this on board, I glanced along the main-deck and up at the compact accommodation block with its towering coloured funnel of Ellerton's *Earl of Bristol* berthed alongside the central grain depot at Inner Dock. The ship was 7,593 grt, 480 feet overall and 62 feet moulded breadth, with five hatches (three forward of the accommodation and two aft) and service speed of a surprisingly fast 17½ knots. She was quite a trim craft, and was originally the first in a series from Swan Hunter that had been built a few years previously, with the others emanating from varying British yards. The vessel was busily engaged in discharging, with disturbed grain dust enveloping all three working hatches making the air between vessel and elevator a smoky grey. Judging by the appearance of the boot topping just below the lapping waves and her after draught mark, she was nearing completion following her recent trip from Huron in Ohio on the banks of Lake Erie. Sage-like supers at the Kremlin forecast that *Bristol* after discharge would sidle down the Thames to my more familiar Royal Docks, then Tilbury, and on to Plymouth completing loading for Far Eastern ports. It was good to be doing my third consecutive trip aboard an Asian-crewed ship whose Indian and Pakistani ratings were generally compliant, after such varied experiences with that mixed European bag who signed articles aboard other ships with perhaps less regal members of the group, notwithstanding the slight initial 'hiccup' with the serang on my previous vessel.

Reporting to the Mate my delight can be imagined for as he glanced up in response to my knock on his jalousie, he was none other than Mat Synnott, third officer on the old *Earl of Edinburgh* during my round trip to the Far East when I was a second-trip junior cadet. The three broad golden rings surmounted by a triangle on his sleeve seemed somehow strange following my memorised familiarity with a single bar. His beaming smile certainly had not changed much with his steady promotion through the ranks and, after he had rung for customary coffee and biscuits, I threw myself into his luxurious armchair. Delicately sipping from always-welcome cups, we pondered how much water had passed under the bridge since our original meeting many years previously and then discussed old times and fellow seafarers across the globe. The Captain on this trip was Charlie Abel, and one cadet was forecast to join 'somewhere along the line' of UK ports. The third officer, Jeremy Hawkins, had been an Ellerton man since his cadetship days and was commencing his fourth voyage before going up for Mate's certificate at the end of the trip. I recalled meeting the Old Man when he was chief officer during my ill-fated debacle in Tilbury Docks as a newly promoted uncertificated fourth officer aboard the *Earl of Ripon*. Even though this had happened some eight years ago, its memory still educed a slight blush of shame under my suntan. I related the event to Mat working on the theory the Old Man would probably do this anyway – so my version (and excuses) might as well 'get in first'. He merely smiled, while passing the large plate of biscuits. It must have been an hour later when we thought about rousing ourselves: Mat to check cargo progress with Jeremy, who was on deck watch; me to stow away my gear, change into working rig of comfortable battle-dress, and then report to the Old Man.

In response to my knock, Captain Abel, sitting at his desk reading a batch of official papers, gave me a hard look and invited me to enter his cabin. He was clearly trying to work out in his mind where our tracks had crossed. Eventually, he admitted defeat so putting him out of his misery and me into mine, I reminded him of the inglorious *Ripon* incident when he was chief officer and temporarily in command of the ship. He laughed at the memory and stated that if his way had not been overruled by Captain Bassey, the then senior dock marine superintendent, he would have made me remain on board and battle that incident through with the Asian crew. Smilingly, my response indicated pleasure that he *had* been forced to listen to the super. Glancing at my discharge book and Foreign-Going Mate's certificate as I signed Articles, he presumed that crew control was clearly no longer a problem or I simply would not have survived this far.

Saturday night as duty officer on board meant witnessing the high jinks associated with the engineers' party to which, of course, all mates were invited. Nurses from a nearby hospital flocked to the ship and, as the Old Man and chief engineer had shot off for the weekend, the purser opened the owners' suite for the girls to leave their coats and access the heads. With latest pop tunes belting out over the ship's broadcast system – an advantage of including our enthusiastic young radio officer in the bash – and ample supplies of food and booze available in the saloon, our ship offered few social restrictions. As girls and officers had equally few mutual inhibitions the poor old *Earl of Bristol* turned into a veritable floating bordello long before midnight. Remaining ever faithful to my Sue, I joined Mat in 'celebrating the celebrations', as it were, for a few social drinks. We 'old, staid married men' fought off a couple of enthusiastic girls and wended separate ways to our cabins where, ears assailed by shrieks of delight, music and mayhem, we endeavoured to sleep. The ship quietened down sometime in the early hours as party spirit for most gave way to amorous love (or lust). The steward's call on Sunday morning was largely unheeded and only Mat, I and few engineering stalwarts managed to stagger in for breakfast. The purser was not a particularly happy man for, somehow, during the night one of the girls had dropped a bottle of expensive perfume across the owners' best-quality fitted carpet. On venturing inside the door, to sample the promised air, my only reaction was 'Wham!' It was definitely arousal at first sniff and I could not wait to call Mat and a well hung-over Jeremy to share the joke.

Assimilating and making decisions on a raft of varied paperwork was an essential and frequently time-consuming role for the Master of any merchant ship (Courtesy BP plc).

It was 1200 hours the following day when I took stations aft for departing Millwall. It was only a brief trip down river to the Royal Albert Docks (RAD) and a further forty minutes or so in the locks equalising the twenty-foot tidal rise. We anticipated being alongside Number Eleven shed, Royal Albert for two to three weeks loading a full cargo of general merchandise for varied Far Eastern ports. To my sorrow, favourite port Tilbury had been ruled out. Our cargo was to include paint, drums of electrical cables, 300 cases of condensed milk, crated engine parts and assorted machinery and sixty drums of assorted dyes from ICI in the lower holds; together with 'tween deck cargoes of cars, tractors and dumper trucks, plus postage stamps, currency and medical supplies stored respectively in the Master's safe and ship's vegetable room. We would complete with a deck cargo of four railway passenger coaches for the Malaysian railways to be discharged in Port Swettenham, and call into Plymouth on our way down Channel to collect two dumb barges for the Royal naval Base at Seletar in Singapore. 'Quite a mixed bag' was my observation to Mat, who promptly suggested that, as part of my training for eventual promotion, I should have my own stab at the loading plan that evening and compare joint efforts next day. As I was duty officer, this certainly proved an ideal pastime, even if it lasted until the early hours of the morning. We compared efforts after breakfast, after Mat started the cargo and with Jeremy on watch. There were no serious problems with my planning – merely ones revolving around personal preferences – so the consensus was the ship would not have sunk, and DTI examiners would have approved had my efforts been submitted as part of a paper for Master's.

We were delayed for five days due to a dock strike. These were becoming increasingly frequent during recent months, not just in London, but entailing more widespread so-called 'sympathy strikes' across a range of UK ports. Captain Abel put these down to what he termed 'signs of the times' but we could not draw him further, although he did comment that this strike was caused by a petty dispute which even a few months ago would have been settled amicably through negotiation. It was a simple situation that had been allowed to escalate out of all proportion. He did hint that the directors had informed him that these 'unofficial' disputes, which all too frequently became 'official', would have dire consequences with inevitable knock-on effects on jobs as trade moved to the Continent. 'Perhaps these same dockers will soon be out of work permanently themselves,' he ruminated. We felt there was little to add or comment, although our own ratings union had been talking subversive clap-trap about 'offering supportive action to our fraternal brothers the dockers'. We were told when approaching picket lines barring the entrance to the docks to explain that we were seamen and the ship was our home for the duration of the trip. There were no reported incidents and certainly going ashore for local leave visiting the traditional Bent Arms public house and other hostelries, or shopping across the river in Woolwich presented few difficulties. The dockers' action nevertheless left a 'nasty taste in the mouth', as Mat described the situation.

It was interesting to see other ships discharging their cargoes (when the dockers were working) and I recall looking with enhanced interest at an elderly Brocklebank Line ship, the *Mahronda*, which was berthed astern of us, discharging elephants from India bound for zoos and one of the major circuses still touring the country. Virtually half the crew, free from duties, went ashore 'to see the fun', as a junior engineer described it, and even I took time out for occasional moments from my own cargo watch to pop up to the boat-deck and observe events. The four- to six-ton elephants were discharged by use of slings under their bodies via the fifty-ton heavylift derrick aboard the ship, rather than shore-side cranes. I imaged the chagrin of the chief officer at having to rig this monster. The whole procedure went without any hitches – apart from some stridently complaining trumpet blasts from the cargo – and the ungainly animals were led into what looked like reinforced horse boxes, apparently none the worse for their voyage or man-handling experiences to date.

We often exchanged anecdotes after lunch over coffee in the smoke-room about other mariners and their exploits, such as the Master on a tramp ship with whom the third engineer had sailed who decided to dismantle and service the Aldis lamp on the bridge during an apparently interminable trip across the southern Indian Ocean between Africa and Australia. I had experienced such a voyage myself so felt particular empathy with the chap's story, even if not the incident. It seemed that father managed to take the lamp apart, but unfortunately was not so adept when it came to putting it back together again. The only way the thing would work was when it was pointing to the deck. In any other position it simply 'gave up the ghost' and refused to click away happily. As it was an integral piece of the ship's safety equipment, the lamp had to be sent ashore at the next Australian port for the nearest optical nautical instrument company to 'do their stuff'. The same chap related also the boredom on the same passage one afternoon of junior deck officers and cadets playing cowboys and Indians, using the parallel rules as a substitute Maxim machine gun. Inevitably, they broke the thing and had to splice it together with sellotape – telling the Old Man that it 'had somehow dropped onto the deck'. There was a rumpus the same afternoon when Sparks found himself handcuffed to the arms of his chair while on radio watch. He had to make excuses to the shore station upon release that he 'had been taken sick with stomach pains and was too ill to keep his watch'. The deck cadet on the same ship had spread a generous layer of treacle over the wheelhouse toilet seat intended for the junior cadet who was on watch with an attack of 'the runs', but unfortunately this was used by the Second Officer instead with disastrous results and a display of anger that roused virtually everyone from their afternoon snooze. As it happened, the humour of the situation was directed more against the mate than the cadet, so perhaps he should have kept more of a low profile and dealt with it summarily. Then there were the deck and engineering officers having a peg, or two, in Sparks's cabin one evening when the third mate glanced up and saw the wake of a passing ship. As he was the responsible officer-of-the-watch, he dived out into the wheelhouse to find the automatic pilot had 'slipped a gear (or two)', and that the wake was that of their own ship. Fortunately, the incident occurred prior to the days of course recorders or otherwise some interesting explanations might have occurred between the imprudent officer and his Master. The third did not mention what the wider engineering department got up to but the stories, which were probably true,

47

gave us interesting insight into things that sometimes happened aboard long-voyage tramp-ship companies.

There was also a tale related by the third mate, perhaps as antidote to such saga's of the sea from the engineers, about an unfortunate and unpopular junior engineer who had upset virtually everyone on board the ship. It seemed his wife drove to the docks to pick up that good man and his gear and, while he completed packing, the deck department manhandled the car onto a pallet and arranged with the nearest crane driver to load this onto the nearest bollard, where it balanced precariously in the breeze. It seemed that the voluble ire expressed by both engineer and his wife more than justified the prank. The junior 'willingly' handed over a bottle of 'hoped-to-be-smuggled whisky' as a bribe for the crane driver to lift the valuably loaded pallet to terra firma.

Then there was the rumour heard from a deck officer who was on a sister-ship of the same company, which was bounded around to bated breath and near-disbelief concerning the stowaway discovered aboard a foreign-flag trader while the ship was on passage from Luanda to Vancouver. He had been landed to the police there, who refused to take him ashore. Similar efforts to offload this stateless person at a number of other ports world-wide proved equally impossible, and he had mysteriously disappeared one dark night in the Yellow Sea. No direct allegations were made, but the pregnant silence meeting this alarming tale indicated something of our own conjectures on that topic.

There was nearly an accident forward during stand-by for departure from Royal Albert. Normally, my supervision aft was from the docking bridge, whose raised height offered an excellent view across the area of operations port and starboard and left me away from the mooring equipment but close to the docking telegraph. On this occasion the Old Man decided unexpectedly to place me in charge forward, putting the Mate in the wheelhouse and Jeremy aft. The third had sufficient sea-time to justify this wider experience in preparation for promotion, hopefully next time out. I noticed as we were singling up that a junior khalasi had placed his foot too near for comfort to the bight of a new mooring rope. There was so much noise from a passing ship exchanging signals with her forward tug that action had to be taken very quickly to avert a possible accident. With no time to shout any warnings, I left the eyes of the ship and dashed to the port winch drum off the capstan, just managing to reach the seaman before the remainder of the crew started to heave in on the rope. I then stopped the proceedings until my station could again be re-established and my greater overview regained. The incident, although probably not as serious as it looked initially, brought me out in a sweat momentarily. It also justified in my own eyes (not that I needed this) the necessity of the officer on duty not taking part by offering a democratic 'pulling on the ropes' instead of supervising others doing so. The serang had been busily occupied with chippy heaving in a head rope leading across the starboard bow so was not aware, until he saw me running down the forecastle head, that anything was amiss. In fluent Hindi he reinforced the need for care at all times when handing ropes, administering an additional rocket to his cassab, who should have seen what was happening. I think it was as well my handling of Bazaar Bat Hindi was not up to the standard required to comprehend fully what was said, but it was the first time I had ever seen an Asian sailor blush!

The serang on this ship was a very unusual man. He was always immaculately dressed in navy blue drill uniform with red turban. Woven around his uniform collar draped the silver chains of his office with a bosun's call attached. He was a seaman for whom the entire ship's company of every vessel upon which he served, from Master to lowest topass, had the highest respect and regard. Tabarakullah, the son of Kallimullah, had been decorated with the George Medal for bravery. He had received his award directly from Her Majesty the Queen while attending an investiture at Buckingham Palace. The incident that had attracted this honour had happened aboard the *Earl of Carlisle* some thirteen years previously, a few months after the Queen ascended the throne. The ship was anchored off Mukalla awaiting barges to come alongside for cargo. The first-trip junior cadet unwisely, but inevitably for an enthusiastic and carefree sixteen-year-old, leant over the forepart rails to read the draught, and overbalanced. His shriek while *en route* for the briny could be heard all over the ship, alerting engineers fishing along the main-deck but, more importantly, the Master and Mate chatting amiably on the boat-deck. With that instinctive action for which senior officers are noted, and moving rapidly for the first time in many years, they dived for the jolly boat and had this lowered halfway to the water within minutes of the incident. What they did not see was the large hammerhead shark attracted by the splashing forward as the boy swum steadily for the anchor chain, where he hung on, kicking happily while awaiting rescue. He was blissfully unaware of the danger heading in his direction. Tabarakullah, working his crew on the fore deck, saw the shark torpedoing its way forward alongside the hull and took in the situation at a glance. Without hesitating, he dived in front of the creature. The shark, its passage though the water suddenly impeded by the massive splash directly in front of it, swung off ninety degrees to port and submerged. By this time the dinghy, being rowed more energetically than the senior officers had done anything physical for a long time, had picked up the serang *en route*, proceeding then towards the cadet. The boy was taken aboard. He was completely unaware of how close he had been to probable death until the officers quietly told him what had happened. He subsequently went into a state of severe shock and had to be hospitalised from the next port, Aden, before being flown home. Eventually he left the sea, but returned with Ellerton's a few years later to resume his career. He was a much wiser, if rather apparently aged deck cadet, as the aftermath of the incident sent his hair completely white within a few months.

Both company and grateful parents between each gave Tabarakullah money equivalent to a couple of years' salary, while the senior officers' sent off their report and recommendations on the incident, which were eventually channelled into the correct quarter, leading to the serang receiving, rightly, the highest civilian honour for bravery. The company paid all hotel and air fares for Tabarakullah and his wife to attend the investiture, where they met the boy's family and the cadet whose life he had undoubtedly saved. He seemed to be the 'man of more than one moment', for it transpired just after the Second World War he had rescued two women from drowning when their punt overturned near his native village in East Pakistan. Seemingly, he dived twice into a crocodile-infested river. Later in the voyage, with justifiable pride, he showed us deck officers his George Medal, his citation and an English newspaper report of both adventures. It was truly a pleasure to have sailed with a man of his stature.

Towards the end of our loading in the RAD we were advised that the ship would call into Tilbury Docks after all *en route* to Plymouth to complete 'tween deck loading in numbers one, three and five hatches and would be there an estimated five days – not that we took that forecast very seriously. Interestingly, we were told to prepare to take conveyor belts for Taiwan along with a number of three-inch polypropylene ropes. Man-made fibres were becoming increasingly common throughout the merchant navy, so the idea of exporting them was not quite as unusual, as they replaced or supplemented the manila and sisal ropes still in common usage. They had far greater breaking strains, but were extremely heavy when wet.

We duly arrived at 0330 one wet Sunday morning with a strong wind and very heavy rain whistling around my ears and eyes as, down aft, I dealt with tug and moorings. It was one more occasion when I was glad to finalise the berthing and go for a hot shower immediately upon arrival in my cabin, before staying around for the remainder of the morning as duty officer.

In the absence of cargo work, I wandered around the docks later that day. It was interesting to see the differences that had been made in the 'name of progress' since my first voyages here extending over the years. The new container and timber development just inside and to the left of the main dock entrance had been completed for some months now, and was fully operational, with a range of eager deep-sea and coastal/continental vessels loading and discharging boxes at a phenomenal rate of knots. My Uncle Wag dropped in for tiffin (lunch) one afternoon, after he had found out I was in port, during which he told an interested lunch-time table that one of these ships could load 1,300 twenty-foot containers in around three days, or one container every three minutes, working around the clock. The number of labourers also was drastically reduced. Normally, a conventional cargo ship would probably employ 50 men on the vessel, 18 on the quay and 12 in the shed making a then perfectly acceptable 80 men to load or discharge the average 7,500 grt deep-sea dry cargo ship (like the *Bristol*) spread over an average of 15 or more days. At the container berths, 12 or 13 men only would be employed on an 11,000 grt vessel and complete discharge within a day or so. I had noticed, while stretching my legs as duty officer overnight that Number 4 berth in the Royal Victoria Dock had also been adapted for containerisation and had been working consistently for some months. There was also a gradual decrease in the number of 'conventional' ships using both groups of docks, and many vacant berths in the main body of each could be witnessed where, just a year or so previously, each would have been taken, with ships at anchor outside awaiting their turn. The number of deeply laden ships anchored off Southend in the various anchorages invariably had also fallen, from well into double figures as they awaited their turn to berth, down to about ten. Similarly, the cargo jetty in the River Thames was still in use, but there were fewer ships seen alongside. Even the dry dock was often found empty during my visits, when it had nearly always held a deep-sea ship even as large as one of the Tilbury-based passenger liners of P&O or Orient (or P&O–Orient, as they were gradually becoming known following an uneasy amalgamation), or local craft such as a dredger that would be undergoing repairs or survey and maintenance.

My uncle's contribution was certainly a conversation-starter (rather than stopper) which continued well into coffee over the table, instead of in the lounge, and this was still going strong when I excused myself in order to relieve the third mate on cargo watch. It was good to make the acquaintance of the new chief super in Tilbury, who was considerably more 'user-friendly' that I had found his predecessor, one Captain Bassey, with whom I had 'crossed swords' during an interesting interlude on a previous visit.

An Athel Line tanker, the Athelknight, *passing Tilbury Docks with views of each of a P&O and an Orient Line liner lying alongside the passenger berths at Numbers 33 and 31 sheds respectively (Courtesy World Ship Society).*

As it happened, notwithstanding progress (or perhaps because of it?) we were in Tilbury for the best part of a fortnight, which at least gave me time to shoot off home for an unexpected long weekend of local leave when no cargo was being worked.

There was another 'sign of changing times' experienced while we were outward bound, for it seemed strange passing one mile off Folkestone to drop the South Channel pilot who had taken us out from Gravesend, into a very new high-speed launch, instead of the pilot cutter off Dungeness which had served mariners for well over a century. This wound up the Old Man once more over another lunch-time chat as he referred to 'accountants beginning to interfere with procedures at sea'. He forecast this as the 'thin end of a very thick wedge', whatever that may have meant. We mariners were left to our own thoughts which, it transpired, were pretty sober ones. The future still loomed ahead optimistically, as is the way of youth and young men, but we were well aware that while we were away for months on end, all sorts of dramatic changes affecting our livelihoods were taking place unobtrusively to many areas of our industry.

We dragged a north-easterly gale down the latter end of the English Channel, which accompanied us happily into Plymouth Sound, where we called to collect the dumb barges. These were lifted aboard by a shore-side crane and securely lashed, one immediately forward and the other aft, of our midships accommodation, by numbers three and four hatches. They were slightly longer than our 62-foot beam so about ten feet of barge overhung both port and starboard sides. Once the barges were secured with wires across numbers three and four hatch covers, and bottling screws tightened, we anchored in another Gale Force 8 south-westerly, which was by then luckily decreasing, but blew directly across the Hoe. The storm created an uncomfortable motion which required close attention to our anchor bearings in order to detect possible dragging. As the wind diminished, a compass adjuster came aboard to 'do his stuff' with the magnetic compass. With two sets of derricks raised to their maximum, four railway carriages alongside numbers one and two holds, and the barges athwartships, our poor old compass was the most confused piece of equipment on the ship. Although we were anchored heading due North the compass was reading south of East. It was a first for me both to carry such an awkward deck cargo and to witness an adjuster at work.

To everyone's astonishment, as we had long given up the 'promised ghost', a deck cadet joined us in Plymouth in time to witness the work of the compass adjuster, and so add 'something of value' (as I termed this) into his journal. Reggie Price had received pre-sea training at South Shields nautical college and just entered his final stages of training, with Second Mates' examinations looming over the horizon during his next leave. His open smile was indicative of a refreshingly uncomplicated

Soon after leaving the final coastal port, deck cadets rigged the patent log that was essential in determining the speed of the vessel. On occasions, it was not unknown for the brass rotator, streamed astern of the vessel away from the wake, to be taken by a shark as something of an indigestible meal (Courtesy BP plc).

personality, brim-full of controlled confidence. In view of his advanced cadetship, Mat put him on my afternoon 12–4 watch for bridge experience, additional to the one-hour slot allocated for academic teaching with me every Wednesday just before our seven-bell lunch. He was also placed working with the serang's crew during the mornings, but given responsibility for both lifeboats and for organising small groups of laskari ratings for cleaning and painting the accommodation block, tallying stores and other more responsible work. It transpired that the company had indeed expected him to join us in London, but the young man had been away on holiday with his parents and returned only the previous day to find a recall telegram awaiting him. A quick phone call to the Kremlin led to a hasty packing of deep-sea gear and the next available train from his home town of Seaton, which could not have been much closer, enabling him to join us a few hours before we sailed.

The British Tanker Company's vessel British Vigilance *on passage through the Suez Canal. Tankers, and dry cargo ships with explosive cargoes, invariably headed the convoys (Courtesy Author's collection).*

Local boats of all ships in transit through the Suez Canal were taken on board by the ship's derricks to be used in helping moor the vessel alongside while allowing another convoy to pass in the opposite direction (Courtesy BP plc).

Exhibitions to observe the famous 'dance of the seven veils', and other exotic pursuits, were frequently arranged for ships' crews who were alongside over-night in Egyptian ports (Courtesy Komardoc SA)

Our next port of call was Aden for bunkers and shore leave, following which we commenced the 3,000 mile sea passage towards Penang, our first port of discharge. On our way through the Indian Ocean we experienced an electrical storm. Pundits would doubtless argue enthusiastically that *all* storms are electrical. The thing which made this one different was the absence of any rain accompanying storm-force head winds, which was a very unusual phenomenon of sufficient import to attract a report from the Master to the Meteorological Office, with which the ship was registered as a reporting vessel. As no deck work was possible, Reggie was placed on my morning watch, and we had just relieved Jeremy, who had stirred up this rarity around the middle of his duty. The wind was then Force 7 but, by the time Mat came to relieve me at 0400 hours, this had increased to 10, gusting 11. The wind was so strong that I felt it distorting the shape of my mouth and nose, and pressing back my ears, while endeavouring to keep some sort of lookout in the pitch-blackness surrounding our ship. I put the cadet on radar watch, upon which we relied totally for ship detection, even though he reported the set recording some very bizarre fluctuating reflections. It was unnecessary for me to call the Master to the bridge for he was up there with the first serious motion, ordering an immediate reduction in speed sufficient to keep steerageway, yet reduce stresses on the forepart of our hull. The darkness was relieved periodically by brilliant flashes of lightning: it was the only time in my seafaring to date that I had seen three differently recorded types – the familiar sheet and fork, but also very rare chain lightning during which three or four 'links' appeared in the sky. Captain Abel informed us this was the most dangerous type as the links formed complete circuits. Although the ship was not struck, the chain especially created a very frightening sight, particularly being accompanied by such severe wind. The motion was appalling: the ship pitched and rolled heavily while solid combers smashed along the foredeck almost up to hatch level. Spray was caught continuously by the powerful wind to be swept over the bridge dodger. Our stem pounded heavily into the next valley with such intensity that our stern frequently cleared the water causing our propeller to race wildly. The lack of resistance sent the engines wild and created such excessive forces of vibration that shudders sent along the hull were felt on the bridge. Reggie ended up with even more ammunition for his cadet's journal.

When the weather subsided sufficiently, the chief officer sent chippy and the cadet round the ship, sounding all tanks and recording their readings on the wheelhouse sounding board. It soon became apparent that we had maintained complete hull integrity in all holds and compartments. They reported that the bell forward had been knocked ninety degrees out of true – which was no mean feat considering it was welded to a strong bracket. We blessed the fact *Earl of Bristol* was fitted with McGregor steel covers to all holds, especially those at the very vulnerable number one and two hatches.

On average at least one deep-sea ship every six weeks every year world-wide continued to be recorded at Lloyd's as disappearing without trace, with the loss of all hands. They sailed from port A to port B and were never heard of again, often without having time to transmit an SOS emergency signal. It was popularly recognised that the main causes of these tragic accidents were direct ingression of water into the holds (especially forward) through wooden hatch covers or, equally probable, suddenly shifting cargo, or loss of power, leading a ship to swing beam-to heavy seas and become overwhelmed. Having just experienced the unbelievable savagery of the elements, and man's puny efforts in the face of such an onslaught and come out the other side in one piece, we blessed the good Scottish shipbuilders on the Clyde who had provided us with such a sturdy vessel.

There was an additional problem facing Master and Mate. The barges loaded as deck cargo had shifted in the mountainous seas and were moving gently, but firmly, port and starboard athwartships within their restraining cables. The coaches secured by way of numbers one and four hatches remained firmly secured, probably because they were each lying fore and aft, although they bore scars of more than a few dents. Other than managing to tighten a little more on the bottling screws and using our winches to weave additional spare wires fore and aft there was not much more we could do with the barges except trust that the storm had blown itself out completely, thus reducing subsequent movement to little more than a minimum. The cadet was turned to on deck all day so certainly failed to make his appearance on watch that particular afternoon.

Discharging general cargo in Penang caused few problems, but we were warned that Singapore was 'in a bit of a political upheaval', as it was enthusiastically described to us by the agent. It was fine for him; he was remaining in Penang. We had heard in BBC Overseas news broadcasts that Indonesian rebel forces were creating mayhem that had spilled over to affect shipping. Two or three vessels lying to various anchorages had been blown up by insurgents coming alongside during the darkest hours of the night and attaching limpet mines with time switches to their hull. We were advised to exercise extreme caution as Royal and Malaysian naval forces were unable effectively to patrol the large areas and corridors constituting Singapore harbour. We took this news on the chin, but having been involved in the Cuban crisis and mauled by insurrectionists in Buenos Aires, I felt a little better prepared than many of my shipmates to face these additional perils of seafaring life. Nevertheless, I was not a particularly happy mariner.

I brightened considerably, however, at the prospect of shore leave on this delightful island. It was always a pleasure to go ashore and wander around the market places and side streets meeting the friendly locals and simply escaping the restricted confines of the ship for a few hours. As with most places abroad there was not a great deal to do in the time available, but Reggie, Sparks, myself and some of the engineers managed to visit the snake temple and fit in a tour of the island, both of which were minibus excursions kindly arranged by the agent. All too soon, cargo was completed and with a flourish of telegraphs on the bridge, below and on my docking station aft, we eventually sailed for Singapore.

We discharged our railway coaches at 'Port Swet', as we mariners referred to the place, without any problems and, in return, picked up a small amount of cargo for Japanese ports. It was good to go ashore here for a couple of hours in between cargo watches and visit Kuala Lumpur and surrounding tourist spots. It certainly made a welcome change to go shopping, sightseeing and walking on a surface which actually kept still!

As forecast (it seemed, almost gleefully, but perhaps I was becoming cynical), it proved impossible to sail directly to the north-eastern side of Singapore island upon our arrival and immediately discharge the barges, as we had hoped, at Seletar, the Royal Naval Base by the causeway. Instead the ship was directed to an outer anchorage, which we shared with a considerable number of other dry cargo ships. Captain Abel was informed of the political mayhem which was quickly becoming known as the 'Indonesian situation', as the agent described events around us. He

The scenery of Penang island was frequently breathtaking and, while being driven along the spacious roads, rounding corners often revealed unexpected scenes of jungle and distant sea views (Author's Collection).

A pit viper was typical of the poisonous snakes that frequented jungle spaces. They merged unobtrusively into their background of branches and leaves making detection difficult (Author's Collection).

called a meeting in the lounge after luncheon, when vigilance was urged from all officers and crew, especially us deck officers and particularly during overnight hours. We were to switch on every available deck and external accommodation light, to rig cargo clusters in that dark area of the hull caused by the flare of the bows, and at the stern, and place water pressure hoses at available points on deck. Sparks, who had served on tankers (much to my continued envy) observed, not very helpfully, that were we a steam tanker then superheated hoses would have been available. His remark, not surprisingly, brought forth an appropriate (if rather restrained comment under the circumstances) from Father. Our radio officer was not perhaps a very 'bright spark', for it had taken him three years to complete his Post-Master General (2nd class) training, with a Board of Trade Radar Maintenance certificate, the legally recognised Sparky qualifications, which was a period twice as long as normal. We gave him full marks for perseverance if nothing else. In London, the fourth engineer, Jeremy, Reggie and I had invented our own version of cards, which was a mixture between gin rummy and knockout whist, into which we had attempted to introduce Sparks. Either our teaching was at fault or we had made our rules too complicated. It made little difference, for Sparks was unable to follow the game, even though the cadet very soon acquired sufficient expertise to beat us occasionally. Mind you, as we refined, amended and introduced variations, the game became so complicated that at times we had to think carefully before making moves especially as, due to watch-keeping all four of us could rarely manage to play simultaneously, and so ended up with just a pairing. The convoluted game passed away more than a few otherwise tedious evenings while in port or at anchorages. We were fortunate in inducing also the second and third engineers into the rules. This opened the available opportunities and increased the number of evenings available for play but, inevitably, brought additional refinements of which the newest players were unaware. This led to further complications. The entire pastime was aided and abetted by indelicate quantities of sherry quaffed enthusiastically from half-pint tumblers, with customary lack of finesse. It was hardly surprising that, during some games, clubs began to look suspiciously like spades, thus adding additional confusion to a game already fraught with its own complexities.

About 0300 hours the second morning the sound of an almighty explosion woke up the entire crew apart from Reggie and me, who were on anchor watch anyway. A Norwegian cargo ship had been blown up and we caught sight of dense smoke and vivid flames surging into the leaden skies off our starboard bow. With five ships' distance between us there was little effective help we could offer. The area was soon awash with launches and belated Malaysian naval vessels scurrying around importantly. The next night another ship was blown up, this time the Swedish vessel dead-ahead of us. The force of this explosion caused us to pitch violently, straining our cable to such an extent that we feared we might unwittingly have dragged anchor. Once again, the Old Man rushed out on deck followed by every officer and rating. So severe was the motion that many on board thought it was our ship under attack, thus causing considerable panic amongst our Asian ratings. Luckily, Tabarakullah soon had the deck crew knocked back into some sense of order. His positive actions had a salutary effect upon the engine-room crew, enabling their serang to regain control within a short while. We lowered a lifeboat to go alongside the heavily listing Swede as it was painfully obvious she would be unable to lower her own boats. We checked also our own cable, which had held, but ran out another shackle to consolidate the anchorage.

I was put in charge of number two boat and we were soon lying off the victims' port side, gazing with wonder as water surged around and into a massive hole in way of number three hatch. The rising panic in my crew was almost tangible, causing me to cover my own apprehension and appear as if our action alongside a stricken vessel at 0320 hours was the most natural thing in the world. I knew of old that the slightest visible sign of concern across my features would have a devastating effect upon them, so submerged the butterflies' cross-diving in my own stomach. The dryness of my throat was not helped by the pungent smoke occasionally wafting our way as Malaysian light airs haphazardly 'boxed the compass'. Soon, we were surrounded by launches and sundry Royal Naval craft on this occasion so, working on the theory that as our presence was both ignored and superfluous, I ordered my suddenly very enthusiastic crew to return alongside our own ship.

The following morning an exquisitely uniformed Royal Naval officer graced us with his presence, making enquiries about any possible sightings of 'darkened craft' or other denizens of the night which we might have observed. Our negative responses were at least met with an expression of thanks for lowering a boat. There was little more to say or add to the night's adventures. In the cool light of day, however, the Swedish ship looked an even more sorry sight than the spectacular firework display of the previous night had led us to believe. She was not sitting on the bottom of the anchorage, so her back had not been broken, but had developed a magnificent port list. Luckily there were no direct casualties, but we suspected it might have been a very different story if the bomb had been attached directly under the midships accommodation or aft.

With a delightful sense of timing as the lunch gong sounded, the pilot's launch came unexpectedly alongside. Captain Abel wisely escorted him to the top table, thus allowing us lesser minions to follow his eminently excellent example by having our meal immediately before going on stand-by. It was a smooth passage around to Seletar enlivened only by passing close to the pathetic sight of the Norwegian vessel sitting on the bottom of the harbour with her midships accommodation and superstructure showing forlornly above the waves. Already salvage vessels were attending with procedures in place to raise the ship and tow her into one of the dry docks for subsequent repair and return to service.

There were a number of frigates and a destroyer alongside and, what with the base ward-room and those aboard these vessels, we mutually entertained Royal naval officers aboard our ship and in their varying wardrooms, thus savouring the delights of someone else's cooking and catering. Needless to say, a few parties developed, proving merchant naval hospitality equalled that provided by our brothers (and especially sisters) in the 'Andrew'. Nevertheless, it was a relief to discharge the barges and lower the derricks to normal but, of course, we had to anchor in the bay upon departure from the base for another compass adjuster to pop out and do his stuff.

I suppose there is truth in the adage 'familiarity breeds contempt' or, at least, if not contempt, certainly for me a feeling of staleness as we traversed these familiar Far Eastern ports in Malaysia, 'Honkers', Taiwan, Japan and the Philippines. It was a good run, but having seen the sights so often, the voyage for me had degenerated into little more than a lengthy bus trip! Certainly, with fast, modern motor ships cutting the duration of sea passages and the increase in containerisation with many ships, reducing the length of time in port, voyages nowadays were considerably shorter.

I saw from a recently posted house magazine while we were discharging and loading general cargo in Honkers that Peter Dathan, my old friend and mentor from Keddleston Navigation School, had been promoted to temporary command of the cargo–passenger vessel *Earl of York* while she was on a coastal voyage. He had passed his Master's certificate about four years previously, while I had spent too much time deliberating whether or not to attempt mine, and had served previously for a few years as chief officer. Clearly he was now being geared for stardom on Ellerton's coastal and continental voyages until a permanent vacancy arose on a deep-sea cargo ship within the group. I guessed that would not be too long in coming. I genuinely wished him well and, while penning a few congratulatory lines in an air-letter, reflected how strange it would be were we to serve together at sometime in the future. No particular problems could be foreseen, were that situation to occur, for my assessment determined he would make a first-class Master under whom I could serve. It was with something of an odd feeling, however, that I addressed the envelope to 'Captain P. Dathan'.

Other correspondence of note came from one of the junior engineering officers who, having received a 'Dear John' letter from a girlfriend in the UK, posted this on the ship's notice board so we could all enjoy and share his newly found freedom. He certainly did not seem over-upset by the parting and the manner in which she described ditching him made interesting reading, to put things mildly.

Stand-by for departure from Osaka had just been called and I was fitting on my gloves and grabbing my VHF to go aft when the second engineer appeared at my cabin jalousie clutching his hand. I noticed that blood was seeping out from the cloth wrapped around it more in hope than in expectation of stopping the flow. It appeared he had been working on turning metal on a lathe in the workshop below when he had slipped on the deck and his hand had fallen into the iron-filing residue. It was covered in the small pieces of metal but not bleeding as profusely as the cloth indicated. We adjourned to the sick bay while I sent the cadet, who was passing to work forward with the crew and Mate, back to the wheelhouse to let the Old Man and pilot know there would be a slight delay. Once in the sick bay, I cleaned around the wound as best I could and, in the absence of anything better than literally first aid, slapped a generous couple of spoonfuls of cold poultice on the wound and bound it up, telling him to come and see me once we were under weigh. I then popped down aft, telling Captain Abel by VHF radio of my progress so far and, perhaps cheekily, informing him he could now take his ship away to sea. Of course, immediately having to go on watch once stand-down was announced, I forgot all about the poor old second's mishap so effectively that it was not for a couple of days when he came along to sick bay while I was on duty seeing to the often imagined illnesses of the Asian crew. With mounting trepidation, wondering what on earth I was going to see, I gently peeled off the dressing, only to find that all of the filings came away attached to the wad of lint and that the wound was perfectly clean, if a little puckered around the edges. I am sure my sigh of relief must have been heard all over the ship. The second remained totally unperturbed as I neatly re-dressed the wound, commenting only that over the past couple of days, 'his hand had felt a bit funny'...

It was with something of a surprise when we arrived in Port Swettenham homeward bound to load rubber, to be informed that we should lay on the berth for a few days awaiting delayed delivery of this cargo from 'up country'. Inevitably, we rearranged duty watches to give each of us two days completely free of duties. Reggie and I took advantage of an invitation from the agent to plan a savouring of the delights in a Malaysian fishing village but, at the last minute, the cadet was detailed for some extra work, leaving me to go on my own. I took a local bus to a nearby beach and started to walk in the direction of a village which the agent had advised would welcome visitors and was 'about three hours' trot' from the stop.

Within a short space of commencing my walk, long before I reached my destination, my eye seemed drawn magnetically to the grey, slender trunks of endless miles of wiry palm trees, lying at haphazard angles, bowed before the monsoon winds. I liked the way their subtle colours, dotted among the green and black hues of thick lush vegetation, clashed imaginatively with the pure-white, finely sanded beach. Brown-blue boulders and threads of rich green weed lay half-submerged, stretching as far as I could see, gently kissed by the varied blues and greens of the undulating ocean. This enormous watery expanse seemed to flex and ripple its muscular waves as if warning of the powerful reserves which I knew only too well lurked within its surging yet momentarily quiet depths. I noticed the blue of the hazy sky was littered with woolly puffs of scudding cloud through which the sun struck down in blazing heat. I had long discarded my shirt and walked only in shorts, although the banging of small backpack against naked skin was a minor irritant. The sweltering temperatures a couple of hours later and the quiet water was too much of a temptation so I found a space among the palms and, sitting on one of the horizontally growing trunks lying just inside the fringe of trees and shrubs, took a heavenly rest. Laying aside my bag, I stripped off and went for a gentle, effortless swim, afterwards lying on the warm sand drying off. Lazily I listened to the cheerful sound of birds as their musical calls blended in harmony with insects rubbing and calling, and the crash of gently smashing surf intermingled with an overhead whisper of palm fronds blowing sibilantly in the short, refreshing breezes.

Feeling much refreshed, I brushed the sand from my body, put on my dried shorts and continued the leisurely meander along the deserted beach until I reached the isolated fishing village and object of my walk. My arrival coincided with tiffin and I was greeted by the excited shouts and calls of children as they left the bus which had brought them from the small school further inland. Gradual and shrill, like a powerful overture they breached my mind's repose, but were not too unwelcome, for the presence of these lively youngsters completed the feeling of carefree joy and innocent simplicity which was so much the ethos of this small, more-or-less self-contained community. The picture developing in my mind was restricted purely 'to the East' and my Western mind, bogged down with shipboard issues and everyday concerns about home life, seemed harsh and cold in comparison.

The shy, friendly people invited me to join them in their meal and to spend the remainder of the afternoon with them, languishing in this new-found and unimaginable paradise of carefree mankind and nature. I observed and studied their way of life, simple yet so happy, and realised that it was in their very poorness and near-poverty, compared to the affluence of the towns and my own Western existence, that the secret of their contentment had its existence. It seemed the less they had materially, the less they demanded or required. One very amusing incident related by the head-man was the occasion when the village had elected to try experimental roofing to one of the huts. This consisted of corrugated iron sheeting that was duly fitted and seemed fine until one night, at about two o'clock in the morning, a coconut fell from a height of about eighty feet, hit the roof and rolled onto the ground. The

Very soon after leaving the coastal villages in Malaysia, deserted beaches and lush tropical jungle appeared, with the varying moods of the sea either smashing surf upon the beach, or gently lapping in detached repose (Author's Collection).

entire village was awoken by the reverberating clang; I assumed that the 'boing' must have sounded like 'one of the hammers of hell' going off!

In late afternoon, having enjoyed a meal of delightfully 'fluffy' rice and curried fish, and refilled my freshwater bottle, I made reluctant farewells and set out for the beach and my journey back to the ship – or 'home', as I referred to it. Again the entire village turned out to wave me off and a small group of delightful children went some way outwards with me. Finally alone, I meditated a veritable kaleidoscope of thoughts and images, somewhat enviously, of the simplicity of life-style experienced in such an idyllic setting.

It was soon growing dusk and, as the sun set across the horizon in a fiery ball of rich golden red and yellow, I plodded my way through the fine sand towards the bus stop and reality. Passing that place where I swam and rested 'a year ago', I experienced a feeling that all was not quite well. It was a strange, nay eerie, sensation at the back of my mind that was difficult to define. Suddenly a cloud passed across the moon, and the atmosphere enveloped me fully in an almost dark shroud. This brought me up in my tracks momentarily, leaving the short hairs on the back of my neck rising slightly – a most bizarre feeling. I tried to rationalise and analyse the reasons supporting my disturbing thoughts. The jungle so welcoming and beckoning in the heat of the sun seemed somehow forbidding and very black in its pitch-darkness. The buzzing, chirping birds and insects momentarily stopped their rubbings and unknown callings and even the stronger smashing surf seemed subdued, as if forced into submission by some sort of greater power. Everything was still, perfectly so, and very, very quiet. Suddenly the mystery clicked into place – as if by the turn of a key. The short breezes, so gently refreshing earlier in the day smoothly began to blow, fanning the palm fronds, trees and bushes, but especially the tall, oppressive trees. The branches started to sigh and sing as if watching for something indefinable to happen: something that emanated far back in the dank, terrifying jungles of the interior and from within the stinking, rotting mats of vegetation, mangrove swamps, and living unhealthiness densely covering the tall, satanic mountains. With the awful breezes the night life returned to normal, as it had always been, but I was aware that somehow nature had chosen me to feel another side to the contrasting picture that is essentially Malaysia, and reserved only for a sensitively imaginative traveller to experience.

With a cold shudder in the warm night air, I left my haven of the morning to the mocking satanic jungle and as quickly as the dragging sand would permit, hurriedly continued my journey towards the distant lights of the rapidly and gladly approaching friendly town. I was strangely subdued and in an odd mood as, missing the last bus, I gladly negotiated a fare with a local taxi driver to take me back to the ship. He was talkative and friendly, so I had to answer his questions and make general discussion with him which forced me consciously to shove these confused deeper thoughts to the back of my mind.

Once back in the safety of my welcoming cabin, I relived and reviewed the conflict of turbulent emotions that had beset me during the day. I had experienced every aspect of peacefulness, contentment, awe, disquiet and even vague fear. But of one thing I felt sure: however varied my future travels might be, the conflict within would not be readily appeased; that something in this country would spread out like a magnetic field to draw me back, daring me to explore more deeply the vast contrast of tumult and peace that I acknowledged existed in terrifyingly wonderful abundance in this country.

The feeling lasted for a few days until familiarity with shipboard routines re-established my own real world, but often at night in my sleep, a confusion of disturbed dreams encouraged me to relive the combination of pleasure and uneasiness experienced in the hollow on that otherwise beautiful beach. I supposed the event was little more than romanticism, but I was quite certain there was something more to the incident than mere imagination – even if I remained vague concerning exactly what this might be!

Along with general cargo, we collected a missionary from the next port, Penang, and it remains one of my endearing memories to visualise her stomping around the boat-deck dressed in the chief officer's greatcoat with a Bible tucked under her right arm in the midst of a Force 10 storm in the Indian Ocean. She was quite harmless, however, and made no efforts to convert the unrighteous whom she encountered amongst certain of our officers in the lounge over coffee after meals. It was good having a female on board and added a sense of civilisation to our often outrageous efforts at entertainment. Luckily, seeing as she was berthed in the owner's cabin and was far removed from officers' territory, her presence did not prevent us holding the occasional SODS opera in a mate's or engineer's cabin. I often wondered what she made of the aromatic tang associated with her quarters!

Three days into our crossing of the Indian Ocean, the senior officers and I were invited by the serang to join their Ramadan feast. This was indeed a singular honour and Tabarakullah did us proud by arranging for the deck bhandary to prepare for us a particularly delicious and not-too-spicy-hot lamb curry. It was strange sitting in the decorated crew mess alongside the men with whom we normally worked, but everything went off without a hitch and a grand time was had by all.

We had a problem with the electrician while approaching Aden, or, more accurately, the electrician found himself with an unexpected difficulty. He had been asked by Mat to pop up the mast serving number three hatch to change a complete set of fused electric lightbulbs serving the two lights which shone down into the hold. These were frequently supported by clods of cargo clusters at the corners of the hatches, but the additional lighting shining from the masthead made a major contribution when working overnight cargo watches. He managed to get aloft without too much difficulty and hoist his bag of goodies up the mast, aided and abetted by an able and willing (euphemism for a co-opted) cadet Reggie. The problem arose when he went to come down, for he lost his nerve and was unable to put the first footstep onto the rung of the ladder. We could quite appreciate his predicament. The ship was rolling and pitching only moderately in a gentle head swell but at the top of the mast the movement was accentuated considerably. Mat and I were watching him from the wheelhouse windows and it took a few moments before we realised he was in trouble. We saw him on his knees and then lying horizontally on the mast truck. The Old Man joined us and after a few moments decided that the guy needed help and that his predicament fell into the category of a medical emergency. Inevitably, therefore, I was detailed to grab a messenger rope and pop up to help him down, as it were. I appreciated the movement of the vessel once on the mast truck and, gently tying a bowline around his armpits, coached him even more gently to put a foot onto the ladder, keeping the rope taut and hopefully giving him the requisite confidence to make the descent. It must have taken all of ten minutes for him to clamber awkwardly down the ladder successfully and, once on the main-deck, he was violently sick. I am sure that the missionary's fervent prayers aided our efforts, but on any future occasion I suggested to Captain Abel that we could perhaps send up the cadet, in order for him to gain much from the experience.

Coming into Little Aden for bunkers, we had to sound the customary whistle for the pilot boat, but unfortunately the damn thing jammed. The engineers reckoned they were unable to do anything constructive to stop the racket echoing off the nearby cliffs so, fitting the cadet with double ear-protectors, we sent him up the funnel ladder to thump the siren control with a heavy hammer. This seemed to work, for at least the raucous signalling stopped and, having attracted the attention of the whole of Little Aden maritime and civilian population to our arrival, we settled to take on board our allotted intake of fuel oil and diesel.

Mooring to a buoy often entailed use of a local line boat while the vessel took on bunkers or sometimes loaded a range of diverse cargoes (Courtesy BP plc).

We had an Asian crew-change upon our arrival in Tilbury to discharge. It was very strange for me to be once again in my favourite dock and berth with its proximity to Gravesend, the riverside town which had played such an important part in my desire to go to sea in the first place. It was stranger in another respect, for this was the first time I had entered Tilbury homeward bound as normally it was the jumping-off point for me to go deep-sea. If I had any visions of being relieved these were scotched immediately by the dockside super, who told me I was to remain on board until Hull or even Newcastle, where we were to complete the UK discharge before the ship went to continental ports for completion and loading. At least I was allowed local leave to pop home for the weekend as no cargo was being worked and I was invited to bring Sue back for the coastal run, for which neither of us required a second bidding.

As second mate there was not a lot for me to do regarding the crew change. I was on cargo watch anyway, but it was interesting to watch the old crew leaving the vessel, bloated with good food and living, with an inordinate amount of luggage, including sewing machines, bicycles, prams and seemingly countless boxes, suitcases, bundles and bags. I wondered if the plane repatriating them to various airfields in India and Pakistan would have sufficient capacity to cope with all of their traps and trimmings. The Mate arranged for the crane-driver serving number five hatch to offload cargo slings and nets with all of their valuables which were then unceremoniously loaded into a large furniture van. The Indian welfare officer was on hand to see 'fair play' – not that there was much for him to do. After a gap of a few hours the new crew joined, looking somewhat emaciated. Mat reminded me of a jingle – one could hardly afford it the title of poem – which had appeared in our house magazine some months previously directed at crew changes:

> *In Liverpool, we get new crew,*
> *Serang, cassab and tindal too.*
> *They come on board with box and bundle,*
> *Butler, bhandary and a tindal.*

The doggerel reminded me of the quality of what passed for verse among my fellow mariners, but I assumed I had been spoiled by continuing to read much quality poetry usually after turning in coming off watch and prior to settling for sleep.

Relief followed as promised (for a change) in Hull, so Sue's short coastal passage was precisely that. At least her name was included on my travel warrant so our thanks went to the company for this generous act. It was good to have her on board along with the wives of a few other officers so we had a civilised passage up coast. She stated how much she enjoyed being on the bridge and seeing me performing what to me were my usual duties. Seeing me there and on cargo watches removed much of the imaginative mystery that had previously shrouded her views of what I actually did on board ship.

I was much bemused, while coming towards the end of my leave, by a directive to join the head office recruiting team for two months covering youngsters hoping to join Ellerton's and the wider group as deck cadets. This proved rather a surprising appointment but was welcomed because it would allow me extra leave with my Sue and I rather liked the sound of the challenges in the job. Apparently it was company policy that suitable serving seagoing officers of senior rank should correspond with the young hopefuls by inviting them to attend selection boards following their initial enquiry, addressing them about events of the day when they were invited as a small group to attend the Kremlin, and then sitting in on the interviews with the marine and personnel managers. The co-opted officer was encouraged to ask a few questions, and finally contribute opinions regarding the suitability of the applicants before the panel either rejected them or arranged for the successful lads to visit the medical officer and then proceed to pre-sea training colleges. What made selecting officers 'suitable' was never fully explained but, seemingly, it was to do with 'preparing them for greater things', although again it was left to the imagination of the individual to determine what that might mean. It seemed I would be looking for an undefined 'potential' as much as actual ability. The job was not particularly onerous; in fact I enjoyed doing it for what extended into a few months although, as I confessed to Sue, I would not like it as a permanent number. For one thing I soon tired of the daily scramble to arrive at the office by 0900. I had done this while working just around the corner with another shipping company before going to Keddleston, but I was younger then and the travelling seemed part of 'the big adventure of life'. Now I was older it proved to be little more than 'a pain'.

The work on the selection board was not without its humorous side. There was the sixteen-year-old boy who was a sound candidate on paper. Unfortunately on appearance he turned out to be painfully shy and was clearly not ready for any selection board, let alone one to determine his potential as an officer. Personality-wise, he really had little to offer and we all 'bent over backwards' as the saying went to find something constructive which he could discuss with us. The conversation was like drawing teeth, but finally, we managed to elicit that he had been involved in school amateur dramatics. At last we all breathed a sigh of relief; here was something for him to put himself into the picture. We asked him what part he had played and then held our breath, not daring to look at each other, as he explained he had been a 'navvy's assistant'. The Marine Super, as chairman of the selection board, smothering our collective gulp, asked him if had performed other roles. He replied that in another production he played the part of a 'garden gnome'. This time it was all too much and we collapsed with spontaneously unrestrained laughter across the table, to our collective horror, and a delightfully blank look on the face of the candidate. We could not accept him for training, but felt failing him was not particularly fair, especially in the light of our own behaviour. The situation was saved by the super, who signified that the boy should reapply in twelve months' time. He also kindly made gentle suggestions concerning how the lad might improve his interview techniques in preparation for next time round.

3

FINALLY MATED

I was aroused from my reverie by a gently toned voice asking me if a meal would be required as one was shortly being served. The question was accompanied by a delicately brushing hand against my right shoulder. Rousing myself, yet still delightfully fuddled with sleep, my automatically affirmative reply was followed next by the task of fiddling with the rather stiff catch of this ridiculously small table on the seat back in front of me.

Having looked up the mv *Lady Varma* in Lloyd's Register, I found her to be around 18,000 grt and some 210 metres in length. She was a veritable monster compared to the *Earl of Bristol*, my previous ship. Admittedly, returning to the bulk-cargo-tramping trades was not at all my preference from the more stable (one might even say 'civilised') Asian-crewed Ellerton Line vessels, but the move offered promotion to chief officer, so was worth accepting. Although the ship was three years old, I knew her to be the latest in a class of four representing Empress Shipping's newer mini-bulk carrier constructions, complete with two slewing cranes and a few traditional five- and ten-tonne derricks. Empress had been dragged, some years previously, almost 'kicking and screaming' into part of the parent Ellerton Group, not through any measures of directorial love, I was led to understand, but from motives of unequivocal economic survival. Both pieces of information had grown out of fleet gossip passed by radio officers, which managed to reach all areas of the globe. It had not taken me too long to accept this appointment after Captain Henshaw's suggestion that, as Ellerton liner vacancies were not immediately available, I could either take a little more leave or, alternatively, do them 'a very real favour' by accepting this unexpected job and so return deep-sea. Inevitably, of course, my by-now regular request for appointment to a tanker (even as Second Officer under training) had proved unsuccessful because on this occasion, there were 'no deck officer vacancies on the two ships currently in service, even though our Viscount Tanker Company is continuing its policy of building larger supertanker class vessels'. This story, with its mere hint of future optimism, was passed in a suitably neutral voice that left it open to me either to accept or decline the proffered appointment. I decided there was little mileage in the latter so, hiding my disappointment yet again, smiled ruefully and signed the contract with a flourish, witnessing my agreement with their former proposal.

In the manner of Captain Ford, with whom all my previous dealings as third and junior Second Officer had been negotiated, Captain Henshaw had been extremely persuasive so, put in the tone it was, I really had no option but to accept this job. The problem was easy to appreciate: in keeping with the merchant navy generally, all companies constituting the Ellerton Group remained so short of officers across all departments, and in all ranks, that they were grabbing junior and even senior officers from nautical colleges before the ink was dry on their various certificates in order to get ships away to sea. Again my daydreams were interrupted. This time by the air hostess bringing me the customary plastic delight which passes for meals on short-hop flights, usually consisting of either a minced concoction or chicken. The BEA Hawker Siddeley Trident I had joined a couple of hours earlier at Heathrow was taking me to Tel Aviv airport, and thence to join my ship, which had been lying in Haifa anchorage for a couple of days awaiting a berth alongside. According to the Kremlin, the previous Mate had become involved somehow in an obscure shore-side rumpus in New York, during the course of which he had been stabbed – not fatally, but sufficiently seriously to require hospitalisation. This left the Old Man, second and third mates between them to take the ship on her 5,200 mile passage from the States.

As the agent's launch approached the ship, now my ship, I experienced a veritable jumble of thoughts, possibly arising from a mixture of that slight apprehension usually felt when confronting the unknown. Even in the gloomy light of an overcast afternoon, I absent-mindedly took in the smart lines with all accommodation aft, but her rust-streaked hull clearly resulted from inattention aggravated by a ravishing, doubtless, from rough Atlantic seas during the crossing. The funnel also was badly in need of attention, with the Empress yellow crown looking decidedly faded. The hope simultaneously entered my thoughts that being short-handed of navigating officers had not left the Old Man feeling too disgruntled. After all, he was very much an unknown quantity, as were the existing crew, and amongst all lesser mariners it was common knowledge that Captains, concurrent with putting up the fourth ring, tended to get bloody-minded and most definitely did not like taking regular sea watches, especially for a long fourteen-day stretch across the Atlantic and through the Meddy. I hoped that turning to regularly had not affected his delicate system and made him too difficult, and tried, comparatively successfully, not to view the situation with too much cynicism – especially after seeing the appalling state of both hull and superstructure.

There was nobody to meet the launch – a lack in itself sufficient to set alarm bells ringing in my ears. The ship looked like a twentieth-century version of the *Marie Celeste* – abandoned and rejected by officers and crew. Vague reminiscences of joining *King William* in Montreal began humming distinctly through my mind. I hoped there was not to be a reoccurrence, but gained confidence from feeling a definite surge of fortitude and resolve at the prospect sufficient to banish all fear. I supposed it was a sure sign of my maturity as an officer and arrival as Mate. Clambering up the rope pilot ladder with its wooden spreaders, I lowered a messenger to hoist my gear on board, after explaining to the boatman that lashing the rope end to the handles of my holdalls was not a particularly sound idea, and encouraging him to at least make a lashing around the cases themselves finished with an appropriate ('granny', as it turned out) knot before I hauled them unceremoniously up the ship's side. It had been known for handles to part from cases at most awkward moments leaving the poor mariner with no gear as it either disappeared smartly through the gap between ship's side and boat, or ended up being deposited in a mangled heap on the bottom boards. My valuable sextant in its stout wooden box I had tied before ascending the ladder and had hauled this up with extreme delicacy after my arrival on the main-deck. Waving a farewell to the launch skipper, I paused and looked around me. The decks were unswept for which there was no excuse, and littered with cardboard boxes and wrappers from the steward's stores which had been blown around the foredeck and left there to rot. The contact houses were filthy, unwashed and in dire needs of undercoat and a lick of white paint or two. The few derricks had been topped ready for discharging, but swung uneasily from slack guys and preventers: in fact, the entire ship was a nautical shambles. Even more alarming was the total absence of any crew, for I would have expected the lads to be not only turned to, but out and doing, especially as the ship had been anchored for nearly two days now in comparatively calm weather. I felt my hackles rising. I would have at least expected overside painting to be going on, and had never in my entire nautical career seen a ship in such an unforgivably slovenly state, apart, that is, from occasional sightings of some eastern-Mediterranean tramps owned by unscrupulous owners.

Grabbing a bag in each hand and with my precious sextant looped over a finger I struggled to the companionway on the port side and, lowering the bags, threw open the door. The smell of polish and neatly swept alleyways met me, leaving thoughts that at least the housekeeping department was functioning on most cylinders. I picked up my 'magic box' and wandered up three decks to the chief officer's cabin. It was, of course, locked, so returning below to the Mate's office, I took the key from the open board with its missing door, collected and dumped my holdalls, and then initally went to the wheelhouse assuming whoever was doing the anchor watch might just conceivably be there. The place was as deserted as an out-of-hours

A BEA Hawker Siddeley Trident was one of the regular aircraft serving flights from London to a range of foreign destinations, including Mediterranean countries (Courtesy J. Arthur Dixon).

The port of Haifa, below Mount Carmel, was the major point of Israeli import–export cargo handling (Courtesy Palphot Ltd).

bordello, but reflecting my assumption had reminded me of a witticism from my old English master Mr Harber at grammar school. How did it go? Ah, yes: 'Never assume anything, young Caridia. If you do, you'll only end up making an ass out of you and me.' Very droll, I reflected with amusement – quite witty really, though, the old devil. I spent a few moments wondering what he would think if he knew his star pupil was Mate aboard a deep-sea cargo tramp ship, and then popped below to the Master's cabin to see if he, at least, was on board.

As it happened, the fears generated during my flight and approach to the ship quickly proved groundless, at least in one respect, so far as the Old Man was concerned. Captain 'Bert' Mitchell was alarmingly pleased to see me and, after introductions, offered a seat on his settee and a whisky peg of truly magnificent proportions. It appeared I was the only navigating officer on board. The newly promoted third mate in New York had gone ashore first night in and had not been seen since, and the second (acting chief) officer had been sent home immediately on arrival to have a stab at Master's. With a momentary pang of conscience, I wished him well. The third officer had been uncertificated and elevated from a deck-hand. This plainly unproductive move had been made in the absence of an officer, merely to nod an acquaintance to DTI requirements enabling the ship to sail from an out-United Kingdom port with at least (in theory) her full complement of mates. 'He was more bloody trouble than he was worth' seemed to be the overall verdict of the Master. I ruminated quietly about my own experience with this very practical implication arising from officer shortages. It reminded me of my previous encounter with a specimen of the now all-too-common 'uncertificated mate' species – dear old Waclaw on the *Lady Vedera* – although I was quick to note that Ellerton's themselves, as the main company, employed only certificated mates. It transpired Father had not kept a watch on the crossing coming over, but had exercised his prerogative as Captain by leaving his deck officers to do their normal stints each between them, plus the Mate's share, for the entire eighteen-day crossing. Apparently, however, this six-hours-on, six-hours-off routine had not proved the unmitigated success anticipated, and it was an effort to keep my face straight as Captain Mitchell related how his new third mate had called him to the bridge every time he picked up a ship on the radar PPI (plan position indicator). This included (on one occasion in the middle of father's afternoon 'zizz') a target at 22 miles distance, passing well open, clear and steaming in the opposite direction, down the starboard side.

It seemed the crossing, complete with some atrocious weather, had been for them both a proverbial 'yo-yo' with the Old Man popping up and down from his cabin to the wheelhouse like a living – or livid – version of 'Bob in the bottle'. It was good to have received confirmation that at least my assessment of the weather had proved accurate – and rather explained the contribution of the previous officers to the state of their ship. I asked him why the company had sent off the second mate for his ticket without sending out reliefs, but it seemed there was no answer to that question. I did not consider it appropriate to ask him why he had allowed the third mate to go ashore with them in the launch, so leaving himself bereft of any deck officers, competent or otherwise, for clearly there would equally be no effective answer to that one. Concurrent with these quiet observations I simultaneously nursed my by-now empty glass, wondering if another was going to be offered.

'Don't know where the bugger has got to,' Captain Mitchell said, meditatively referring to his absent officer – or, at least, that was my supposition as I moved from my gentle daydream. 'Admittedly, he was not much good and I was going to get rid of him anyway, but at least he was a pair of eyes and hands. Not only that, but we've got a crew change across all departments lined up as well. The company is getting rid of the English crowd and we have Spanish ratings joining us from Corunna.' He paused. 'I must admit my supervision of the deck crowd lately has not been too rigid.' He glanced pensively at me while delivering this latter gem, leaving me a golden opportunity of mentioning that I had noticed the appalling state of paintwork, littered maindeck, plus the absence of a duty watchman at the gangway. Father glanced at me over the top of his glass and, noticing mine was empty, absent-mindedly passed across the bottle, by way of an answer. I grabbed it happily before he could change his mind, and enquired if there were any deck crew aboard at all and if so, what was happening in that direction. I was quite wasting my time. The old man clearly had no control over his ratings for, glancing ruefully down at his desk, suggested for my first duty it 'might be useful' if I popped down to their accommodation and arranged some sort of work rota for the lads. Following my train of thought. I found myself asking if the ship had received any news concerning coming alongside. The frown on his face provided my answer long before he focussed his thoughts on the question – or perhaps the frown was the result of his focussing…

'I was thinking, in the interim, sir, that it would be a lot easier to effect a crew change there than out here in an anchorage?'

His weary response eventually confirmed my fears. He was not completely 'shot', however, for he added with a spark of humour his view that as we were in Israel going alongside seemed as predictable as the Second Coming. I smiled in return, acknowledging his wit as he continued telling me the ship was carrying grain in all six lower holds, with articulated lorry cabs in the 'tweendecks. The lorries had to be discharged prior to going alongside Haifa grain wharf and there were, at the moment, no general cargo berths available. He paused and yawned, while grabbing the bottle from my side of his coffee table and refilling his and my glass automatically. Then he announced his intention to turn in as, having done the last couple of all-night anchor watches as well as being up and about all day, he felt 'absholutely bussed' – a comment which required little by way of amplification from me.

I left Father to his well-deserved sojourn of the clearly far-from-sober stand-down and returned to my cabin to change into uniform and take the anchor watch in the wheelhouse and chartroom. I was staggered to find myself listing a little as I left his cabin, but then reason asserted itself that in the space of an hour I had consumed as much alcohol as I would normally in the best part of a week. Not yet having had chance to unpack, and not one to live out of a suitcase, it was probably I who felt most disgruntled. First, looming over the horizon, was the slight problem of touching base with the bosun and organising some sort of order amongst the crowd. Regardless of the *laissez-faire* approach to crew control exercised by my good Captain, now I was aboard it seemed correct for me to show at least some interest in this area of mutual shipboard responsibility.

Our initial meeting could be described only as an engaging encounter. Bosun was in the mess room with the carpenter and who, I assumed, were most of my deck-hands. The place postively reeked of alcohol, and each of them was more than slightly sozzled, doubtless resulting from the array of empty and partially full beer cans literally floating around the place. My appearance was clearly the last thing they expected, although I was surprised that the crew grapevine from other departments had failed to lived up to its normal effectiveness. An unshaven, thick-set figure who I assumed to be the bosun levered himself from his chair, glanced at my sleeve rank – and suddenly realised he was now blessed with a chief officer. There was what is known in the trade as a pregnant pause while he eyed me blearily up and down prior to greeting me with a 'burp' – and then the following bland utterance:

'You will understand, chief, that the present old man and previous officers have left me to organise the crowd, so I naturally assume, sir, you're gonna let this con-tinue.' By way of response, I met his look equally pointedly and paused for think-ing time by introducing myself so there could be no doubts concerning status. This rather handed me the initative because he mumbled his own name in response and introduced the carpenter, who looked at me as if I was a maritime ghost who had walked through the bulkhead, complete with three heads. Quietly I thanked the fates that had landed me with a few experiences of mixed European crews and, indeed, a potentially difficult Asian one. Watching how senior officers handled the former delightful lot certainly paid a few dividends now, even if the situation was marginally different in that it was I who had to cope with this happy band of apolo-gies for mariners. Waving an arm invitingly, I suggested he accompany me onto the main-deck, where, tapping the rust-streaked plating before us both, I encour-aged his myopic glance towards the state of contactor houses, masts and just about everything else that, even in the twilight-shadowed deck-lights, clearly required a rubbing-down and coats of paint. Even as we spoke, a stray piece of the *New York Times* wrapped itself lovingly around our feet. With completely serious expression I congratulated him on his enthusiastic efforts over the past two days to remedy matters. I then told him point-blank that once he had welcomed me on board, he could equally enthusiastically assume a new and more focussed eye on his duties by organising the crew immediately to tidying up the main-deck, and then arrange a gangway watchman throughout the remainder of the day and all night. He could also organise the two deck boys into cleaning up the deck-hands' accommodation and restoring this to something approaching habitual living. Bose lurched into the alleyway muttering and swearing vehemently, but at least telling one of the quarter-masters to go to the gangway. He then told off another one to relieve the gangway at midnight and stay there until 0600 the following day. Following him in and shunt-ing him gently to his own cabin, I then suggested that he might enjoy taking the remainder of the lads onto the main-deck and commence an immediate tidying-up session which should last until the entire area was completely clean. I also reminded him that I would be watching from either the wheelhouse or my cabin and expected him to work until the decks were completely tidy, without overtime, and turning to after supper if this proved necessary. I also mentioned that if any litter remained when I did evening rounds I would log him and the entire crew, ensuring they each received the delight of a 'Double DR', or 'decline to report for ability and conduct' in their discharge books when they signed off in a day or two's time. Considering this sufficient success for the immediate future, I returned to the wheelhouse.

So far as the crew (my crew now, I reminded myself) were concerned, I could possibly see at least an aspect of their point of view. Following a very rough crossing, there had been no shore leave while in Haifa as the Master and agent between them had not made available a suitable liberty boat, and the Old Man (by his own admission) had been more than a little lax in not only failing to organise their duties but criminally so in leaving them totally to their own devices. With the second mate doing regular watches and the third completely useless there had been little time for crew supervision, or even, it seemed, inclination in this direction, which was not the fault of the bosun, although any chief petty officer worth his salt would have acted on his own initiative anyway, but with a more positive attitude. I silently called a few blessings onto the head of my acting predecessor, who could have at least organised something useful during the comparatively calm Meddy crossing. That mitigating thought allowed me to relegate crew supervision to the back of my mind and concentrate on other aspects of my duties.

After the comparative compact conciseness of previous wheelhouses, I was amazed at the 'roominess' available. It seemed quite a stretch from port to starboard sides with equipment far more spread out than I had previously encountered. It was quite a walk from the centre-line steering and bridge-control monitors to the wheelhouse entrances, but I was relieved to notice that all bridge gear was pretty standard stuff – at least there were no surprises or shocks there. The ship remained lying quietly to anchor in a calm sea with light airs and no swell. Such currently excellent weather was probably the reason why I found the Captain in his cabin and not on the bridge, was my charitable thought, even if this did not leave me completely convinced – or even partially so. Absent-mindedly looking through the Mate's rough log-book and noticing it had not been filled in since the ship's arrival directed my thoughts to the non-appearance of the Master as duty officer, let alone a rating watchman, when I had boarded. It had seemed at the time a bit unusual as I always made it a point to be around, at least on the bridge wing, when other boats came alongside – for safety as much as curiosity. It had not been unknown for ratings to have accidents coming on board following some debauched revelry ashore (said with all the punctilious self-righteousness of a happily married man – smug so-and-so). The accidents were usually the self-imposed type and were often remedied by the throwing of a well-aimed lifebuoy. There was also, of course, another, more altruistic reason for the duty officer keeping a low profile. It had not been unknown for conscientious but very unwise duty mates personally attending the gangway to be clobbered by disgruntled crew members bolstered by 'Johnny-Walker-induced' courage. This compounded their original offence with that of striking a certificated officer – still, even in these enlightened days an offence under the Merchant Shipping Acts. Anyway, as eagerly proved aboard the *Lady Vedera*, the offence was punishable by imprisonment and I was content to remain (happily) far from being a fully paid Member of the Heroic Club for Deck Officers. It was all rather academic really, I reflected, in the light of my new knowledge.

It was with such comforting thoughts that I watched the crowd working sluggishly around the decks, but at least working, and wandered below to my cabin. I met the chief engineer and other officers over coffee after supper and enjoyed exchanging some interesting comments about the Old Man, deck officers generally and our ratings. Later, I stowed away my gear and, before popping onto the bridge for a quick check around, went on deck to offer the promised inspection and check that the gangway now remained correctly manned. The decks were in acceptable condition, so I told the quartermaster to call me if the weather deteriorated or in any other adverse circumstance, and returned to my cabin and prepared myself for an interesting day on the morrow.

Before going to the saloon for breakfast the next morning, not having seen any signs of life let alone movement from 'the lads', I went to the new quartermaster, who, I was pleased to see, was not only on duty but, he told me, had tried to turn

Lorry cabs proved a popular import from the United States and were invariably carried for safety during an often rough Atlantic crossing as a 'tween deck cargo chained to the deck (Author's Collection).

to the crew without favourable response. Going along to the bosun's cabin, I steeled myself for 'what I did not know', but with grim determination to log the lot if necessary. Again my reception (not surprisingly) was far from cordial. The remainder of my deck department from bosun, carpenter to lowest deck boy clearly retained monumental hangovers and were to a man truculent and quietly aggressive. I felt my patience snapping and looking bosun directly in the eye asked him if he wished to set his crowd to work on deck directly, or whether he might prefer to do so via the Captain's cabin, where I would perform the promised logging session. I then stood with my back to the bulkhead, and along with an interested gathering of ratings hanging from their cabin jalousies and in the alleyways, awaited events.

Chippy was the first to move, asking me what I wanted him to do. I thanked him for setting a sensible example and suggested it might be an idea to start sounding all tanks as I had noticed that the sounding board in the wheelhouse had not been touched for three days now and there was no record of whether or not water existed in tanks where it should be, or more relevantly, where it should not. The bosun, his bluff called and seeing Chips setting off to collect his sounding rods, ralllied his happy lads, who then turned to with all the enthusiasm of tumbril inhabitants heading for the guillotine. As he lurched past me, I suggested half his crew could be organised overside on stages for hull-cleaning prior to painting, with the remainder placed inboard commencing a smartening-up process on the contactor houses, and that they could 'chip, undercoat and paint…chip, undercoat and paint, and continue doing so until the day came for them to leave the ship.' Retaining the initiative and as a final couple of shots across the stern, I told him to set the deck boys once more to continuing clearing the deck-hands' accommodation by clearing all bottles and beer cans from the mess room, opening all jalousies and portholes, and then soogeeing every square millimetre of paintwork. I then confirmed that he had made arrangements for the quartermasters to be set on gangway watches throughout the day, and remainder of the our anchorage stay.

Inevitably my first crew of deck-hands required an extremely close eye kept on them to prevent the traditional twenty-minute smoko developing into one of an hour's duration, combined with a generous three for lunch. I was not exactly flavour of the month each time I made my appearance in the crew mess to encourage bosun to get the lads started again but, after nearly ten years at sea, was by now far too thick-skinned for those occasionally pained looks which romped my way to penetrate too deeply into that vulnerable area between my shoulder blades. The thought did cross my mind, however, whether they might have had something to do with the signing-off condition of the previous chief officer. I did not voice that particular thought to Father, but merely related events that had resulted in him becoming suddenly aware that he now had a working deck crew. In the interim, I turned to and shared with him the twelve-hour anchor watches for the next couple of days, telling him that I would appreciate him keeping his crew up to scratch while I was turned in below – which, to give him his due, he fully supported. I suspected he was glad that he was now the proud possessor of a chief officer to at least organise this apsect of what were, after all, the Mate's responsibilities aboard the ship under his command. The third mate never showed up and the agent ashore seemed unable to find us temporary officers, lending confirmation to the old adage that it was not only in the UK where the road to a navigator's hell was paved with good intentions. There are no prizes awarded for deducing which one of us did the 1800–0600 stint. I did mention to Father gently that he might consider it relevant to report the third to the police through the agent as a deserter, but remained unconvinced that he did so.

Four days later saw the promised crew-change. Once I had seen that the crowd were responding, with the ship slowly beginning to take on a smarter appearance, it seemed appropriate to meet them halfway by offering the carrot of a few hours' unofficial, hence unworked, overtime all round, with an extra few more for 'my good bosun and carpenter'. This at least had an encouraging effect and when finally we parted company, it was on relatively amicable terms even if not much love was lost on either side.

With much raucous cheering, the deep-sea British crowd left the vessel upon which they had served for fifteen months – obviously as delighted to go as the second engineer and I were to see the back of them. He apparently, but not surprisingly, had been experiencing considerable problems below with his lads. Two hours after they had left we received a message saying rating replacements had been held up in Spain for twenty-four hours for reasons never clearly explained, but having something to do with flight and visa problems between Spain and Israel. Naturally enough, as the old crowd could not be recalled, the ship was left entirely without ratings for a day. We officers found ourselves doing the catering additional to the deck and engine-room watch and day duties normally undertaken by them. This was not so much of a problem for me as much of the deck work could easily be left, but the engineers had to shift around a little as the engines were ('technically', as it happened) on stand-by for immediate going alongside.

For myself, I meandered happily if somewhat confusedly between occasional catnaps in my cabin to catch up on the night's lost dreams; anchor watches on the bridge, and moving around the main-deck doing those essential things normally attended to by the duty man. The Old Man had gone ashore with the agent to sign off the crew and had not returned. It dawned on me while moping around the forecastle head that I represented the only member of our deck department aboard ship. There was not even a cadet with whom to share the work. I was reminded of a doggerel ditty which had been published in a recent copy of the house magazine (although Heaven alone knew why), under the title of a chief officer's Lament':

> *Most officers like an (Asian/Spanish etc.) crew,*
> *But I wonder if you truly knew*
> *The only thing I really miss*
> *Is not having an Apprentice.*

As poetry, of course, it was lamentable in more ways than one, but I certainly appreciated the feelings that motivated the composition of the jingle.

Cooking lunch in the galley was quite humorous. I raided the fridges and stewards' dry stores to see what was available, namely whatever took my fancy conditioned, of course, by what I could actually cook. Yet again there was cause to be grateful that my Ellerton cadetship had been served aboard their 'old timers', where cadets, 'in the ordinary course of their duties', cooked suppers for the duty mate and themselves during twelve-hour overnight cargo watches. It was good to be reminded that old skills had not completely deserted me, for vague memories still existed of burning reasonably effectively steak, sausages, chips and tomatoes.

The mushrooms were off, but so also were many of my clients in the form of the other officers, being happily 'in their cups'. Whatever I put before them would have been greeted with the same degree of enthusiasm. Dinner was to be 'cooked' by the fourth engineer and if I say merely that it was the first, last and only occasion in my life that I have tasted garlic-spiced rice pudding, it will be understood if I gloss over the remainder of his offerings.

O joy, o happiness – during the morning of the following day the new crew reported on board, and it was with somewhat hypocritical glee that I offered cook a similarly effusive welcome to that which I had received in London office, even to the extent of calling him 'chef' – a remark which, being Spanish, appeared totally lost on him. Humming contentedly to myself, it seemed superintendency potential was also being acquired amongst my new chief officer skills. The Master also came back on board with the agent and crew. At least he had the grace to look vaguely sheepish after his night on the tiles as he passed me on the main-deck and invited me up for a compensatory drink.

'You'll have to work with the crew, Jonathan,' he said jovially. This was fine, because that is the Mate's function anyway and this I had been doing since joining, but there was an additional ingredient which sounded alarm bells. Whenever a Captain calls me by my Christian name in a happy tone of voice, I become highly suspicious, based on the assumption that something unpleasant would probably be coming my way that would almost certainly compensate for the familiarity.

'Oh, yes, sir?' I queried, hesitantly, wondering what was coming next. 'Why is that, then?'

'Well, neither the agent nor I, nor, so far as I know, anyone else on board can speak Spanish, so you will have to explain British Merchant Shipping documents to the deck crew before they sign on.'

'You will understand, of course, sir, that I also have no Spanish whatsoever,' I replied, aghast.

'Well…er…do the best you can,' he said brightly and enthusiastically encouraging. 'After all, the second engineer is going to have to do the same for his lads.' As if that was any compensation or constructive assistance to me. The chief steward was Spanish, as it happened, but his English was as lamentably limited as that of the combined crew.

Anyway, my first task was to direct the two petty officers and ratings to their accommodation after working with the bosun to issue cabin keys. Following this, I discussed with the bosun and carpenter our general arrangement plan of the ship in the Mate's office. It was then time to meet the entire deck crew in their mess-room, where valiant efforts were made by both parties to explain and understand the obscurely complicated legal terms contained in both articles and accompanying shipping papers. As intimated to Father, the exercise inevitably proved one of interesting speculation rather than much practical assistance. 'They should have frigging well had this explained to them before they left Corunna,' I moaned to myself in slightly agitated self-pity. Let's face it, there was no one else to offer me sympathy. I did wonder as a more immediate speculation, and perhaps more than somewhat cynically, the extent to which their knowledge of seamanship terms would prove equally proficient.

Following this complete and total debacle, my crew spent the remainder of the day settling into their cabins and acquainting themselves with the routines and equipment of the ship. I returned to my cabin reflecting that first impressions of them were at least favourable enough, but with a certainty of fears established regarding probable language difficulties.

'How did thrings go?' asked the Captain, when I popped up to report progress. I did wonder if my hearing was functioning correctly, but a closer glance confirmed what his speech led me to suspect. Both he and the agent were getting well sloshed, cementing, no doubt, a friendship established the previous evening in some doubtless insalubrious bar-cum-house of ill repute.

'How do you think, Captain?' I asked with innocently suppressed insolence. 'As an exercise in useful communication, it was a total bloody disaster and a waste of their time and mine. The lads have about as thorough an understanding now of their legal rights and duties as they did before they joined.' I added with brutal frankness.

'Silly old devil,' I thought, 'I can get away with anything. He's too frigging bottled at the moment to notice.'

'Oh…goonesh, Mr Caridia. Shit down and have a peg.'

Well, I sat anyway, and poured myself a very generous quickie, before returning for yet another anchor watch. I felt there was little point in giving Father any sort of progress report. It was fairly obvious that before midnight he would once more merely be a pool of alcohol on his carpet bubbling away happily either at *Nelly Dean* or the latest sea shanty.

The bright, sunny greeting of dawn next day gave no hint of the events which were to follow. The old man, red-eyed and very hung over, approached me on the bridge explaining he and the agent were taking the entire crew ashore to sign articles. I looked a bit taken back and enquired, somewhat jadedly, why it was that the Shipping Master could not risk life and limb by popping into the safety of the agent's launch and coming out to the ship – a not unreasonable supposition. I might have guessed the response. Apparently this august gentleman was unable to leave his office. Seeing my mouth half-open to enquire the obvious question, he forestalled me by explaining neither he nor the agent knew the reason, so the only option was for them to take our Mohammeds to the Mountain. There was, of course, no answer to this unexpectedly romantic logic – or, at least not one that I could think of sufficiently quickly.

There were also, it appeared, Spanish Consulate difficulties of an equally obscure nature. The agent, who had spent the night in the pilot's cabin, was still partly 'Brahms and Liszt', a delightful combination which made his attempts at explanation totally exhaust his limited knowledge of English. As the Captain's and my understanding of Hebrew was as comprehensive as our combined attempts at Spanish, we did not feel in a strong position to argue.

I thought ahead to the duties the crew would need to do that morning which were once again, like greatness, thrust upon me along with keeping statutory anchor watches. I had previously set the quartermasters into a gangway duty rota, so ventured onto the main-deck to ascertain that my Spanish ratings had at least turned to, for again no visible signs of this lot had been seen so far from the bridge. They had, for directly they caught a glimpse of me I was immediately assailed:

'Pleasae…Sirra…you a knowa whera are the soundinga pips on this shippa?' wailed the carpenter (clearly having forgotten his introduction to the ship's general arrangement plan sixteen hours earlier). And before I could answer:

'Sirrr…vatta you needa de crew to do?' Came a contribution from my bosun.

'Thosea lasta b******ds…they steala or ditcha halfa my frigging deckastoressa,' lamented the storekeeper.

'Oh, hell,' I thought, wondering which request to sort out first. 'Give me strength…'

Then I suddenly realised that strength was indeed coming, but most certainly not from where I expected it, nor quite so welcoming. For, amidst this jabbering and consternation besetting me, I felt a distinct shuddering as the ship surged at her cable. She began swinging alarmingly around her anchor in the increasing teeth of a sudden wind – common in the Mediterranean. I thought perhaps the Shipping Master had listened to the local area forecast, after all. Then one of the Spanish greasers from the engine-room passed me, swearing violently and followed by the second engineer responding enthusiastically. Wondering casually what might be the cause of this loving technical altercation, I drew consolation from the obvious fact it was not only the deck department who yet again seemed to be experiencing a few problems.

By 0900 the launch with the Captain, a mournfully 'bleary-cum-beery-eyed' agent, and our entire crowd of ratings had disappeared, pitching alarmingly in the direction of Haifa and were soon 'losta to sighta' across the crowded anchorage (as the bosun might have commented, had he been available). I made my way wearily to the bridge, anxiously checking our anchor cable on the way and our bearings upon arrival, as the wind spewed its fury to Force 8, gusting 10. Before he had left the ship, the Master had given instructions that if the situation deteriorated, and the vessel showed signs of dragging her anchor, he should be contacted by VHF. Exactly what my gallant Captain thought he could do from nearly a mile's distance from the jetty, and with seven cables of rough water between us, he did not make clear. It seemed that yet again Caridia had picked up the dirty end of the proverbial stick – the story of my life ever since joining the merchant navy. But at least it kept life from becoming boringly dull.

It seemed prudently sensible to phone our 'ginger beers', advising the situation and putting the engines on stand-by – a conversation harvesting its own crop of interesting problems.

'Sorry, Jon,' stated the chief calmly. 'No can do.'

'Oh,' I replied unconvincingly. 'I thought we were supposed to be on 'stand-by' anyway? We may need the bloody things, chief. It's blowing a bit of a Hooley up here…and increasing.'

'Still can't accept the telegraphs. My engines are not ready yet,' was the response.

Stoically I thought in the light of existing conditions it was hardly necessary to explain my reasons, for the motion below must surely be quite noticeable: 'Helpful buggers,' I groaned cynically. 'So much for the engines – don't quite know what the hell we'll do if we start shifting.'

Before even replacing the phone I noticed that the first ship to drag her anchor was a Piraeus-registered cargo vessel called, rather appropriately, *Fast Wind*. I surmised it was typical of the Greeks to have a name for everything – even if, in this case their choice bordered just a little too close for comfort. The 7,000 grt vessel certainly lived up to the speed associated with the strong gale which was by now blowing as she narrowly missed a Singapore registered cargo vessel anchored two ships ahead of us. The Greek whistled down our starboard side, both literally and metaphorically, her siren letting off like a mad thing as she presumably tried to attract attention from the port authorities. She sheered past the Singapore-registered *Giffin* at an alarming rate of knots – so close, in fact, that from parallax on our radar she actually hit the thing, although there was certainly no visible evidence that this had happened. The whistle of the poor old *Giffin* joined in the fun – even if it did express a remarkably peeved tone.

Making a rapid appreciation, from the frantic signalling of *Fast Wind* in the direction of the port office, I radioed ashore explaining the urgency of the situation and asking for tug assistance to help her: assuming (correctly, as it happened) from the fuss being made that she was unable to make VHF radio contact. I then watched helplessly as she headed for the 'putty' below Mount Carmel. It was certain my relief was more than shared by this errant 'Johnny-ship' as two tugs came bustling out of

Haifa and managed to bring her up. It was a very close thing though – a few minutes later and she would have been aground. As it was, the tugs did not have time initially to put or take a wire on board, but both nudged their charge from port and starboard quarters in order to arrest the momentum of her drift, leaving it until she was clear before sorting out who should be made fast fore and aft.

By this time, our ship almost came out in sympathy, for she was swinging wildly to her port anchor and, when I went up onto the forecastle the cable was bucking and kicking uncontrollably. I then discovered that the previous acting Mate had put only three shackles in the water on our port anchor. It was no wonder poor old *Lady Varma* had nearly dragged, so it seemed prudent gradually to let go another generous two shackles allowing the wind to shift the vessel and lead our extra cable over the seabed. Certainly, if we had continued surging at this rate we would have been the next ship to attack the anchorage like a hot knife through proverbial butter. This quietened her considerably. I shuddered at the thought of letting go the other hook, without power on the ship and with all the implications this manoeuvre might attract. Fortunately, and typical of these waters, the wind soon blew itself out and by the time my esteemed Captain returned, with the crew and, joy upon joy, a Second Officer just flown out of England, it had abated to a more-or-less passive Force 4.

Mike Denton and I shook hands and, with immediate recognition, at least on my part, as I recalled meeting him during a change-over aboard the *Countess Elizabeth* in the West India Docks, London when we were both third officers. It was good to see him again, but he seemed a bit subdued for some reason and I was rather perturbed he did not seem to remember the time we had spent on board together. I assumed, admittedly with some reservations (and no thoughts this time of long-dead English schoolmasters), he was probably merely tired. I placed him on anchor watch and, reflecting on things, suggested he make a start checking all navigational publications plus a mountain of ubiquitous chart corrections. In the absence of a third mate, I agreed to check over the lifeboats. Thus we set our own routines on board, hoping that things would gradually sort themselves out.

Twelve days after I, and four days after Mike, had joined the *Lady Varma*, we received orders to go alongside plus instructions for the next stage of the voyage. After completing full discharge in Haifa, we were to proceed down coast to Ashdod, where we would berth immediately and load a full cargo of phosphates for Antwerp. Mike was definitely not the character I remembered. In fact, he was morose, quick-tempered and uncharacteristically unsociable. This was strange because I knew him previously as a very friendly guy. Now, he did not mix much but kept himself to himself, staying largely in his cabin. I expected him to plot our courses to Ashdod but as time passed and this was not done, decided to do the chart work myself in

Right: Opportunity was always taken by the chief officer during calm anchorages and while the ship was on passage to undertake routine deck maintenance. Here, some Spanish deck ratings clean and oil safety chains for the McGregor steel hatch covers (Author's Collection).

Below left: Lowering the cadet on a bosun's chair suspended from a derrick or hoist was an effective method of accurately reading the ship's draught (Courtesy Captain 'Tinker' Taylor).

Below right: The bosun as chief petty officer of the deck crew, with his wide experience, supervised his men from the sharp end (Courtesy Athel Line).

Clearing the decks of rust and then undercoating and painting were perennial tasks aboard all merchant ships (Courtesy BP plc).

the consolation that at least another job was out of the way. At a push the lifeboats could be serviced there before going deep-sea. I had already ordered from the agents the folio of charts necessary for passage from Gibraltar to Antwerp, along with the appropriate Admiralty *Pilots* covering the English Channel and North Sea. I had also instructed the carpenter to fix a lockable glass-faced security door to the keyboard in my office.

One thing Mike did apprise us of was the shipping situation in the UK. I had heard by listening to the small radio I always brought away to sea that there was a massive seamen's strike taking place in the UK. The ratings union had instructed that all members (which was every seaman in the 'closed-shop' situation) following a 'democratic secret ballot', should withdraw labour and go on strike. Mike filled in a few details which had not been broadcast. He had noticed that ships in his home port of Southampton were moored two and three abreast with others laid up throughout virtually all major UK ports plus a few alongside river berths and jetties. The outer anchorages at many ports were filled with ships unable to dock or berth. We discussed this over breakfast one morning with Captain Mitchell making the sober(?) judgement that this action could 'sound the death-knell of the merchant navy as we know it'. Combined with an ever increasing number of dock strikes, it seemed that the country was going through a tricky time. As officers, and with non-British crews, we were not directly affected but, of course without ratings, officers could not take away to sea their British-registered English-manned ships. In our limited understanding of the situation we were very concerned for the sake of both industries, and the wider economic implications these disruptive moves would have on the country.

It was a great moment when the pilot boarded and we made preparations to go alongside. After testing all bridge gear and doing flags I went below to call Mike for stand by, but it soon became apparent that our manna from Heaven was quite paralytic. He had obviously drunk himself to a standstill the previous evening and was not merely incapable – he could not even be roused from his bunk – such was his total stupor. Reporting this to the Master was what is known in the trade as an 'academic exercise' for he and the chief engineer had also been celebrating some joyful event. They were both undoubtedly 'well away' and were happily sharing a jar with the pilot.

As blandly as possible, I reported on Mike's condition and awaited a command decision. I waited a little more…and then a little more, without response. The pilot looked on benignly, while the chief left – presumably to go below. Suggesting that, although his knowledge of English was 'sketchy' the Spanish bosun seemed to know what he was doing on deck, so it might be best to place him in control of the docking operation aft, while chippy came with me forward (as he would anyway) to interpret my commands to the crew. In the absence of any more viable an option and with the Master smiling agreement, I discussed our berthing plan with the pilot and then shot below to explain events to the bosun and carpenter. It was an unusual situation, to say the least, but having reached quite a good working relationship with both CPOs, the bose agreed to have a stab at taking charge aft. It did not require a 1,000-per-cent gift of perception to see he was defintely not a happy mariner over the idea. I drew a diagram 'refreshing' his memory of what wires and ropes to put out, and in which order, and where the pilot stated he wanted the after tug made fast. Then, grabbing chippy went forward to sort out my own tug and warps.

From my grand-stand view on the forecastle head things were interesting. We nearly hit a Swedish ship while leaving the anchorage. Apparently the telegraphed instructions from the bridge were misinterpreted below, causing the ship to go half-ahead instead of half-astern, thus upsetting the pilot's calculations. It was with some alarm, doubtless shared by the helpless Swede, that I saw our ship and theirs closing at a frightening rate of knots. We cleared the forecastle head at break-neck speed, but eventually our ship brought up some three cables short of their port quarter amidst a series of frightening shrieks from their whistle. My berthing crew were falling about with a laughter that sounded as English as it did Spanish, indicating that at least the warped side of maritime senses of humour were compatible. Once alongside, I went aft to see how bose was making out. There was a complete cat's cradle of wire around the port winch drum – the cause of which it did not seem appropriate then to investigate. He had managed really quite well, but gave a firm impression he would not be prepared to do the job on any future occasion which, I supposed, was fair enough. Up on the bridge the Old Man was cursing about the engineers; the problems of speaking to the bosun aft, having to work the telegraphs himself, as well as doing flags and keeping the movement book. I did not recall my heart breaking for him though. The pilot, for some inexplicable reason, could not wait to leave us and was last seen wandering down the gangway muttering something about 'leaving a bloody English mad-house'.

Immediately hatches were opened, we began discharge of the lorry cabs. This meant that I remained on cargo watch until 0800 the next day which meant a tidy twenty-six hours on duty. Still, as we used to say in Keddleston Navigation School before we had began to understand even remotely the implications of the remark 'If you can't stand a joke, then you ought not to have joined'.

While discharging the cabs I had to work systematically round the hatches look-ing out for breaches of safety regulations as the first consideration, pilfering, espe-cially when a 'desirable' cargo was being handled, and reporting any damage to cases and containers to the shippers. I had also, of course, to keep an eye on the watchman, making certain that he was attending moorings and gangway, as well as looking to draught marks (thus ensuring that the ship kept more or less an even trim). The deck crew were also turned to painting the hull during day time, while a few sundry jobs like taking fresh water and loading stores were also added to my list. Strains of LBB on the cadet-training ketch during pre-sea training were always evoked whenever the latter was even considered, let alone mentioned. Whenever I thought back to those days, I still came out in a sweat and wondered if I should ever lay that particu-lar ghost from all those years back. It was also necessary to assist the bosun in sorting out a certain bundle of wire knitting on the after-deck winch, as well as keeping eye on any boats alongside, such as water or bunkering barges, and looking out for dis-charges from the engine-room. There was much to occupy these watches and, in the continuing absence of Mike, I often wished we had the services of another officer, or at least an experienced cadet to help out. We had gangs working only two hatches at that time so discharging our cabs was clearly going to be a lengthy job.

The Master relieved me early and informed me grumpily that the second mate was still drunk:

'I can't tolerate this nonsense, you know. I'm sorry, but he'll be going tomorrow. I've seen the agent and told him to cable the company and arrange for a replacement for him, and a new third officer, to be flown to us before we leave for Ashdod.'

'I don't know why you should sound so fed up,' I thought. 'After all, your own record on the sobriety stakes has not been all that hot and, anyway I'm the one who has had to do all the extra officers' work, additional to my own jobs – and am clearly going to be the one to continue doing so.'

'I just don't understand this at all, Captain,' was what I really said, and I am sure that something of the mystification I felt came over in my voice. 'I've met this second mate before and never heard of him having booze problems. Do you know anything, sir?'

'No, both he and yourself are Ellerton officers while, I of course have been with Empress Shipping for all of my career. I've had a telephone chat through the agents with the marine super in London and there seems to be a rumour that his wife left him a few months ago. But be that as it may the bosses won't put up with much more of this. He'll be out unless he comes to terms with things sharpish.' He also mentioned that the missing third officer was still absent and totally unaccounted for. We both assumed he might have become 'shacked-up' with a female somewhere, but Father advised he had reported him to the police as a deserter.

I felt really concerned about the second mate, but there was little I could do and not much more for me to say. Practical as ever, I merely remarked:

'I'm going to get my head down now, Captain. It would help if you wouldn't mind relieving me until, say, 2000 hours, thus enabling me to get a decent kip. I'd like to pop ashore as well, but frankly feel too knackered to do so.'

Father agreed to this so I turned in and slept for sixteen hours. The problem was, of course, that being overtired I slept too soundly and woke up feeling even more shattered than before I turned in.

Mooring alongside all berths or jetties invariably followed a routine pattern. Intially a line would be lowered attached to a messenger rope into a boat provided specifically for the purpose fore and aft, which would take the line to the berth, where it was made fast to a bollard (Courtesy BP plc).

Right: Meanwhile aboard the ship, three or sometimes four turns were taken usually on a winch or windlass drum end until the warp was taut. It was then adjusted until the pilot and Master declared the ship to be in the correct position along the jetty…
(Courtesy BP plc).

Below: …when the remainder of the lines necesssary to keep the vessel alongside were put out and secured (Courtesy Ministry of Defence).

At 2000 I went on a cargo watch that was to last until 0800 the next day and then, of course, continue into day work. The Old Man had arranged for the electrician to check all crane contacts and to put cargo light clusters into the holds so that the stevedores could work with those cabs that were in the darker recesses. Around 0200 next morning, as I was enjoying a well-earned supper – after having to cook it of course – and a mug of good strong merchant naval-type tea, when there was knock on the cargo-office jalousie. It was an Israeli stevedore complaining, so far as I could understand, that he could not get the crane that serviced number two hatch to work. To say I was mystified was putting it mildly, so I went to investigate.

I pottered along to the crane, but sure enough it was quite dead. My first action on entering the contactor house was to check the fuses, but they seemed all right. Then with devastating logic, I noticed the cause of the problem.

'Ha! Ha!' I said to the uncomprehending foreman. 'You do not expect the crane to work, do you?'

'Please…?' He responded blankly.

'You do not expect the crane to work if you do not switch on the current, do you?'

'Ah?' He grunted, clearly totally mystified.

I tried again. 'The crane will not work because there is no current coming through. You did not switch on the current. Electrical gadgets do not work without someone pumping some frigging juice through them, will they?' I enquired with the mounting exasperation born of a lifetime of unlimited patience, but smiling to take any sting out of my words.

His reaction was totally unexpected to me. Up went his arms in anger and a heavy frown distorted his features.

'What for you…? Why you say "frigging Jews"?. You bloody English ****'s b****d,' he replied vehemently.

'Oh, no!' I tried to explain, thus making the situation worse. 'I didn't say "frigging Jews". I said, "frigging juice", meaning that there is no electric current.'

I was really quite wasting my time.

'Again you say "frigging Jews"!' he exploded. 'You bloody b****d English friggerman – for you, I no work.'

And with this final broadside, and muttering aloud angrily in Hebrew, he stormed out of the contactor house.

When I followed him, suitably chastened and rather subdued, I heard a whistle blow and saw the head stevedore conferring angrily and heatedly with the by-now assembled gangs. Heat waves of pure vitriol blew towards me and, within ten minutes all the men from the other three hatches, along with crane drivers and tally clerks, Uncle Elijah Cobbly and all were storming their outraged passage down the gangway.

Quite inadvertently, and in all innocence, my phonetical phrases had caused a strike.

I left the contactor house feeling totally bemused and walked along the now-deserted main-deck. Whenever my face was seen on the shore-side of the ship it was greeted with howls of derision, which fortunately, perhaps, I could not understand, although I was left in little doubt concerning the meaning. It seemed my presence was like a nautical pariah: unloved, unwanted and totally misunderstood. Thoughts of the reaction from the Captain and his likely comments assailed my mind.

The *Lady Varma* was again like the *Marie Celeste*, but totally abandoned on this occasion by stevedores and dockers, with cranes and derricks swaying in the breeze, and lorry cabs left in total disarray on deck and wharf – with one unfortunate swinging idly, suspended between ship and jetty.

Cutting my losses, I made my way to the galley, keeping to the offside of the vessel, and making a monster pot of tea, settled down to wait the dawn.

It was about 0730 when the Old Man appeared for his pre-breakfast walk prior to relieving me, and met me on the boat-deck.

'Good morning, Mr Caridia. Good morning,' he thundered jovially, obviously having enjoyed a sound night's sleep.

'Ah, yes…er…Good Morning, sir.' I replied cheerfully.

'Captain,' I pondered, 'I'm glad you're in a good mood, but I don't know how long that will last. You've got a mega-normous shock coming your way.'

He glanced at the length of deserted foredeck from our boat-deck, and finally noticed the total lack of activity.

'Cargo delay?' He asked, a mystified note to his voice.

'Yes, that's right, Captain,' I answered, putting off the inevitable moment. Something in my voice attracted from him a closer, more penetrating look.

'Ah…Gone for breakfast, have they?'

I took a deep breath.

'Well, not really, sir. They've sort of stopped work.'

'Sort of "stopped work"?' The puzzled incomprehension sounded in his voice.

In my mind, I went yet again back over the years to my training ship, facing once more the unbridled anger of LBB.

'Weeeelll…They're on strike, actually.' I replied with a measure of confident aplomb. 'After all, sod it. Let the company sack me if they wanted to – plenty of other companies in the merchant navy.'

'On strike? What, in Israel? But that's bloody impossible,' he stated incredulously.

'Well…yes, sir. I know. It's correct, though,' I replied.

He stood there plainly dumbfounded – looking at me intently and expectantly.

Drawing a deep breath, I launched into my rueful explanation of the night's events. His expression deepened and I waited for the explosion, feeling my cadet training was standing me in good stead once more. It would be true to say that, chief officer or not, I was feeling a distinct sense of *déjà vu*. I had travelled similar courses *many* times since my innocent cadet days.

There was a pregnant silence. He looked hard at me, very hard. Then he suddenly started to grin. This developed into a smile and then a roar of laughter for, even though the stoppage of five hours' cargo was serious, the situation that caused it obviously (and thankfully) clearly appealed to his sense of humour.

'Well,' he said at last, 'the agent will be down soon. We'd better explain to him what has happened and get him to sort it out.'

The long-suffering agent, who was quite intelligent even if his English was a bit lacking, also saw the funny side of things. He soon squared matters with the old and new gangs, who remained fermenting still on the jetty. Obviously they had explained to him the nature of the dispute as he came on board, but now he was able to offer my point of view. I went down with him to face my accusers. Apologies were exchanged all round with much laughter, and the cargo discharge resumed. I reported back to the Captain.

'Well,' was his comment, 'it just goes to show, Mr Caridia, just how careful you have to be.'

I could only concur, as I 'cooked the log-book' by referring to the cargo delay as 'a mechanical problem', which I supposed it was – in a circuitous way.

It was fortuitous that diplomatic relations had been restored with our Israeli dockers because the following night's cargo watch also brought its own crop of uniquely peculiar problems. I had been on watch for about three hours when one of the junior engineering officers came rushing out on deck looking for me, stating breathlessly there was a problem below. I queried blandly what might have occurred, after all this approach could mean anything from a case of sodomy amongst the crew to a full-blown maritime emergency. He reminded me they had recently been renovating below, and went on to explain how a duty greaser was finishing off this task, but had been overcome by paint fumes. He had fallen heavily and given his head a nasty blow and was now slumped inside a tank. In the absence of a second mate, the second engineer wanted me to look at the guy. My immediate reaction was to go below and while doing so I suggested the junior phone from the cargo office for an ambulance. I explained he would find a local directory, which the agent had left on the table, even if the Israeli nightwatchman was yet again inexplicably missing. He would have to cope with the language problems as best as he could. I shouted the last instruction while running for the engine-room entrance in the cross alleyway.

When I got there, it was to find the chief and second engineers had already arrived and the task of extricating their man was well in hand. But it was proving really difficult to remove the chap from the tank due to the narrow entrance and cramped conditions. Jim, the second engineer, thanked me for my concern and I headed for the cargo office to see how the junior was getting on. Even before I reached there my Spanish duty watchman came racing along, waving his arms about in a wild panic announcing that the gangway had collapsed. Of course, there was still no sign at all of his Israeli counterpart. My first concern was to ascertain that nobody was actually on the thing before it began its nose-dive. He offered a customary blank look while trying to decide, but eventually confirmed it was providentially empty of people. Just as I nearly arrived there, the same stevedore from the previous evening came to tell me that our number four jumbo crane had cut out leaving the very last lorry cab suspended in mid-air.

My first priority was obviously the injured greaser, which meant that the gangway had to be dealt with before anything else. I indicated to the stevedore to follow me, indicating by sign language and visually what had occurred, realising how attempts at words were quite inadequate for the task in hand. I was obviously only too reluctant to attempt any explanation. He did so, and did so, in a manner of speaking, understanding even more proficiently when he saw the ambulance arrive for the injured man.

The gangway was a real stinker to sort out. It was by now approaching 0100 hours and I had no option but to turn out the bosun and a couple of deck-hands to assist him. I then went along to the crane with the stevedore and checked the fuses, but there was no way in which the breakdown could be determined by my limited knowledge. The situation was quite outside my jurisdiction. Being extremely careful not to mention the word 'juice', or even electric current, I explained briefly that I was unable to help, and the electrician was going to be called. It was proving quite a night for getting people out of their bunks and, racking my brains, I tried to think of a reason for calling the Old Man, without bringing my own professional competence under too much scrutiny, so that he also could join in the fun.

Sadly, this defied my ingenuity so after seeing Lecky appear to do his version of first aid, I went along to see how the gangway party had progressed. By this time the engineers had recovered the greaser and he was lying on a stretcher outside in the cargo office alleyway. I stopped to see if there was anything that could be done to add to his comfort, but he was quite unconscious and, apart from his tortured breathing, appeared as peaceful as the circumstances permitted.

For some inexplicable reason, the shackle pin had worked loose on the gangway and the whole shooting match, including the safety net, had collapsed into a pile of timber and knitting between ship and wharf. The bosun was well advanced in sorting out the muddle and, shortly after I appeared the gangway was rerigged and serviceable. In the normal course of events, I should have gone with the man in the ambulance to the hospital and reported back when he was settled. As I was the only deck officer this was clearly out of the question so one of the juniors was turned to by the second to accompany their man. I was not sorry to see the last of those blasted lorry cabs, nor that particular watch.

When I surfaced the next morning, the weather was bright and sunny, without a cloud in the sky. There were two new faces in the dining saloon. Hooray! Hooray! Great was my rejoicing. Their shoulder-strap epaulettes signified they were another chief and a third officer. I was a bit bemused by the absence of a second mate, with the substitution of a chief, but more preoccupied with the announcement that they had brought from the agent a veritable stack of mail. I noticed also a deck cadet sitting at the cadets' table, who presumably, unless he had cascaded from heaven, had arrived with the other officers. I nodded across to him and told him to pop into my cabin immediately he had finished his meal. After an unusually swift breakfast, at least for me – I liked to dawdle over the final cup of coffee – I went and collected a very promising pile of post from the Old Man's day room. He was, not surprisingly, also over the moon. At long last, he had a full complement of deck officers and, if first impressions were anything to go by (and at sea they generally were, notwithstanding a few knocks along the way) the new mates looked both sober and competent. However, I remained caustically unconvinced at this early stage, bearing in mind how enthusiastic had been my welcome of Mike, the previous Second Officer, and in the light of ensuing events.

'Good morning, Mr Caridia! Good morning!' came Father's customary jovial welcome.

'Hmm,' I thought, 'his button's been well and truly pressed. What delights have we in store now?' It must be understood that my jaundiced temperament, conditioned by years at sea, had not abated over much.

'Well, first of all,' he began. 'The greaser you correctly sent ashore earlier this morning has some slight concussion and they are keeping him in for a while. The agent will look after him, but we hope that he will be able to rejoin before we sail for Ashdod or, at least come to us there.'

Admitting my concerns over the chap, I agreed this was really good news. He continued:

'The junior engineer sent with him, however, has not returned – probably gone on the "toot" somewhere after he left the hospital. The chief's bloody livid.' He paused. 'You have met the newly appointed mates in the saloon over breakfast? They have taken up their duties with immediate effect. You will continue as chief officer and do that job, while the acting chief mate has signed on as first officer and will do the second mate's job. Due to all manner of shortages, the company are not sure what they want you to do upon arrival in London, but you'll definitely leave the ship in Antwerp. Matthew Deering, the new first officer, will take over from you as Mate. He served with Bank Line, you know, and acquired considerable seniority there but has left them because of their inordinately long two- to three-year voyages.' I knew what he meant, for this company was renowned throughout the merchant navy for its lengthy trips. I did not know about plans for the new first officer, not that it was all that important and, as he was obviously fairly new to the company, had never heard of him anyway.

'You did say the other day that you wanted to have a run ashore, I believe?' the Old Man continued. 'Well, take the rest of the day off. When you return, you'll find the ship over at the grain silos. Discharge should not take too long once they get started.' He paused – it was quite a mouthful for him – and he had certainly not given me much opportunity to interrupt.

'Oh, that's great news, sir.' I replied. 'I won't need further encouragement to do precisely each of those things.' I kept my own council regarding the junior's absence. No point in my stirring things up, but I did think it relevant to mention the missing Israeli watchman.

'Oh, the company took him away two nights ago,' was the response. 'I'm sorry, Mr Caridia, I should have told you but with everything happening around us, forgot to do so.'

'Fair enough,' I thought as, grabbing my mail, I left his cabin before another conversation could develop. Even before I reached the seclusion of my own, I had sorted through the dozen or so letters looking for that special one – from Sue. Actually, there were three – joy of joys!

Everything was well at home and the second one included a photograph of Sue. It was funny how Ma-in-Law never seemed to take a decent snap. This one, for example, was at least in focus, but the horizon was about thirty degrees from the true, making Sue look as if either she or the background were tiddly. I ruminated that the chances of making a photographer out of her seemed increasingly remote.

On my way to change into shore clothes I noticed the cadet standing outside my cabin. I made myself known to him and received his introduction. He was called Adrian Bridge and was just into his second year of cadetship, having been at a nautical training ship in the north-west of England before coming away to sea. I was not impressed particularly as he seemed rather obsequious and just a little supercilious. Anyway, I told him to change into working gear and report to the first officer, who would doubtless find something for him to do. I then popped into the second mate's cabin and made myself known to Mat the first mate, told him he had a cadet to look after and to sort out cargo watches between himself and the third, explaining that I was off ashore having been on the ship since her arrival in Israel.

My trip ashore was filled with thoughts of Sue and how much she would have enjoyed just walking, talking and being together here in Israel. I found myself missing her company enormously and, not for the first time recently felt vaguely homesick. It was strange really that although the local girls anywhere in the world were usually incredibly attractive and full of sex appeal, I had always remained faithful to Sue. Not for me, the customary seafarer's 'bordello-ing around in every bordello'. Even though I remained as randy as when I was a young teenager, first 'discovering the delights' as it were, I seemed able now to exercise far more self-control, even if the occasional wet-dreams were still as messy as they had ever been. Despite (or perhaps, in spite(?) of all my efforts, I had been still a virgin when I met her – as also was Sue, a fact discovered…'

These most intimate thoughts were rudely shattered, as was I almost, by the car that pulled up sharp, with squealing brakes and a torrent of screeched abuse from the driver. His comments were in Hebrew but (once more) the meaning was all too clear. Rapidly recovering my wits from a very pleasant reverie, I set about enjoying the remainder of my time ashore. I planned a trip into Acre, just north of Haifa, a place high on my list of 'those to be visited', following an encounter with a member of the St John's Ambulance Brigade while renewing my first-aid certificate a few months previously. I was not disappointed by the ruins, but not very impressed by the Arab population there, who seemed friendly enough but, for some reason a little wary. My subsequent visit to Jerusalem on another day was far more impressive and thoroughly enjoyable.

At 0300 the next day I found myself back in charge on the forecastle while the senior mate went on the bridge in order to gain additional first-hand experience of controlling the ship. The Dutch third mate, who was proving to be quite a character, took charge aft, to the relief of my bosun, so he also could gain additional experience. I placed the cadet with me on the forecastle, putting him to work as a member of the crew. We were to go alongside the cleaning berth before departure as our orders required us to commence loading immediately on arrival at Ashdod. It seemed my first serious cargo plan as chief officer was not going to prove very demanding.

I singled up to a head rope and back-spring forward and instructed Chippy to commence weighing the starboard anchor, which we had lowered to assist in coming alongside. I could hardly believe my eyes as a length of wire came up with the hook, being fouled over the flukes. Using my recently charged VHF set, I explained to the Master what had happened:

'Might I suggest, sir, that we drop the anchor again to shake off the obstruction. It's too dark to ascertain exactly what it is. Probably the remnants of a parted mooring as a previous vessel had come alongside, but it could be a power cable of some kind… perhaps it's better to be sure…?'

With three deck officers available to keep the invariable twelve-hour cargo watches, there was inevitably adequate time alongside or at anchor for shore leave, which was spent in a variety of different ways. Often 'sightseeing', acting as a tourist was a good method of passing away the hours. In Israel this allowed trips to the old city of Acre or to Jerusalem (Courtesy Palphot Ltd).

The Captain and pilot were quite happy to agree we were better rid of it and my suggestion was accepted. I told chippy to let her go and then we reweighed. This time the anchor came up quite clear.

Going alongside the cleaning jetty, on the other side of the harbour near the breakwater, we surged ahead slightly and took the dolphins in way of the engineers' flat on the port side. No bump was felt on the ship at all, but the incident was reported by the linesmen on the quay. I had by this time brought her up with four shackles on the starboard anchor against the dolphins and popped out the customary wire spring and three head ropes.

By the light on the jetty, Father and I were able to make a preliminary assessment of the damage. This turned out to be merely a couple of sharp dents on the port quarter. From the ship's plans we deduced that it was just aft of web frame No. 30, with a second dent in way of the lap weld between Numbers 31 and 32 frames, aft of the port freshwater 'dom' tank after bulkhead. Captain Mitchell suggested we should call in the local Lloyd's surveyor to be on the safe side. So I got hold of the agent to arrange this and, in a later survey, the Lloyd's man suggested welding over the dents and providing a couple of cement boxes before sailing deep-sea, in order to preserve water-tight integrity of the hull. The welding was done very efficiently in Haifa before we set sail and the cement boxes were completed in Ashdod. We certainly had sufficient time. Contrary to information received earlier in Haifa, we did not go alongside immediately upon arrival, but instead spent six days swinging idly around our cable in the anchorage. Of such incidents is seafaring comprised.

I was definitely not enamoured of cadet Bridge. I certainly 'had my apprentice' as the lamentable jingle of early days had suggested, but now I was not so sure. Frankly, I had 'never met a more arrogant little bugger in the whole of my life', as I described him both to the Master and first officer. He was full of his own importance and spoke in far too familiar terms to the too easy-going third mate. I metaphorically stomped on him good and hard which brought him up with a jolt a little, and set him to deckwork tasks with the Spanish bosun for much of his time, merely to get him from under my feet. Comparing notes with both other officers, we agreed that he really did need a lot of hard work to bring him round to that state of mind more appropriate to a cadet and little less like a Master Mariner, a position he was far from achieving. I told the third mate that I insisted the cadet refer to him as 'sir' – something I had never done or heard of with Ellerton's before, and in another unique move cancelled the cadet's two afternoon study periods and academic session with the first officer. I purposefully gave him hell for the one-hour slot on which I took him after breakfast on Saturday mornings, and cancelled all shore leave until he could repeat word-perfect the rule of road I had set him to learn (as was customary for all cadets during weekly chief officer training sessions). When I reported his behaviour to Captain Mitchell, he agreed that from his observations the boy needed 'bringing down a peg or two'. It transpired he was the son of a director of the company and had been offered a cadetship with Empress Shipping purely on that basis. He was undoubtedly capable academically, but I asked the Old Man how he thought the boy had survived his first year with a variety of officers, but received only a shrug of the shoulders in reply. Not much joy there – not that I really expected any.

By 1930 on the seventh day we were safely alongside the phosphates berth, but were unable to start loading because the hold inspectors found remains of grain, clogged, wet and smelly on the beam-bracket spaces in number four lower hold. He found also some soya beans from a previous cargo – oops! – in number two. This had probably been shaken out during heavy weather while crossing the pond from the States, but we had to turn to the crew (and cadet Bridge) anyway, who, with the aid of clusters, swept out all beams and recesses so that we could be passed fit to load. They were not a happy bunch of mariners.

Whether the announcement by two of our Spanish ordinary seamen of their intention to resign upon the vessel's arrival at Antwerp was influenced by this additional work, I do not know, but I had a heated dispute with these two regarding overtime payments and adequacy or inadequacy of same, dependent upon one's point of view. Perhaps my period explaining the articles earlier in Haifa had not after all been totally wasted. It had certainly rebounded on me with considerable interest. That there seemed very few dull moments aboard this hooker was my yet-again rueful reflection, which was shared completely by the second engineer even more vociferously, seeing as he was sorting out similar problems with his own engine-room crew.

Anyway, we commenced loading the next day and, by 1935 hours of the following, had taken aboard 16,015 tonnes of phosphates and prepared the vessel for sea. Johannes, the third mate, had taken the draught all round and found that we had a mean of nearly ten metres.

It was just before sailing that cadet Bridge finally broke down and tearfully confessed that he 'had been a bit of a prig, but was not sure why he had acted so childishly'. In the light of this humble confession, I was quite happy to meet him half-way and to 'test the waters', as it were, to see how things might develop in the future. We had a lengthy heart to heart chat in my cabin and as a result, I reinstated his two study afternoons and teaching session with the first officer. He had been having lengthy chats with the second engineer and Sparks, and I think it was as a direct result of their gentle intervention that the boy had come to his senses. I did not classify the incident as too much of a trauma – at least to me – but was glad that the impasse had been broken. Matthew also was delighted, for he would be taking on this young man once I had left the ship in Antwerp. The Old Man also told me that he had seen 'signs of improvement' in the cadet's attitude so reinforcing my decision to relent. It was not an incident that I regarded as being particularly positive from any point of view and was one I was pleased to relegate to the area of 'experience'.

The next day saw us out at sea with the ship moving easily and comfortably on a course of 286 degrees True and Gyro (T & G). We were keeping traditional merchant naval sea-watches, which meant that I took the Mate's watch so was on the bridge between 0400 and 0800 and from 1600 to 2000 hours each day. This was a useful arrangement because it enabled the bosun to check each morning for the day's maintenance programme and deck work. A steady routine of lookout duties with sights and electronic position fixing, along with assisting on an accrued mountain of ubiquitous chart corrections were soon routines of the day. I had long ago found time to write up the Chief Officer's log-book covering the rough entries for the period from arrival Haifa and had of course kept this updated from then.

The third day out saw a considerable change in the weather that stopped all deck work dead. The wind increased to a north-north-west Force 4–5 and the ship began pitching and rolling moderately, shipping spray and occasional green seas in way of numbers two and three hatches on the starboard side. The visibility was still quite good and an increasing number of vessels were observed as we approached the shipping lanes off Crete. I put the crew to washing and painting accommodation and store-rooms for the chief steward.

By the next day, the wind had increased to Force 7–8 and the barometer fell rapidly. The ship began to pitch and roll severely and we shipped continuous heavy seas over the forecastle head and down the starboard side. We had run into a typical Mediterranean gale: in itself nothing particularly out of the norm nor worse than the kind of sea experienced on virtually any passage. As it was coming from the direction in relation to the ship's head, however, I found it a very unpleasant motion and, for a while, felt slightly ill. As the wind increased to full Storm Force 10, gusting 11, and the vessel pitched and rolled violently, we had to alter course to 310 degrees True until we were well inside the Malta Channel, in order to ease pounding and severe rolling of the vessel.

At 0507 on the fourth day at sea, we experienced a total power failure. Everything died: steering, radar, and gyrocompass. There was a total shut-down with the ship completely hove to at the mercy of the storm. I did not have to call the Captain to the bridge – he was there before I even had a chance to pick up the phone.

'Hmm,' he said laconically. 'Trust this to happen in your watch.'

'Well, yes, sir,' I replied slightly cheekily. 'We have to engineer things for you to do, you know, to stop you becoming bored.'

He took that on the chin quite well really, and relieved me so that I could go to the locker abaft the bridge in order to get out and rig the 'Not Under Command' lights on the monkey-island halyard and wait for the engineers to sort themselves out below...

'What to do now, sir?' I enquired.

'Well...what do you think?' He responded.

'Well, not much we can do, I suppose, except to let it blow itself out. I could get onto the second and obtain a progress report, or, on second thoughts, might be best not to pressure them just yet, but wait for them to contact us when they're ready?' My observation was posed half as statement and half as a question.

'Yes...we'll give them a few more minutes and...'

Before he could finish, the telephone rang. I went across to answer the thing.

'Bridge. Mate here,' I said.

'Ah, second here, Jon,' said the voice. 'Bit of a problem with a generator spilling oil and so overheating. It's the only one running, as we've got the other one dismantled. We're sorting it out, though, if you could let the Old Man know. Be around two to three hours, I reckon.'

I dutifully passed this snippet to my illustrious Captain. We had to hang on really tightly as the rolling of the ship was quite considerable. 40 degrees to one side and 45 degrees to the other, according to the inclinometer. The difference of five degrees was caused by swishing in partially filled tanks below. As the ship rolled, the water had a delaying moment until it rushed over in the opposite direction. I had to admit that since leaving Ashdod the Old Man had laid off the drink to act extremely competently and with authority.

I had been watching through binoculars the lights representing the antics of an approaching cruise liner which seemed to be closing us at a very near collision angle on our starboard quarter. My feelings became increasingly perturbed; the more so as the angle between her masts opened only very gradually. It crossed my mind if she did not alter course soon a very real danger existed she might well clout us. As ever in tense situations, my mind seemed to run along parallel tracks yet again as thoughts of Sue 'thinking positively' on an occasion when she investigated a course in Pelman-ism, while in personal development phase. Luckily, neither lasted very long. Anyway, as I consoled myself, the breakfast menu on that hooker would almost certainly be a damn sight more exotic than ours. I voiced my concerns to Captain Mitchell:

'I think, Captain, that bloody liner over there is closing us too finely?' I half-posed again.

'Yes.' He said bluntly. 'Well, Mr Caridia, what action do you want to take? After all, now you have returned from looking after the NUC lights, I have not relieved you. You're still the officer-of-the-watch, you know.'

'All right, you cunning old devil,' I thought, half-vindictively and half-respectfully. Without voicing my thoughts – yes, I was learning some common sense at last – I grabbed the VHF:

'Liner, fine on our starboard quarter – this is the mv *Lady Varma*, how do you read me, please? Over.'

Silence. It was quite safe to use the thing for this purpose. After all, its range was comparatively limited and, so far as I could see, we were the only two ships around this stretch of the sea. Use of the radar would have been particularly effective in this situation.

'Captain, would you please flash that liner the letter 'Delta' on the Aldis while I continue to attempt radio contact?' I asked.

Give him due, he did not make any comment, but just went over to the lamp and sighted it. Shortly after, I could hear him clicking away happily.

'Little things please little minds,' I quoted to myself, 'while this bigger fool continues, not so much to look on, but to make verbal contact with this floating whorehouse.'

At last the VHF broke into life.

'Halloo…*Hady Warmer*. This is the liner *Brilliant Days*. Receiving you loud and clear. Go to Channel 67, please. Over.'

I went from 16 to 67, as requested.

'Hallo, *Brilliant Days*. This the *Lady Varma*, repeat *Lady Varma*,' I replied, spelling it out the second time phonetically. 'We are showing NUC lights, old chap, with an engine breakdown, and cannot get out of the way. Would you alter for us, please? Over.'

'Bloody ignorant Dago. And what a stupid name for a ship,' I thought vindictively. 'You are the giving-way vessel anyway and, as such, should have altered for us long ago. Anyway. No need to be too unpleasant just yet – see what happens.'

'Hallo, *Laddy Warma*. According to our radar, we should pass clear astern of you.'

Hallo *Rilliant Ways*. Fine, but you are closing us too closely for comfort. I request again, please, would you open up to starboard a little for us, in order to pass well clear beyond our stern.'

Yes *Lady Warmella*. Our plotting shows we will pass clear of your stern, but will open up wider to save embarrassment. Over.' Came the rather caustic reply.

The Old Man, on hearing this, was not impressed.

'Hmm. I agree with you, Mr Caridia. She is closer than I would have considered healthy. Still, it looks as if she is coming round wider now.'

Years of experience told us both that yes, she could have passed very closely astern but, with the entire Meddy at their disposal, a one-mile-or-more closing is by far preferable to the less-than-half we had estimated, especially with the ships yawing so violently in this weather. I responded to the other ship's action and message.

'Thank you, *Brilliant Days*, for opening to a safer passing distance. Much obliged. Pleasant voyage to you. Over and Out.'

'OK, *Laddy Wardma*. Good trip to you also. Over and listening Channel 16. Out.'

'Ships that pass in the night,' said the Old Man.

'Yes, sir. At least this bugger did pass,' I responded with feeling.

Nevertheless, it was a relief, both physical and psychological when, after a couple of hours, the chief engineer phoned to let us know that all was well below that we could now resume our passage.

In consultation with the engineers, we set off gradually at around a hundred revolutions, which was roughly two-thirds our normal cruising rate. I placed my deck man on the helm steering magnetic courses, until the gyrocompass resettled, and told the third mate when he came to relieve the watch to take a few azimuths, ascertaining any error.

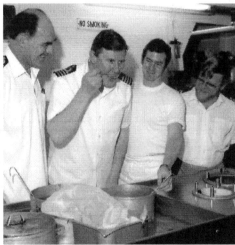

Saturday-morning inspections of the accommodation by the Master and senior officers were routine aboard most merchant ships, which included visits to the galley observing the hygenic way in which food was prepared and often sampling the luncheon fare being provided (Courtesy BP plc).

The next few days passed uneventfully. I was relieved by the third mate at 2000 hours, and can still recall his bubbly personality and inexhaustible fund of dirty stories prior to handing over the watch. He seemed a likeable character and highly competent officer, who was apparently due up for his Dutch Mate's ticket in the near future, hence the Kremlin transferred him within the group for just a short trip, allowing him to leave in Antwerp. He was certainly capable of doing a second mate's job and it seemed he had agreed to do this trip 'as a favour', which sounded very familiar somehow, notwithstanding the mutuality of the arrangement. I was pleased to see the cadet up there with him learning more about his chosen profession and gave him an encouraging word or two before I shot down below. In view of his limited experience, I retained him on deck work with the crew, but told him he was always welcome in the wheelhouse to gain bridge experience – with no pun intended. Saturday-morning sessions were also less of a strain to either of us and he learnt his sections of the collision regulations and was able to discuss sensibly simple applications and implications of these.

We cleared the Sardinian and Algerian coasts and the storm steadily gave up the battle and blew itself out. It had to be in my watch of course that we ran into a fog bank. I was able to call the Old Man – at half past five in the morning.

'Trust you to do this to me, Mr Caridia,' he said. 'I remember you saying the other day that you would hate me to be bored. You've certainly found a real pea-souper for me this time.'

'Do you know, sir, I haven't heard that expression for years. It was a favourite of my mother's,' I said.

'You needn't add insult to injury by dating me *too* much,' he replied, pleasantly, adding, 'There is always a lot of shipping about as we approach Cartagena.'

The shipping, as if to call the Master's bluff, refused to co-operate because, from the time I called him until the end of the watch when the third mate came up, the only ships we saw were all radar-identified only; well over, and passing clear. Still, Department of Transport regulations required me to notify the Captain, and for him to at least make his appearance, in such severely restricted visibility.

It was shortly after I had relieved the first officer the following morning that the radar packed up. I was changing range from three to twelve miles for a look-see, after following a ship down and clear, when the picture faded. I had, of course experienced this kind of mishap before as a very new third so, although very annoying it was not a total shock. Usually, it was found if the thing were left switched off for ten minutes or so, the problem generally solved itself.

By 0445, however, there was still no sign of life. As we were in the busy shipping lanes that approach the Straits of Gibraltar and the visibility was around three to four miles or so, I decided to turn to Sparks with his little box of tricks, to see if he could do anything to rejuvenate the poor old thing. I went to the phone:

'Haaallooo, Rupert,' I murmured with a silky, sexy voice into the mouthpiece. 'Sorry to disturb your nocturnal dreams, about which I shall say no more, but the radar has gone on the blink and, as we are approaching Gib. in not too good vis. it would be useful if you grab your tool – sorry, tools, and pop along to see if you can do anything to help your little friends in the deck department.'

How could he refuse such a desperately loving appeal? Still, it took him one hell of a long time to make his appearance and, when he did, I swear to this day that it was his liver that came through the chartroom door first.

'Jon, what the frig have you been up to now?' He questioned crustily, as if it were my fault.

'Sorry, Rupe.' I said in a consoling tone. 'Here you are, mate, I've brewed a cup of coffee for you, exactly the same as your dear old mum used to make when she dangled you on her knee – just before you joined the *Lady Varma*,' I comforted him.

'Oh, very bloody funny, but thanks for the coffee, you cheeky sod,' was his endearing reply.

I left him to his labour of love and, of course, his coffee and continued my lookout duties. It was coming to the end of my watch when we passed through the Straits, still radarless, I might add, so it was back to the steam-and-coke work of electronic navaids, supported by good old-fashioned visual bearings as a sensible back-up. I let the Old Man know, but he did not grace the wheelhouse with his presence so, in the absence of any problems shippingwise, I left him to it – safe in the knowledge he was always on hand if needed. The strong current caught us as we approached and, boy, we went through the narrows like a cork popping out of a well-shaken gaseous bottle. In fact, we managed at least four knots above our normal cruising speed, even though this was soon lost once we cleared Gibraltar and set course for Cape St Vincent. The third mate was suitably impressed when he saw the run for the watch as I entered it into the log-book upon being relieved.

We had a few problems on passage up the Portuguese and Spanish coasts. The traffic separation zones rounding Ushant had removed much of the potential stress experienced in earlier days, not only in this area, but also up-Channel and in the Dover Strait. I recalled my first voyage as third officer – seemingly light years away – on the *Earl of Gourock* going from the Royal Sovereign light-vessel up towards Dungeness and Dover Strait in the congested waters with ships passing at every conceivable angle (like training ketches, of course) and never quite certain what sort of multi-vessel collision situation would be met until the occasion happened. Watches in those days were rarely completely without incident, but it was an element of the old-time 'bucko-Mate' happy days that I for one was pleased to see ended.

We reached Ushant on schedule and had just given notification of readiness to the company and our engineers when we encountered dense fog. Without mentioning 'pea-soupers', I called the Old Man to the wheelhouse and awaited his instructions. He was very different from the Captain of Israeli days. Clean-shaven and totally sober, he assumed command with a poise and professional competence unrecognisable from the Master of just a few weeks previously. I felt I was seeing the real person behind the drunken facade and, while recalling some psychological talk of Sue's about human metamorphosis, rejoiced in the newly found man. There was little really for either he or I to do all the time other vessels observed their obligations under the collision regs, other, of course, than to maintain a strict lookout by all available means. The radar behaved itself admirably, gyrocompass ticked away merrily and our watches changed without incident. It was tempting for us to be lolled into a sense of false security. Luckily, professionalism paid its own rewards for, just after I had handed over the watch to the third officer and even before I stood down from the bridge, a fishing vessel suddenly cut across our bows from port. I had been watching his progress on the radar along with every other target, but he had kept his course and speed without problem. The first time anyone knew something unusual had occurred was on hearing the third drawing a quick intake of breath, uttering a loud series of justifiable Dutch-cum-English oaths and telling the Old Man, near the forepart of the wheelhouse by the telegraph, to throw the helm hard to starboard. Father's reactions were instinctive and devoid of worries concerning protocol. He shot quickly across to the steering console, knocked out the auto-pilot to manual and threw over the helm. I also moved to the forepart of the wheelhouse awaiting developments and on call from the third or Master upon request. I was also, of course, professionally interested, relying so far only on guesswork, but pretty certain of what had happened. I looked aft as we swung to the impact of helm and engines. Just visible in the thickening gloom was the outline of a trawler. He cleared our stern by only a cable or two, possibly more, but in the heat of the moment it seemed so close, and as the third officer followed him down on the radar reported that he was heading inshore. It was a very close call. Collison had been averted only by the prompt action of the third mate. To say we were all shaken would be an understatement of the first order. I still felt a sense of disquiet once below and it took some time before my metabolism could settle and allow me to sleep. And, tragedy of tragedies, I could not even concentrate properly on my usual pre-snooze read!

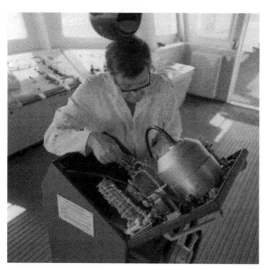

The radio officer was qualified not only for communications control aboard ship, but also to service and repair the main and secondary radar sets. His brief invariably extended to examining and repairing other items of electronic bridge gear, including occasionally servicing defects in the Decca Arkas steering console (Courtesy BP plc).

When next I appeared, to relieve the watch, we were clear on track, although well behind schedule. The fog had cleared and the vessel sailed serenely through a dark night with clear atmosphere and good visibilty. Once the first officer had left the bridge, I checked our position and, finding all in order, settled to a quiet watch. There was much traffic overtaking and being overtaken, but each vessel behaved itself. I guessed we had had our excitement for this particular stretch of the trip but, in the light of recent events, was reluctant to lower my guard. I called the Old Man to the bridge as instructed in his night order book once we had cleared La Basseurelle light-vessel and straightened the vessel on course off Cap Gris Nez. He came up just as we were abeam of Boulogne and chatting quietly I told him about the tide rip I had experienced previously in these waters off the Hinder and Ruytingen banks. He was unaware of this unusual effect on a ship's course and we enjoyed an interesting discussion airing possible causes as thoroughly as we were able. As it happened, the tides behaved themselves according to predictions and it was a few hours later that we approached Flushing pilots. Inevitably, of course due to the weather delay we had lost our berth to another vessel so had to proceed to anchorage. It was two days later that the pilot was waiting for us at Flushing and, by 2300 hours nearly seven days after clearing Gibraltar, we were firmly alongside No. 10, 160 Albert Dock, No. 3.

'Sounds more like the telephone number of the local bordello, doesn't it, Sir?' I wittingly engaged the Old Man.

'Don't you ever let up?' he asked, almost admiringly. 'I would hate to do a seventeen-month voyage with you. I think you'd drive me round the bloody bend. But you will listen to what I have to say to you now,' he concluded authoritatively.

'I have never got round to thanking you for all the extra work you did for me and the ship in Haifa when we were short-handed. I've mentioned this in my report on your Watch-Keeping certificate, if you'd like to collect this from me when you sign off. I'm going to let Captain Biddle, the chief super, know as well. Won't do your career any harm for it to have a boost-up, you know, especially if you intend to stay in the company. The group needs Captains desperately, as you are only too well aware, and I think you might make the grade if you keep your nose clean.' He paused, eyeing me carefully before proceeding, 'and, of course, get a few more years experience – and,' he paused meaningfully, 'your Master's certificate. Anyway, I've also recommended that Ellerton's confirm your promotion to chief officer to help you gain enhanced experience in senior ranks. The super had told me in Haifa that it will be in that post you will rejoin your next ship after a week or two's leave, although I do not know what that will be.'

With that parting broadside he walked off the bridge and down to his cabin, leaving me soberly to pack up the bridge gear – and with one hell of a lot to think about.

At 1530 later that day, I was stood down by the Master to sign off articles, and left the *Lady Varma* at 1700. Travelling to Ostend by taxi, paid for by the agent, I caught the last day-sailing to Dover literally by running down the ramp with all of my gear seconds before the ferry departed.

'That was a close-run thing,' I mused, as I allowed my breath to catch up with me, and as I was once heard to have said in Haifa.

4

PLANE SAILING ON A SUPERTANKER

Captain Henshaw greeted me effusively, urging me into the comfortably padded chair but evoking in me (inevitably I supposed) only ungraciously cynical wonderings: 'What has gone wrong?' and 'What does he want now?' After the engaging trip aboard Ellerton Empress Shipping's *Lady Varma* any future appointment, I felt, could only be an anti-climax. How wrong I was to be proved. Once we were firmly ensconced with a tray of coffee and biscuits his smile grew wider:

'Mr Caridia…Jonathan…' He paused, somewhat dramatically.

'Now is this for effect?' was my immediate spontaneous thought, 'to allow use of my Christian name to register, or has he choked on a biscuit crumb, or is he perhaps drawing breath for an announcement of monumental import? It certainly cannot be promotion to Captain, mindful that I have insufficient sea experience having only just been elevated to chief officer and, equally important, have showed absolutely no enthusiasm in going for Master's…'

'Jonathan. We have for some years now recorded in your personal file, in fact ever since you joined Ellerton's after your first trip as a cadet, your desire for a posting aboard one of the group's tankers. I am pleased to inform you that we are now in a position to appoint you to such a ship. And what a ship. We should like you to serve as Second Officer aboard Ellerton Viscount Tanker Company's 300,000 summer deadweight ton (sdwt) supertanker, or very large crude carrier (VLCC) *Viscount Gwendoline*.

He held up his hand to stop what he clearly recognised would be my instinctive reaction, explaining the move was not demotion, because the directors had instructed their superintendents to confirm my promotion to chief officer within the group and that I would consequently be joining the ship as first officer, on the slightly lower salary scale of that rank, but doing second mate's duties until I had gained wider highly specialised cargo experience and indeed familiarity with this new class of ship. My pause for thought was only momentary. Having awaited a tanker appointment for so long this was my opportunity. I wanted this ship and recognised it would be totally foolhardy to reject the offer. He glanced at me closely during these deliberations, obviously wondering what would be my reaction now 'my bluff had been called'. Without further delay, and with excited images of grand tankers floating across my mind's eye, I confirmed acceptance and enquired further details concerning the vessel and its proposed officers.

Apparently she had recently been launched and was now in the fitting-out berth at Lindo yard of the Odense Steel Shipyard in Denmark. It transpired the ship was fourth in a new breed of group supertankers that would eventually number some fourteen craft. This one was to be the largest, hence flagship of the fleet, with a loaded summer deadweight capacity of 286,000 tons, and some 340 metres or approaching a third of a mile in length, a beam of 180 feet or about sixty metres, and loaded draught of over 22 metres, or about seventy feet. She was a veritable giant compared to anything upon which I had sailed previously, or even with envious eyes merely observed on distant horizons. It seemed the theory behind my appointment was if Captain, ship and I related as forecast then, after a number of tours, each of roughly four months' duration, when all parties considered my experience was sufficient, I would be appointed chief officer in my own right. I would then either sign on another leviathan already in service or (a more remote possibility in view of my forecast recent promotion) stand by and join one of the other vessels whose constructions were under way, shared between yards in Denmark and Japan. There was an experienced Captain on board *Viscount Gwendoline* who had served until recent retirement as fleet Commodore with a major British international oil company, and he was accompanied by supertanker experienced chief officer, chief and second engineers. Were I happy with this offer, then Viscount Tankers would in a few days arrange to fly me to Odense for the final stages of fitting-out for deep-sea; the sea-trials, maiden and second voyages – totalling some six to seven months.

I sat in silence for a moment, overwhelmed as much by the sheer enormity of the ship offered as by the realisation that my constant requests for many years had finally come to fruition. It goes without saying that I was bursting with enthusiasm and excitement on the train home to Sue and could hardly wait to relate my news. That she was pleased for me was obvious, but I sensed also slight vibrations of concern.

In recent years there had been a number of widely publicised horror stories concerning explosions aboard this class of vessel which had resulted in loss of life and extensive damage with, in one case, the ship having sunk. We discussed Sue's very real fears and I did whatever was possible to reassure her, even offering (with bated breath) to cancel the appointment and return to conventional dry-cargo trading. This, of course, was the last thing she wanted. Eventually we agreed I should sail on the good *Viscount* and continue trusting whatever guardian angel had kept me safe at sea so far in the various escapades into which circumstances had frequently projected me. Certainly on occasions these had not been without danger.

So it happened, a couple of weeks later in company with our radio officer and a deck cadet, I found myself after an uneventful flight from Heathrow, aboard a Fokker Friendship aircraft between Copenhagen and Odense, flying directly over the ship we were to join. From the height of a few hundred feet, as we came in to land the first glance showed us a vessel which, quite frankly, looked enormous as she lay at her fitting-out berth. She seemed almost like a small elongated island and I felt a distinct spasm of not exactly fear, but certainly an unexpected wave of apprehension at the thought of actually navigating her at sea and the challenges of practising unfamiliar cargo routines. We were met at the airport by the agent, who promptly whisked us into a minibus and out to the lodging house, about a quarter of a mile from the ship, where we met the Master and other officers already standing – by our supertanker. Captain 'Tommy' Anson was an ex-Commodore Master with the Esso Tanker Company who had graduated to VLCC class ships as these were systematically introduced into that fleet. He greeted us warmly, introducing us to the chief officer, Derek Ellington, and senior engineers, who had been advised that we were joining. We were directed to sparse but comfortable single accommodation before joining the others for supper.

Sparks was a lean fifty-year-old, experienced Marconi Marine man who had served only on cargo ships, product carriers and liners in his previous existence. Jason Ewen-Smith, our cadet, was just nineteen and this would be his third trip to sea. He was an Ellerton Company lad originally from the London Nautical School. He had served previously aboard the Earl class dry-cargo ships for voyages of thirteen and eighteen months respectively, so was certainly not green, and this appointment was his first venture also into tanker life. The third officer was Jeremy Richardson, an Ellerton man until he had been appointed to Viscount's first supertanker *Viscount Angelina*, a vessel of 205,000 sdwt, so he brought with him the experience of some three tours aboard VLCCs. My first meeting with the Captain was extremely favourable. There was yet to be appointed another deck officer, who had experience aboard Caltex Oil's large tankers and would sail as extra chief Mate, so the ship would sail with four navigating officers. I was surprised at this and, seeing my raised eyebrows, Captain Anson assured me that Viscount Tankers made regular appointments of four deck officers to this class of ship, freeing up the Mate for permanent day work of which, he also confirmed with a smile, 'there was aplenty'. The Master impressed as friendly, with that relaxed and engaging personality that emanated from lifelong experience aboard tankers. I could foresee him as a man firmly in control of every situation, and already began to feel respect for his rank and person.

*The cross-section midships deck service piping invariably appeared
confusing upon initial appointment to a supertanker ...*

*...while the distances along, and mass of pipework on the main-deck
proved equally impressive (Author's Collection).*

Above: Inspections of the usual thirty-three cargo tanks were quickly 'taken in the stride' and became a matter of routine within a few days of joining the vessel (Victor Pyrate).

Left: A deck cadet walks aft from the forecastle head along the catwalk, which is a legal requirement allowing safe passage during rough weather (Shell International Trading and Shipping).

Below left: Visual tank inspections following the launching of a VLCC invariably uncovered a number of defects, which were reported to the builders and rectified (Shell International Trading and Shipping).

Joining the ship next day my first impressions were ones of absolute sheer size. If she had appeared large when viewed from the Fokker Friendship, seen closer she was gigantic. As the minibus drew alongside, we were confronted by a cliff of black steel. We left the bus and entered a makeshift lift that took us on a lengthy journey to the main-deck. As the lift brought my eye to deck level, I was confronted by a maze of massive blue-grey piping behind which 'grew' an enormous expanse of white accommodation, adorned with a strident red 'no smoking' notice splattered across the front. I mentioned to Jason, our subdued cadet, 'Let alone the Mate, there appears to be work aplenty to keep us all busy with this little lot,' as a relief to feelings of complete awe aroused by the sheer immensity of everything around me. The view of the main-deck leading to a distant forecastle was almost overwhelming, spreading into a seemingly distant landscape. My thoughts began to freeze again at the idea of taking this small island to sea. The very notion seemed preposterous. We walked towards the accommodation, feeling totally insignificant alongside the four 5-metre-high cargo pipes alongside a catwalk surmounted by a series of nine red fire monitors.

On entering the accommodation block and taking the lift to the navigating officers' cabins below the wheelhouse the Old Man chattered away happily, plainly in his element and seemingly unaware of the effect his command was having on at least three of his officers. Entering my cabin, sandwiched between that of the first and third mates and opposite to the jalousie leading to the wheelhouse, the idea of spaciousness was perpetuated. A double-sized bunk and large blue Formica-topped desk, adorned by a lonely telephone and angle-bracket lamp confronted me. There was a blue softly covered armchair and settee, or 'day bed', as we at sea referred to the thing, with a toilet-cum-shower room leading off to the port side. Two large windows offered a panoramic view over the foredeck, which lost nothing in dimension when seen from above. In fact, about two-thirds of the ship forward was spread out before me and I felt lost by the maze of pipework, separated by a wide catwalk, with white derrick arms and what could only be described as a series of lamp-posts (for that is what they were) heading to the far-away forecastle head.

My reverie was broken by the sudden appearance of Derek popping in from his suite of rooms on the port side of our deck and throwing sets of General Arrangement and Capacity plans onto my previously lonely desk. He invited me to go to the wheelhouse and 'get my series of shocks over with at once'. I knew only too well what he meant, but it was reassuring to appreciate someone else understood the maelstrom of thoughts doing a tidal race in my mind. He continued, 'The plans are for you to keep and are provided for each deck officer by the Lindo yard.' He paused, eyeing me pensively before continuing, 'Don't worry, Jon, you'll soon get used to her. Especially once we are under way, for you'll be surprised how the sea will cut her down to acceptable proportions. You'll soon find she'll handle more or less like other ships, although perhaps a bit slower than you'll have been used to. You must remember that you have moved on a bit from your dry cargo carriers. In the meantime, after your wheelhouse visit, look through the plans there, and then go on deck and acclimatise yourself with the vessel. Take the cadet with you and go everywhere, finding your way about her and starting the process of learning the function of the deck cargo and service pipes, remembering that tomorrow you'll be "down to work".'

As instructed, I went up the companionway to the bridge, on the next upward deck, already prepared for the vista that would doubtless be stretched out before me. The chart table fronted by a thick black curtain confronted me as I entered but the latest Mark 21 Decca Navigator and ubiquitous Marconi Lodestone direction-finder were identifiable at a glance – along with many familiar navigational instruments and the traditional poised angle lamp. Somehow they made me feel more a part of this colossal venture. Captain Anson was on the starboard side of the massive wheelhouse explaining things to the cadet, so I simply moved in and enjoyed listening to his explanation of the salient features of this very impressive tanker. He glanced up and smiled as I joined them.

'Don't be concerned, Mr Caridia, about the size of the ship. You will soon adjust to that, more quickly than you think,' was his reassuring comment to me.

Returning later to my cabin, I moved the telephone and spread out the large General Arrangement plan on top of the Capacity plan across my desk, noticing that their four-feet lengths fitted comfortably onto the available space, and intently studied them alternately. Reassuringly they were little different to any other plans, but the ship's third-of-a-mile length and 262 feet or 80 metres or so from keel to top of funnel still seemed enormous. From the plans, I deduced that the cargo tanks consisted of five mains, each with two port and starboard wings, and two slop tanks aft to collect the residue from tank-cleaning operations, which was later discharged ashore, or, perhaps, had new cargo loaded on top. There was a separate ballasting system with its own sets of powerful pumps, with numbers two port and starboard wing tanks being sub-divided, with the after parts designated for permanent ballast, thus never used for cargo. Two of the main cargo tanks were also designated for extra ballast water in the event of need caused by excessively heavy weather. The four main cargo pumps collectively, once worked up gradually, discharged at a rate of ten thousand tonnes per hour, which meant theoretically the VLCC could discharge her full load in about thirty hours – although events proved this was rarely achieved in practice.

By the end of my studies, I realised that my stock of superlatives had run dry, and started from that moment to view my new appointment more objectively. About twenty minutes later, I went past the Master's generously lavish suite of cabins on the starboard side of our deck, to the cadets' cabins running aft, and invited Jason to join me in venturing forth for our 'recce'.

It took us two solid hours to complete visiting the main-deck, about which we walked for a good hour or more before venturing below in number two centre, the largest cargo tank on the ship, relating much that we had seen on the General Arrangement plan to the reality before us. Climbing over the tank coaming and descending the ladder leading below was an eerie feeling. The bottom of the tank seemed 'one hell of a way below', as Jason commented breathlessly, probably more from awe than effort as we took the first steps downwards. A series of vertically staggered ladders, each with its small landing, offered opportunity to glance around at the tank construction. Obviously we had both seen diagrams of tankers previously, but it was interesting to see for ourselves the girders, swash bulkheads and brackets. Light shone feebly in beams from openings for the tank-cleaning machines as well as from the tank top entrance, so the scene was not in gloomy darkness, but painted in an almost spectral light, enhancing the cathedral-type atmosphere. I estimated (probably pretty accurately) that one of our smaller cathedrals, such as Rochester, could easily fit into this cavernous hole. Once we reached the bottom below the stringers and started to walk about examining the construction, the feeling of awe increased. Yet again, the very idea of taking this monster vessel away to sea, from all that we had seen during our morning, taxed my imagination. I could think of no improvement on my earlier comment of 'simply preposterous', so making mockery of my earlier good intention 'to be objective'! In order to reach the next section we had to clamber through manholes which separated the various tank verticals. All too soon, after we had been through twenty or more of these, it became second nature to twist our bodies into contortions by putting through one leg first, following this with a twisted trunk and finishing off with the remaining leg. Clambering up the tank ladder was exhausting and we needed every landing to retrieve our breath. It must have taken us all of five minutes to reach the vast main-deck which, after the comparative scope of the tank, still seemed extensive. Looking down from the forecastle head, the distance to the jetty seemed immense and the superstructure aft appeared quite diminutive. The accommodation block loomed high above as we stood in front of the Butterworth locker by the manifolds, while the way to the forecastle head in the opposite direction again seemed an impossible distance. We compared notes like a couple of excited schoolboys as we concluded our trip with a visit to the funnel top. By the time of reporting to the Mate's suite, we had visited just about every deck compartment space there was and it was time to leave the ship and go back to our lodgings for lunch. The galley and crew accommodation were not yet ready for handing over, so we would be unable to take meals on board for the next few days. To keep 'body and soul together', we had equipped ourselves with thermos flasks and biscuits so something of a mid-morning/afternoon 'stand-easy' was possible as and when, wherever we found ourselves ready.

The conversation over lunch inevitably ranged about 'the ship'. We compared notes and listened to the Master's observations. I declared to Derek that the cadet and I were ready to do something a bit more constructive than merely walk the deck once back on board that afternoon, but was told that first it would be more profitable for us to visit the engine-room, taking in those very few places which are a deck officer's responsibility in the chief's equally impressive domain. Two particular aspects I recall were entering the steering gear compartment, and then wandering around looking in on the rudder pintle with its series of lubricating tubes at the top of the rudder. The distance along the propeller shaft seemed to go on for ever, while the six-cylinder steam-turbine engine towered through four decks.

The senior officers were quite correct: by the end of the day a myriad of observations and emotions led to a strange feeling of familiarity consistent with one aspect of the Mate's and Captain Anson's 'cutting the vessel down to size'. This gave me a boost in confidence that other things mentioned such as, particularly for me, watch-keeping at sea aboard such a monster would be conquered equally automatically. Thinking back to our day, I felt that seeing the whole vista of ship and surrounding fitting-out berth from the seagull's view at the top of the funnel, it was unlikely that familiarity with 'my supertanker' would be allowed to degenerate into contempt.

The cadet was turned to next day and given spaces on the foredeck and an instrument designed to test the thickness of paint. He was to go about the allotted portions and take notes of his readings, comparing these afterwards with a maker's manual in the Mate's office, where the specifications for thickness on each part of the deck were recorded. My job was to take my brand new notebook and go around the deck, looking for anything which appeared it might need attention from the dockyard. I was to mark these with a piece of chalk and note them, afterwards handing the list to Derek who would add them to a growing sheet of other items and point them out to a representative of the builders to 'attend and mend'. It was a pretty wide brief and I set off quite happily, even if blissfully unaware of what I was really supposed to be doing. I soon found out. My meanderings within a couple of minutes found an entrance to a wing tank for a Butterworth portable cleaning machine which had over it a piece of metal protruding from a nearby pipe support. It had not been completely cut away and would prevent the machine from being lowered. Once I had focussed on the possibilities open to my piece of chalk and notebook, my enthusiasm knew few bounds, and before long I had recorded a number of similar obstructions and overlaps. The same afternoon involved inspection of numbers one and three port-side wing tanks, where in number one I noticed a number of buckled plates. By the end of the day, moving around inside the tanks was second nature.

Next morning, Derek instructed me to inspect the web framework of the ballast tanks aft. This entailed taking a specially constructed gas-proof torch, stuffing

Gaining access to inspect ballast tank areas was through a rat-hole in the main-deck. Moving around the confined spaces proved cramped and claustrophobic in the protective gear that it was essential to wear (BP plc and Jotun Paints (Europe) Ltd).

my boilersuit pockets with spare bulbs, batteries and a ball of small stuff similar to string, plus a packet of white chalks. Once I lowered myself through the rat-hole on the main-deck aft of the accommodation port side, with the cadet standing by on deck, I then descended the various layers through a system of subsequent manholes and rat-holes, tying my ball of string to the entrance and marking the way back with a chalk arrow. My mnemonic 'arrow heads point to safety' helped me keep a sense of direction in what was otherwise pitch-darkness. It helped me also to prevent a rising panic and so retain my sanity. I found the experience totally disorientating and perhaps one of the loneliest jobs I had ever undertaken. I was seeking for any 'apparently noticeable defects', which covered as pretty wide a briefing as my previous deck meanderings. Certainly, so far as I could ascertain, all was in order, but it was with a total sense of joy that I followed my string- and chalk-trail back to the normality of the main-deck. My venture below had taken me just under two hours, I was surprised to note, but was reassured that on the starboard side the third mate was doing a similar contortionist job under the passing eye of Peter Dawson, the newly appointed extra chief officer. Jeremy also reported similar claustrophobic feelings to my own.

It was later the next evening that the Old Man informed us we could move aboard in about four days' time even though the ship would not have been formally handed over from the yard to the owners. Everything would be ready for us to join by then, as that was the day the crew were due, flying in from Pakistan and Indian ports of Calcutta and Goa. It seemed that we would soon be back to sea-going routines, an exciting thought which appealed to me immensely. Contrary to his forecast, it was only two days later that the yard ship-owners announced we could move aboard the next day. We greeted the news with unrestrained joy. We were fed up with living in lodgings and catering for ourselves, particularly as the price of food in Denmark was twice or even three times the cost of a similar item in England. It was annoying to keep asking the agent for additional funds to help us maintain body and soul. We were also equally tired of having to make time to buy groceries and meats and then take it in turns to cook the stuff in the ridiculously small kitchen and then, of course, wash up the utensils and clear these away afterwards. I supposed that we had all become accustomed to being waited on at sea in the 'manner of officers and gentlemen' and had so become delightfully lazy over such chores. Much as we were tempted, we could not realistically leave it all to the cadet to do (although he received something approaching a generous lion's share).

I was busy over the next few days sorting out navigational books, instruments and a ship's technical deck library in the wheelhouse, as well as composing brand-new chart folios from the accumulated mass of nautical publications that arrived in two containers, which included also steward's dry stores, paint and general deck stores. When the doors of the first were opened on deck we could not believe our eyes that everything was jumbled in together with no semblance of order. We had to rake everything out and sort it in piles on deck. We thanked our lucky stars that the weather was warm and dry, baulking at the very idea of doing this sort of job with strong winds and heavy rain descending upon us. As it was, it took us all of two days before we emptied the damn things and it was annoying having to reload and lock them up at lunchtime and overnight, protecting the stores from the covetous eyes of sundry yard workers. Fortunately there was a large deck trolley which helped enormously with the task and provided our cadet with considerable steering experience, while the third mate stood on police duty as we navigated between accommodation block and containers. As it was, we left much of the deck stores locked away until we had a few ratings on board. The lift from main-deck to wheelhouse proved invaluable, for the packages were of awkward shape and heavy. All of the nautical publications and instruments I left for the arrival of our deck crew.

During sea-trials all gear was tested thoroughly including the fire-fighting monitors and equipment, both for water use and foam (BP plc).

Within a few days all officers and crew had shaken down and settled into regular shipboard routines. Numerous 'teething troubles' had been ironed out in all departments and it was good to have a working galley and catering department under the excellent control of an English purser, and highly competent Goanese butler. Our officers' steward was quite superb and looked after us in the manner to which we Ellerton men at least had become accustomed.

Ten days after we had been in Odense, the ship prepared for sea trials under the command of a Danish Captain, officers and ratings. I found their presence extremely useful while alongside and later under way for it was professionally encouraging to have experienced supertanker officers with whom to discuss such things as turning circles, timings for ship response to helm and engines, and numerous technical niceties. Sea trials were conducted by belting around the Kattegat testing everything that was capable of being tested: fire hoses with water and foam, all cargo gear including manifold connections, pumps and valves; the entire engine-room equipment not forgetting main steam turbine engine, and generators, with auxiliary machinery. We ran the windlass and all winches, and filled/emptied all cargo and ballast tanks beyond capacity so that sea water ran over the main-deck. Upon departure for trials, it was interestingly instructive for me to watch the Second Officer from the yard take charge aft with his crew of Danish seafarers. I took my tindal (or assistant bosun) aft with me for observation purposes as he would assist me in charge of the khalasi seamen who would constitute my mooring party. I had noticed from my inspections that conventional rope and chain stoppers were not used

The view from the wheelhouse on a supertanker was uncluttered proving very useful during visual watch-keeping and lookout duties, compared with that from the bridge of a dry-cargo vessel where masts, cranes and derricks created a number of 'blind sectors' (Author's Collection).

on a ship this size, but that all mooring wires and ropes were attached permanently to self-tensioning winch drums. It was strange initially to handle plaited eight-inch, eight-stranded mooring ropes, with four alternate left-hand and right-hand strands that allegedly would not kink. They may have indeed had that advantage but later they proved extremely heavy when wet. Massive 'cobras', or rope and cable mixed wire, acted as a forward and aft back spring possessing sufficient flexibility with a considerably strong breaking strain. Being accustomed to mainly three-inch nylon with their breaking strain of twelve tons, or polypropylene with a breaking strain of eight tons that had superseded manila and sisal ropes in general use aboard most deep-sea ships by now, these monsters were a further initial surprise. After my observation visit, I was confident, however, that the idea of handling the situation aft would soon be mastered, which was just as well seeing the next time we were in action aft I would be in charge of things, responsible to the Master. All docking and tug operations would be taken far more slowly than with a smaller ship, not the least of the reasons being the broad expanse of after-deck presenting difficulties in keeping an eye simultaneously on everything taking place.

We returned to anchorage off Helsingor and the Master and chief engineer pronounced they were satisfied with things in most respects. To the chagrin of Sparks and the engineering officers who for some reason had been excluded apart from the chief and second, we deck officers, including the cadet, were invited to the handing-over ceremony and sumptuous dinner party with a ready flow of alcoholic drinks. It was a feast *extraordinaire*, as the French would doubtless have pronounced the lavish meal, rightly celebrating taking into Ellerton's Viscount Line Tanker fleet the good ship *Viscount Gwendoline*. We were joined for this by the chairman and board of directors of both Ellerton's and Viscount Tankers, along with numerous superintendents, including our own direct bosses, although the cadet super was absent sorting out a serious problem aboard one of the company's cargo ships in the Japanese port of Sasebo.

We changed national flags from Denmark to the Red Ensign and next day, eleven days after joining the tanker, signed articles. The time we had spent working aboard, 'standing by', was recorded in a special section in the centre of our discharge books so that the sea-time could be accredited for examination purposes. This was particularly important for those of us who still had certificates of competency looming ahead. For much of the next three days until the tanker proceeded on her maiden voyage to the Arabian Gulf (as it was now known) for loading our first cargo, I was busy sorting out the long-awaited nautical publications from those 'damned containers' as we termed the conveyances, and also preparing voyage plans along with their essential chart work. Once we sailed, I held the traditional 1200–1600 and 0000–0400 second mate's navigational watches but was on duty forward with the Mate for weighing anchor. This took an inordinate amount of time, and confirmed my view while watching the Danish Second Officer at work aft that many operations which had appeared so 'slick' on smaller vessels certainly would take at least twice the time on these monsters – something I was well able to live with seeing that it could not be changed. Once stood down from the forecastle I was on watch while we navigated the Kattegat with the pilot, while occasionally Captain Anson popped into the wheelhouse to 'see how things were going'.

We dropped the pilot at the station off Skagen and settled to seagoing routines. It was a strange feeling to be on the bridge alone with just my secunny as lookout. The expanse from port to starboard wings and of the foredeck ahead still seemed enormous. Navigational routines were reassuringly familiar, and it was quite easy to settle to radar and visual lookout duties interspersed with 'putting a dot on the chart' every thirty minutes. I quickly found, as we rounded Skagen point leading from the Kattegat into the Skagerrak, and shortly afterwards into the North Sea, that the supertanker indeed handled like any other vessel, as I had been told. That she required much more thought before taking any action to alter course was also true, for the ship initially was slow to respond to her helm. Once she gained slight momentum and answered, she came round fairly quickly and required counter-helm almost immediately to bring her up and retain control. Very often during this (and subsequent) voyages, I knocked her off auto-pilot, or 'Mad Mike', and steered her myself, mainly to test the reaction on the helm so physically gaining a 'feel' for the vessel.

While not on bridge-watches the second day out, I established a work pattern which lasted for the remainder of my time aboard. I turned to for a few hours each day, engaged on various administrative or operational duties: on one occasion with the serang and cassab tallying the after stores lockers; variously with the pump-man in the pump-room in the depths of the ship forward of the accommodation block, on stand-by operating valves in the cargo control room while we shifted ballast water between tanks, and frequently merely familiarising myself with various gear and equipment. Often I worked with the Master or Mate on deck supervising the crew at various tasks or, for much of the time, checking the Whessoe gauges which indicated the ullage (or how much oil/water was not in individual tanks!), which had an irritating tendency to stick. Weekly fire and boat stations were exactly the same as on board any ship. I was in charge of the Mate's boat, while he was either on station with the Master in the wheelhouse, or holding a watching brief on the main-deck, to which we invariably lowered the boats, as opposed to merely swinging them out. My second emergency duty was in charge of a five-crew party taken from the deck and catering departments and we exercised fire party drills at the monitors along the catwalk. For variety, we also practised smoke helmet and resuscitation drills, or were in various parts of the ship practising with the stretchers or hoses/extinguishers. On one occasion we lowered a stretcher down one of the tanks and brought up a straw-filled dummy called Charlie – a formidable exercise which brought back a train of unpleasant memories from a previous voyage between Russia and Cuba where a docker had been killed. For our maiden voyage we carried a group of Finnish workers who ferried around the tanks in a rubber boat fitting zinc anodes to each permanent ballast tank. We also carried a guarantee chief engineering officer from the builders' yard whose job was to iron out any difficulties occurring largely in the engine-room, although his brief extended to any other department where 'contingencies' might occur.

We encountered thick fog on our maiden voyage while thirty miles off Orfordness, approaching the northern part of the Dover Strait, which continued throughout the passage off Dover past the Varne and Dungeness. I was off watch by this time, but the Master was in the wheelhouse virtually continuously. All bridge gear worked extremely well, and we were particularly pleased with the Marconi main radar. This was sufficiently sensitive in calm seas and low range to detect gulls taking off from the water. It was fascinating to see the 'V'-shaped echo returned, while on this low half-mile range the entire outline of the tanker appeared as a distinct trace. With the height of the scanner some two hundred feet above (or about 62 metres) the waterline, depending of course on the draught, we picked up ship targets at seventeen miles or more, while solid land-masses frequently came in at maximum range outside the space beyond the maximum ring on the physical edge of the screen!

The chief officer had no tank-cleaning duties, of course, during our maiden voyage but, from the first day, tested various instruments and operated the tanks, supervised his cadet and did the hundred-and-three jobs normally within his orbit. Such a range of duties kept him busy and very much out of mischief. We three deck officers took the normal navigational watches, but there were few scares or problems. The ship was indeed being 'cut down to size' but personally I at least never became completely familiar with this vast bulk of ship and always felt a sense of awe when looking ahead from the wheelhouse windows and seeing the vast expanse of foredeck. The forecastle was such a long distance away that when the crew were working there (or anywhere on the main-deck forward of the manifolds, for that matter) I needed the binoculars to keep an eye on their safety. At night the check light from the main-mast could often, especially in my early days, be mistaken for the stern light of another ship because it was so far away. Even after a couple of months, during the occasional instinctively quick 'shuftie' around the horizon, a glimpse of this still caused a momentary attack of palpitations, until once again common-sense prevailed.

We started taking sights once the Decca range had been exceeded in the Bay of Biscay, which produced a further subtle realisation of the size of this ship. Normally on a dry-cargo ship the height of eye above the sea would be around 50 feet, or 16 metres, but on the VLCC in ballast it was 110 feet, or 34 metres. This measurement was essential for corrections to sextant observations while making celestial astronomical sight reductions.

We ran into a Force 8, gusting 9 or 10 south-westerly in the Bay of Biscay, which was interesting to test the response of the ship to rough seas. I was on watch when the first breezes developed within a couple of hours into a full storm and was not surprised to find that the vessel rolled moderately in ballast but pitched quite violently. As I mentioned to Jason, who was in the wheelhouse on duty, 'We'll have to ease her revs down a little or we could pound the forepart to pieces', telling him to get the engine-room on the phone so that I could inform the duty engineer of events. There was a continuous problem of vibration when the ship was in ballast, which was so severe that it introduced minor errors in the sextants until we pleaded with the engineers to provide us with thick sorbo wedges upon which to lay 'our trusty guns' to cushion these adverse effects. They readily complied, having at least a vested interest in seeing the ship make somewhere near her destination. Captain Anson often popped on and off the bridge sorting out paperwork and stopping for a casual chat. The more I had dealings with him, the more I respected the man. He never swore or used bad language, which was unprecedented for a mariner, but if something ruffled his feathers a little he would simply say, 'Oh, my goodness, Mr Caridia…' and then comment on whatever it was that had aroused his ire. It was the weather on this occasion which attracted his interest and he agreed with the action I had already taken to reduce speed, but suggested a further reduction in revs 'to be on the safe side'.

My first stand-by for coming alongside Las Palmas passed without incident. Once stations had been called, I went aft and saw that my tindal had already organised my crew and patiently awaited orders as these were relayed from the wheelhouse via the handy 'walkie-talkie' two-way radio set. We took a tug aft in precisely the usual way and then ran out our lines to the waterline for the boats to take ashore. Once the back spring was made fast I winched this in from the drum and made variations as the ship closed the jetty or according to instructions (literally) 'from above'. The six other warps followed and within an hour or so the vessel was in position and made fast. We called in at this port for bunkers as they were considerably cheaper here and more convenient than taking them from a UK or continental port.

On my first passage off Sierra Leone I witnessed two fishing fleets up ahead, whose haphazard wanderings around the ocean made their courses difficult to determine accurately, so I continued to hold my course and speed until the situation clarified itself. By then, of course, it was too late to make any bold alteration, and I found the fleets suddenly altered course and converged instead of continuing to diverge, with the result that we went through the middle of both! Captain Anson, having a chat with the chief in his own day cabin, suddenly looked up in the middle of conversation and realised that he was looking directly at a trawler seemingly very close on the starboard side. Shifting his glance forward, he saw others ahead and on the port side at varying angles. Momentarily forgetting all about his plans for the garden next time home, he came up into the wheelhouse to see what was happening only to find his ship surrounded by a complete vista of fishing vessels. I was aware of the wheelhouse door opening but was concentrating to such an extent on moving this massive tanker in between the trawlers that I did not even turn round. Sparks (whom I subconsciously thought it was) and his weather reports suddenly seemed small fry. The Master apparently stood by the chart table observing but not saying anything, obviously ready to step in if it seemed necessary for him to do so. It was a strange experience and I was grateful that I had taken the helm earlier for rounding the coast and course alterations and, as my duty man was below calling his relief, I felt very confident altering course manually. I still retained much respect by the manner and speed in which this large ship manoeuvred within arcs of ten or twenty degrees of port-to-starboard helm. Seemingly a lifetime later the last trawler crossed our starboard bow and I visibly relaxed, catching sight of the Master as I did so. By then, the extra chief officer had appeared to relieve the watch and both he and Captain Anson just stood there looking at me silently, as well they might. It was obvious that now reaction had set in I was visibly shaken, so the Master simply told me to write up the log-book and then hand over the watch, and go below. When in my cabin below *en route* to the duty mess for a slice or two of buttered toast and a healthy cup of tea, my stomach felt as if 'the butterflies were turning somersaults' and my mouth was very dry. It was later, while coming for a post-midnight trip to his bridge for a cup of thick ship's-speciality cocoa and a chat before turning in, that he asked the inevitable question:

'Oh, my goodness, Mr Caridia, what happened earlier this afternoon, then?'

'It was really quite simple, sir. I made an error and misjudged the situation.'

'You know what you should have done?'

'Oh, yes, Captain. I should have opened wide to starboard earlier and left them to sort themselves out and not become involved.'

'Yes, well, hmm. Well, you'll know another time, won't you?'

There did not seem to be much more to say, and the situation was allowed (to my relief) to die a natural death. I at least learnt more about the handling capabilities of the ship, which would stand me in good stead with future manoeuvrings, but it was a hard lesson to have learned in that manner – even if the circumstances were entirely of my own making.

The shipping situation paralleling the African coast remained very busy with high densities of assorted vessels, mostly passing open to port but with plenty of diverse crossing situations requiring more immediate attention and often action. Running down the coast off Columbine light heading towards Cape Town, I saw ahead a col-

Taking stores from a helicopter while under way off Cape Town was far more efficient than the old launch service, and prevented the ship from slowing down or even stopping in bad weather to provide a safety lee for the transfer operation (BP plc).

lection of cargo ships almost in accidental convoy and, with a previous lesson learnt, altered course to starboard taking the entire fleet down our port side. It was appreciated how much the height of the radar scanner above the sea-level detected targets early, giving ample time to deduce possible courses and distances and for any necessary avoiding action to be taken almost imperceptibly by altering our course only a few degrees.

Passing Cape Town saw the arrival of a helicopter with stores and mail, plus a change of films and library. It was interesting to pick up the plane on the radar and watch the echo zooming across the PPI on the screen. Captain Anson told us that the helicopter was a new arrival, for previously on his visits to this port the ship had hove to in order for a launch to come alongside and perform the same operation at a much greater delay to the ship, something of the order of two or three hours by the time the vessel had reduced revolutions and then increased afterwards once the thirty-minute operation with the launch was over.

The main radar, our pride and delight, decided to pack up just as we cleared the Strait of Hormuz, or 'Quoins', as it was known to 'tanker types', marking the entrance-cum-exit to the Gulf, and we set our course towards Kharg Island for our first loading. Sparks came and gave it some first aid but the poor old thing failed to respond reliably. Luckily, we had the Marconi secondary radar for navigation and collision avoidance but we were by now well-spoiled with the sophistication of the newer model.

'Oh, my goodness, Mr Caridia, it is like driving a Mini-Minor after a Rolls Royce' was the Old Man's accurate description of the situation. We sent a radio message ahead hoping that the manufacturers' agent could send a technician out to the vessel upon arrival.

A direct effect on the secondary radar PPI caused by atmospheric instability had disturbing consequences, especially for me, new to navigating these large ships within the Arabian Gulf. An echo would be detected directly ahead, moving down the heading marker so indicating the presence of a vessel under way directly ahead towards us, only to disappear when it came to within a couple of miles of the centre-spot of the screen. Initially, I found the experience most unnerving in the conditions of poor visibility frequently experienced when visual contact with binoculars was impossible, and occasionally came very close to altering course to starboard for what was, after all, a spurious, non-existent echo that suddenly faded!

Coming alongside any port was usually a slower operation than aboard smaller vessels requiring much patience and professionalism. Self-tensioning winches were the norm as the wire and ropes were too heavy to be used with bitts and stoppers in the conventional way aboard smaller vessels (BP plc).

On our maiden voyage, coming alongside the jetty at Kharg Island after a couple of days at anchor was a nightmare. It was, of course, my second stand-by aft and was celebrated by the shore-side lines party entering a 'go-slow' for some reason never satisfactorily explained but something to do with overtime payments. It meant that our berthing operation lasted for a phenomenal five hours. It was difficult to comprehend why the men were there one minute to accept our lines and then disappeared. The pilot was left fuming on the bridge, but the Old Man (not surprisingly to me) retained his remarkably calm demeanour. All he said over the walkie-talkie was, 'Oh, my goodness, Mr Caridia, I feel we are going to be in for a long haul.' His forecast proved correct, but the company had to incur the cost of keeping seven tugs in attendance continuously to prevent us moving off the berth, until we could secure head and stern lines, as well as back springs and breast ropes.

Loading our first cargo was uneventful. We were to take a full load in all tanks of Iranian heavy crude, some 286,000 tons in all. Fortunately, the tanker had been fitted with Inert Gas System so considerably reducing the dangers of potential explosion. 'IGS', as it was familiarly known, was one of the greatest safety devices invented in the twentieth century for all tankers, let alone ships of this class. It was a veritable lifesaver. We finally departed with the laconic statement 'Kharg Island towards Land's End for Orders (LEFO)' in the log-book as we were not issued immediately with a discharging destination. That came later as we rounded Cape Town when, on this occasion, we received orders to proceed to Finnart in Scotland and then complete discharge at Milford Haven. This was to prove a popular sequence over subsequent voyages, intermingled with calls to Europoort and occasionally Wilhemstad or Le Havre for variety.

An understandingly benevolent Fate often allowed the challenges of both outward and homeward bound passages of the Dover Strait to fall during my watches. Trips aboard the supertanker in this favourite stretch of water were completed in all weathers from fog to good visibility, and storm force winds to light airs at all hours of the day and night. Passing the Varne and Sandettie light-vessels, for example, invariably evoked a veritable host of memories. I recalled navigating these waters as a sixteen-year-old officer cadet aboard the training ketch, and then as a watch-keeping officer on the bridge of numerous deep-sea dry cargo vessels. My initial passage (related in *Mariner's Launch*) was unique and important, for it proved to me and others, including (very much against his will!) my erstwhile Skipper that I showed some promise in my chosen profession. Each class of vessel, with varying lengths overall and height of wheelhouse above the sea, demanded slightly different responsible emphasis in the application of navigational techniques and ship-handling.

Invariably, I was alone on the bridge for most of these passages apart of course from the narrowest stretch of water. Homeward bound, with deep-draught restriction signals already hoisted, once I had rounded Le Basseurelle light-vessel and straightened my partially-loaded supertanker on course for a position with Cap Gris Nez some five miles abeam, I would phone the Master:

'We have just rounded Le Basseurelle, sir and are on course for Gris Nez. The traffic situation in the separation zones ahead is quite heavy with the usual run of cross-channel ferries, a few fishing boats and pleasure craft, but no potential problems at the moment. I am going to VHF CROSSMA (the French traffic control authority) advising our cargo, destination and intentions.'

Inevitably, he would reply: 'Thank you, pilot (the alternative name for his main navigating officer) – I am on my way' and appear in the wheelhouse as either Les Ridens light or Boulogne came abeam. I also phoned his steward and arranged for a tray of tea and biscuits to be made available either in his cabin or the wheelhouse wherever he happened to be once the steward appeared. If the activity of the ubiquitous French fishing fleet was sufficiently numerous for any particular passage to look even potentially threatening, then I would knock the steering off automatic and place my duty quarter-master on the wheel, turning to the stand-by man for continuing look-out duties.

Upon arrival, Captain Anson would survey the situation, and take the small radar on the 6 or 3-mile range, monitoring targets I fed to him from my overall view on the main set operational on the 12 or 6-mile range respectively, and he would order course alterations as these became necessary. Meanwhile, I continued keeping an eye on the quarter-master, in following our voyage plan and, as we were so close to land, 'popping a dot on the chart' every twenty minutes by each of radar, Decca and visual bearings. I would also look after the telephones or telegraph and keep up-to-date our voyage records, as well as keeping 'one ear open' for relevant announcements from Gris Nez's CROSSMA but especially Dover CNIS coastguard service.

Our main intent was to navigate the VLCC within the deepest water available consistent with our sometimes reduced sixty-feet (18 metres) draught. Occasionally, we came up the Strait drawing nearer the maximum seventy-two feet, or 22 metres. Whilst obviously mindful of our obligations under various rules contained within the International Collision Regulations, we were nevertheless unable to manoeuvre outside the deep-water channel without risk of stranding – something unthinkable with between fifty and eighty million gallons of crude oil on board! Even a lateral course deviation of merely a quarter-of-a-mile was difficult to contemplate because of the potential problems this might create. It was dangerous therefore for us to give-way to crossing ferries, yachts and cabin cruisers, or those unfathomable courses steered frequently by trawlers. Generally, we had to stand-on and rely that other craft would alter course for us, even if (very occasionally) a terse reminder had to be offered them by CNIS! Also, there was some risk attendant with the squat of our vessel, and the lesser (but not unknown) scouring effect of tides upon wrecks previously submerged on the sea bed that might suddenly 'sit up'!

These dangers were found not at all worrying, but stood merely as examples of 'maritime things to be borne in mind' whilst manoeuvring not only this stretch of water, but many similar restricted areas of the world's oceans. There was always much to do, invariably demanding intense concentration. But there was more than such abstract professionalism might imply, for navigating these magnificent ships appeased something indefinable within me. Entering the wheelhouse to relieve the watch was literally a walk into the unknown. Yes, it was undoubtedly challenging, but the very ethos proved inherently satisfying – and excitingly interesting! The sense of achievement allowed a host of what would prove contrasting experiences to become established deep into my memory bank and I admitted (even then) to a perfectly happy acceptance of the undoubted romanticism blending itself within this process!

I made a number of voyages aboard the supertanker, each of the promised roughly two months' duration covering the 22,000 mile return journey between the Gulf oilfields including Mena al Ahmadi and Ras Tanura, and discharging generally at Europoort before heading for final discharge at No. 4 Jetty, Coryton, in the River Thames, following our Mobil charter. There were many officer changes during this period, but Jason it is pleasing to report, served out the remainder of his time and, during the final year, took charge fore and aft under the first officer's and my supervision respectively, until he had gained in confidence, but not over-confidence. In my cynicism I observed that if the latter situation were to arise, that would probably come when he was a new officer in his own right.

Numerous and varied situations arose during these trips. It was necessary on a subsequent voyage for a round 180 degree turn to be made. We had left Sete, in the Gulf of Lyons, opposite Marseilles, after discharging heavy crude from numbers two and four centre tanks, and light crude from numbers one, three and five wing tanks at Frontignan Single Buoy Mooring (SBM) to lighten ship enabling us to make the English Channel and Dover Strait passage to Europoort and Coryton. The discharge was undertaken without any problems and the vessel duly cast off and proceeded on passage. After steaming for about four hours and in position twelve miles south-west of Cape Creus, the engine-room notified that trouble was being experienced in the stern gland. It seemed that the inner seal packing the propeller shaft (containing lubricating oil) was leaking at the alarming rate of a gallon per minute, and this could be fixed only by returning to Sete and stopping the engine, with the vessel coming up to anchor. We put the helm hard over to starboard from course 195 degrees (T&G) to steady up on 015 degrees (T) and cover the 55-mile-distance back to Sete fairway. The turn took forty minutes to make. After the initial quick response to about twenty degrees from hard-over, the ship was extremely sluggish in making the remainder of the turn largely due to her massive beam bulk area. We put up NUC (Not Under Command) signals in accordance with International Regulations and proceeded on reduced speed. Once anchored and the examination undertaken, the engineers found the seal had not broken after all, but had merely become dislodged. This was reset, cables sent to the Kremlin and the vessel returned on passage. It was another interesting example of the vessel's turning ability.

There was an incident in which a new third officer learnt his lesson the hard way. I relieved the bridge to find us in the St George's Channel heading for Milford Haven having offloaded at Finnart in Scotland sufficiently to allow entry into the former port. I saw the third mate busily engaged in tuning-in the Decca navigator at a time when the reception was affected by sky-wave variations. The obvious thing would have been not to have attempted changing channels at night. As it was, I entered the wheelhouse to see the duty secunny desperately trying to attract his attention, and a small coaster looming ahead fine on the port bow being overtaken. Once I had assimilated the sight, I immediately went over to the automatic pilot, knocked it onto manual and went over to starboard. The ship responded after her usual breathtaking (in this instance) pause before I checked her swing and brought her round gently to miss the coaster by a closer margin than I would otherwise have wished. The luckless third mate, meanwhile, came to the forefront of the wheelhouse and watched the coaster gradually passing down our port side. His face was as white as the circumstances permitted, as he told me his lookout had reported the vessel but he was far too engrossed in his task, and had 'simply forgotten about it'. I could sympathise and appreciate, but that did not alter the fact that a near collision had occurred. Looking at the coaster through binoculars indicated that there was no one on deck or, more importantly, manning the bridge. They would never know how close they had come to a collision, and probable sinking.

Although most officers and cadets appointed to the vessel were of sound quality, we encountered a few who fell below the company's traditional standards. They soon found themselves 'walking the proverbial plank' at the earliest opportunity. There was the third officer whom we quickly discovered was a rampaging alcoholic and was completely intoxicated when I relieved the watch at midnight the day after he joined us in Coryton. When I went into the wheelhouse while we were still crossing the Bay of Biscay, he was seated on the settee that we used generally as a dumping ground for an assortment of gear, with his head in his hands. He clearly did not know whether he was on board a supertanker or the Royal Scot. I went below to the Old Man's cabin and suggested he came up to the bridge for a moment. He queried the reasons for doing so, but I merely repeated my request that he should go into the wheelhouse and then, returning, waited for him to do so. He popped in about ten minutes later and joined me when I pointed out the third mate, who had not moved from his position since I had come in. There had been no question of taking over the watch from him in the normal way: he remained totally incapable of doing his job and was a menace to us, other shipping, and even himself. The Master managed to arouse him and ordered him below. As the chief officer was on day work, the Old Man next morning rearranged our watches until Las Palmas. Derek was asked to stand-in and keep the third mate's duties, while arrangements were made to fly the guy home and have another officer standing by for the tanker's arrival there. This duly happened to the relief of us all – plus, of course, the alcoholic mate!

We had a further problem of drunkenness with a Second Officer who was acting in his rank following my seniority promotion to acting chief officer and taking the first mate's watches. He was an ex-tanker type from British Petroleum Shipping (or BP, as it was known colloquially) and was duly welcomed for his wider cargo experience but, unfortunately on his first trip he was 'under the influence' in Mena al Ahmadi and allowed oil to seep out of number three port-wing tank. He had apparently failed to shut fully the inspection and access hatch and permitted cargo to exceed the 98-per-cent capacity level. Luckily, the duty cadet at the time (Jason had long since been relieved, certificated and sent to another VLCC as third officer) noticed the seepage, and reported this to the Mate, who stopped cargo immediately before oil was allowed to enter Gulf waters. It was then 'all hands available to the permoglaze' cleaning fluid, and a full-scale mopping-up operation. He was another one who was soon 'on his way'.

On every voyage, after discharge of cargo the routines of tank-cleaning occurred in preparation for the next cargo, often from the Arabian Gulf. This involved lowering tank-cleaning machines into the tanks, allowing the crude oil adhering to the tank bottom and sides to be washed into slop tanks aft (BP plc).

Cargo was loaded and discharged by computer, enabling the considerable stresses and strains on the hull to be assessed and taken into consideration, while ullages were measured by mechanical machines until they jammed when resort was made to traditional methods of using a sounding rod (BP plc and Athel Line).

Standing below any supertanker either before launching or, more usually, while in dry dock provoked an eerie feeling in the knowledge that a few hundred thousand tons of ship were immediately above (Shell International Trading and Shipping).

Then there was the deck cadet with an engaging smile, who joined full of promise until the elementary book *Teach Yourself Navigation* was espied in his personal library. It appeared he had been recruited from Regal Supreme's Hull office without any formal educational qualifications and nothing other than an Outward Bound Sea School course behind him for pre-sea training. These schools were excellent but very practical for, in the space of just twenty-six days, there was no opportunity for any academic input. Any potential navigating cadet attending them needed to have something a little more educationally substantial supporting his cadetship, otherwise he would simply be unable to cope with these rigorous demands of his training. It was a mystery to us aboard the ship why Viscount Tankers accepted the youngster as a group transfer from Regal, but 'ours not to reason why'. As it still remained my lot to take him for one hour per week's tuition, his shortcomings became all too apparent within the first session. He had no knowledge of plane trigonometry; had studied general science and not the individual ideal subjects of physics (especially), chemistry and the lesser requirement of biology at school, and was generally incapable of understanding even the elementary first-year Merchant Navy Training Board's syllabus content. I think we could still have done something with him, but his Saturday morning session with the Mate revealed his inability correctly to memorise even the most fundamental of the collision regulations. At the end of a two-month trip, he had still not progressed accurately beyond the second rule. He was, alas, not the 'brightest knife in the drawer', as the chief officer described the poor lad. Even while the ship was homeward bound, his parents were called in to London office and an agreement made to terminate his cadetship at the end of the first trip. It was suggested that he be returned to Regal recommending they send him away aboard one of their tramp ships as a deck boy, hoping he could fare better there. We lost track of his officer 'career' following departure from the VLCC, but the memory lingered of *Teach Yourself Navigation*.

An interesting meteorological phenomenon was observed on another trip that owed its origin to the abnormal refractive effects often experienced in the Gulf. On one voyage, we were all intrigued to see the masts, superstructure and hull of a tanker superimposed on the distant sea-line off the port bow that offered the appearance of a ship proceeding upside down. Of the original parent vessel there was no sign as it was hull-down below the horizon.

Perhaps a revealingly interesting development of my service aboard VLCCs was the unique friendship that developed between Captain Anson and me. It meant that I served aboard a truly 'happy ship', but definitely not a slap-happy one! Apart from a disastrous encounter with a Master on the *Earl of Nottingham* in Tilbury docks, (examined in *Mariner's Voyage*) a partial relaxing in relationships had occurred with previous Captains that was always correct and had never bordered on familiarity. It was the recognition of such specific boundaries on my part that doubtless made this possible. Captain Anson was always totally at ease and friendly with most officers but, as we served together over a number of voyages, and each became increasingly aware of the other's professionalism, a deeper level of mutual respect occurred almost imperceptibly. He became, without exception, the 'best' Captain under whose command I ever served: which, although 'all things to men' as a definition, remains no mean accolade.

Whilst on watch during day-time coffee or tea breaks when my watchman was away for his 'smoke-oh', or working together on deck tasks, it slowly became a matter of course to speak naturally of leaves just spent or anxiously anticipated. This gradually developed into talk of family and friends, interspersed between wider or perhaps more parochial issues of the day and of course, exchanged experiences of ships, mariners and incidents covering the globe. The Captain was a 'tanker-type' through and through from his cadet days aged sixteen years and had never served ashore or on board dry cargo ships. Encountering such smaller vessels whilst on various passages, he raised frequent and often penetrating questions regarding issues of cargoes/stability, derricks or cranes, ship-handling characteristics, and of course navigation-seamanship. He expressed particular interest in crews and seemed absorbed in sharing varied experiences with what he termed "the vagarious nature of the human condition". As well as proving an expert navigator and ship-handler, Captain Anson was also very much a "people's person" – attributes, of course, that do not always prove easy bed-fellows with more closed temperaments. In turn, I learned much concerning supertankers that could never be gleaned from text-books, or even limited experience serving aboard these impressive monsters.

Inevitably, that own little imp which accompanied me wherever I went could not be subdued for I soon learnt that any expression, however slight, indicating approval for the Labour Party was guaranteed to 'get him going' until, equally as inevitably, he 'cottoned on' and threw the teasing back onto me:

'Oh my goodness, Mr. Caridia, I do believe you are trying to 'wind me up'!'

'Oh come now, sir, would I do an unspeakable thing like that?'

His sideways smile of recognition and warm eye contact indicated the sharing of a similar sense of fun and even of the ridiculous that encompassed everyday situations ashore and on board ship. Frequently, the wheelhouse resounded with countless warm chuckles and a wider spread humour sandwiched between commands, often intensely technical discussions, and navigational or cargo remarks.

Towards the end of my second four-monthly tour as we chugged up the English Channel, having just passed Ushant and settled onto our new course; given notice of arrival to Europoort and readiness to our engine-room concerning easing back the main engine, Captain Anson surprised me by announcing his intention of retiring after signing-off at Coryton. I was surprised and, to be honest, just a little sorry because I was beginning to mould myself to his methods, liking what I saw. I expressed this mildly to him, but he stated how adamant he was, so I took this on board and already began to wonder about who might replace him. Of course, I might have guessed – for it had to happen. Due to unpredictable movements of these very large tankers and their frequent delays within or arriving at various ports, before we sailed from Coryton on the River Thames, officers gathered together at a hotel in London for a couple of days prior to joining the ship. Only when the vessel had actually tied-up alongside Number Four jetty were we conveyed in a couple of minibuses to the refinery. I found this a very handy arrangement in many respects. It enabled new officers to become integrated before joining the vessel; helped any who suffered to quell their inevitable homesickness, and allowed numerous sundry things like latest chart corrections/Notices to Mariners to be delivered from the London office before we joined the ship, as well as facilitating exchanges of current ideas and information concerning our voyage and possible cargo, invariably from the Middle East. It was also possible to arrange visits to various shows or to sample London hostelries which otherwise we could only have dreamt about.

As I entered the hotel in readiness for my third tour, wondering who would be in command, who should I see propping up the bar but Captain Anson. Yes, he had agreed to return to his ship. It became quite a routine over subsequent trips for him to make the same announcement more or less at the same time on passage in the same serious tones until, eventually, I told him:

'Do you know, sir, I have heard *some* modest mention of this before on previous trips, but I think the only way you will ever leave this ship will be when they carry you down the gangway and along the jetty in your box!' This proved a comment with which, to give him due, he met with an open chuckle, an engaging grin, and a ruefully shaken head agreement!

A further perennial voyage topic was the frequency of house moves that he planned for each leave, most of which were initiated by his very restless wife. He had married late in life and, whilst undoubtedly very much Master of his own ship, I was not so sure of the extent this became reflected when he was at home with his 'good lady'. Certainly, on those rare occasions when she visited the ship, occasional imperiously demanding tones could be heard emanating from the Master's day-room, calling him by name and dragging him away from a quiet beer with the chief or casual chat between his deck officers. He responded to these 'royal commands' with all the alacrity of a junior cadet being called by his Captain: a source of considerable secret amusement between us all!

Even whilst serving aboard *Viscount Gwendoline*, and consistent with my earlier views, I never took for granted or lost my allure for this class of ship. The supertanker always retained strangely unique mixtures of detached professionalism and the

A 300,000 summer deadweight, one-third-of-a-mile supertanker typical of those of the early 1970s, which were built in major shipyards in the Far East and Europe (Fotoflite).

impressively romantic. Apart from dimensions, her sleek lines and enormous funnel dwarfing seven-tiers of accommodation block never lost its charm (and, indeed, it never has!) I view still in my mind's eye broad expanses of fore-deck seen from wheelhouse windows with crew members working on deck looking like diminutive ants. More appreciated were clear unhindered views of the horizon, making watch-keeping a delight as *my* supertanker ploughed serenely through calmly untroubled waters. And there was always of course, the sight of smaller ocean-going dry cargo vessels pitching, cork-screwing and rolling wildly in Storm force winds and seas to link my own days aboard these with the stable platform from which they were placidly observed.

5

CAPERS ON THE COAST

'Good morning, Mr Caridia. Come in, please. Good to see you again. It seems such a long time ago since you and I chatted. The last trip was highly successful, I believe, judging from Captain Anson's reports? How are things with your good lady and yourself? Have a son now, I have heard? White, with one sugar, as I remember?'

It was good to see Captain Henshaw had not improved with time so, while I sorted out this little lot in my mind, he rang for his secretary and, on her appearance, ordered coffee and biscuits.

'Well, sir.' I parried, wondering which question to answer first, and finally deciding to supply a blanket coverage. 'All is fine at home with wife, but there is no son, white or otherwise, or, at least, if there is I certainly know nothing about him, so I am not quite sure where you got that one from – as it were. Yes, I suppose the last time we met was just prior to my rejoining *Viscount Gwendoline* before my last tour. So far as I know, things went well enough. At least Captain Anson seemed satisfied…oh… and…one sugar, please!'

I stopped. It seemed the logical thing to do. I was also wondering why I had not received joining instructions for the next supertanker voyage from the company. I had continued to rub along extremely well with the Old Man (as well as other officers) and knew he was doing the next trip. This was certainly the case when Captain Anson had telephoned just three days previously. He had been his usual jovial self, obviously looking forward to rejoining his ship, and had spoken enthusiastically about my sailing with him again, this time as his chief officer, the rank I would now hold for subsequent voyages. He had even promised (or threatened) to bring to our hotel the latest copy set of cargo bills, and tanker regulations governing the carriage of crude oil so I could cast an eye over these before joining. I had liked the sound of this, in all respects, and it was good to have confirmed his views that things were progressing so well in what had previously been a very new trade for me. Duly inspired, I felt confident of rising successfully to the challenge of loading, caring for, and discharging a full crude-oil cargo. The only jarring note had been his casual comment, reinforcing what he had mentioned a number of times while at sea, to the extent that I really ought to go for my Master's Foreign-Going certificate as soon as possible – certainly if I wished to obtain my own command of a VLCC 'in a few years'.

When two days afterwards I received an unexpected summons to the Kremlin, I was bemused, to put things mildly. I wondered what Captain Henshaw knew that I did not. I guesssed it could not be too serious or he would not have offered coffee, for his approach under any severe circumstances would have been more formal. I guessed it was probably something like potential study leave, so waited patiently for him to continue, watching to see if any posible outcome could be deduced from his expression. He began by apologising for his error concerning the non-extension of the Caridia line, at least by Sue and me, sensibly stopping before swimming further into potentially deep waters. He then confirmed no complaints had been received from the Master, rather the contrary: Captain Anson had praised my ability, sobriety, temperament and character (which covered just about all options of the human maritime condition), and had indeed requested my services for the next tour on promotion as Mate.

The group had called me in as they wished to discuss another appointment with me. Once again he paused while I waited expectantly with increasing interest and slight trepidation, particularly in the light of his unexpectedly formal reference to 'the Group' as my employers. I certainly experienced a distinct sense of déjà vu. While speaking, he picked up his desk telephone, requesting an unknown person, to 'Come in now, Tony'. While I waited, a battery of alarm bells rang stridently in my mind, probably concerned with subsequent events. A few moments later the door opened and through it came a tall, broadly built man, supporting a magnificent 'set' of beard and bushy moustache. Drawing up a nearby spare chair, he took his place at the end of the desk, between Captain Henshaw and my highly suspicious self. His smile developed into a warm, open grin as he sat. The super introduced us. He was Captain Hillier, marine superintendent of London and Chatham Shipping Company, the group's coastal concern. Another pause followed after which drawing a deep breath, the newcomer explained they had serious manning problems aboard their coasters. He assumed I was aware that the group, of which Ellerton remained the main company, managed various fleets. As well as the dry-cargo ships and supertankers upon which, obviously, I had served, they owned a number of approximately 1,000-gross-tonned, low- or light-air-draught coasters, a fleet of about twelve smaller craft and five 3,500-tonners engaged on middle-sea trading. The long and short of it was that he wanted me to serve aboard one of the medium-class ships as chief officer for a short trip of just two to three months' duration before, he guaranteed, I would be relieved. He paused and I noticed he and Henshaw exchanging glances as he continued, 'We are making considerable efforts now to ascertain correct manning of these ships and think very carefully prior to making appointments.' He paused and looked as if he were going to add to his comments but stopped, after exchanging a further glance with Captain Henshaw. I pondered that if they 'thought very carefully now about making appointments' how had they managed in the past, but refrained from contributing this aphorism.

I did comment that he made it sound as if both supers, and, of course, 'the Group', as I referred to them sarcastically, made service aboard their blasted coaster appear as both an honour and privilege. I stressed not being so sure and, grabbing the intiative, interrupted him by asking Captain Henshaw about my appointment to the VLCC. It seemed pertinent to remind him that Captain Anson was firmly under the impression I would be rejoining and that we had both discussed this probability. It seemed relevant to mention also the promise of my promotion as tanker Mate. So, I parried – it might be added with desperation – that were I to sail aboard the coaster then 'the Group' (heavily emphasised) would still be a chief officer light on the supertanker, and that frankly, however friendly Captain Hillier might appear (I smiled disarmingly in his direction), the last thing I wanted was to go into another new trade, one of which I had neither knowledge nor any desire to investigate. That argument was soon put to a quick death as Henshaw (ignoring my thinly veiled sarcasm) explained he and Captain Anson had discussed this problem only the previous afternoon before calling me to the office. Henshaw was also well aware that the Master wanted me to sail on future voyages as chief officer at least for the next tour and, were I to do this coastal voyage for the group, they would guarantee that the time away would not stand in way of my promotion aboard VLCCs. I noticed how the personal pronoun had made again subtle change to the collective 'we', as corporate responsibility intervened. Probably, this was 'superintendenteese' intended to soften this kind of bad news. I filed the technique away for future reference, pondering, perhaps, if I might be a superintendent myself one day in the future – even though the thought passed without too much optimism, conviction or even enthusiasm. My visions of a supposed bliss were interrupted by Captain Henshaw confirming the supertanker Master had indeed not been a very happy mariner upon hearing their plans, but had agreed to my release for a tour of about ten weeks' – once he had understood the group's various needs were presently more urgent than his own.

I frowned and felt my features harden as the light dawned that the verbal parrying, like ancient barons in the joust resulted in this particular *fait* becoming well and truly *accompli* – as it were. Captain Hillier then took up the mace to this fallen knight requesting me to at least 'hear him out' as he put it. This comment was stated quite firmly, but with more than a hint of request in his voice. There was no option left to me really, after all there was still a small matter of a few months remaining on my contract to serve and, as I was well aware, it would only be a matter of time before it was pointed out that this was with the group, as opposed to Ellerton's Viscount Shipping, who operated the supertankers. Reluctantly I agreed that he might as well continue, but my lack of grace was all too evident. It appeared that London and Chatham's *Prince Albert* was lying fully loaded with 1,340 tonnes of china clay at Par in Cornwall, which was wanted urgently at Dordrecht, near Rotterdam, and that it was imperative she sailed on the next available high tide. While he spoke, they both glanced at the clock, as Hillier explained:

'Hmm… It's 1100 hours now so it'll be too late for today's high water. We have no spare officers across all ranks, but an abundance of ratings, and as we are desperately short of qualified Masters and mates at the moment, we haven't anyone capable of acting in this rank available – at all. I'm afraid that we must ask you to join her today in order to get the vessel off the berth. She's got a Master and second mate aboard, but in view of the recent exploits of the *Prince Henry*, of which you've undoubtedly heard…?'

He broke off, glancing sideways at me, begging me not to make him repeat the story before adding, 'Anyway, we dare not sail her short-handed.'

Although not a 'coasting' man, I happened to know what he was talking about. There had been a major stink, which had hit the shipping and national press with something of a bang. Captain Anson had related the incident to me with considerable hilarity as he passed a message just received from a jubilant Sparks, while we were homeward bound off Ushant. Apparently, one of the company's five larger 3,500 grt coasters had sailed more than short-handed from Oslo bound for London; she had been positively and definitely undermanned. The second and third mates plus two crew had missed the sailing, probably 'savouring the delights' somewhere, but the Old Man had decided to sail anyway, sharing the bridge watches with his chief officer. Unfortunately on the way over the Mate, overcome with exhaustion following only a few hours sleep after loading the vessel and before a seven-hour bridge watch, had fallen asleep and run the ship into the side of a deeply laden 50,000 grt bulk carrier lying in Southend deep-water anchorage waiting orders to discharge at Tilbury Grain terminal. The first the Mate, and everyone else, knew what had happened was when there was a 'mother and father' of a crash and he was thrown across the wheelhouse to receive more than what was euphemistically known as 'a rude awakening'. It was then that those aboard the coaster became aware of the carrier's siren blowing frantically, but clearly to no avail. Luckily the coaster hit one of the bulker's frames instead of her shell plating for, with the momentum gained at the speed she was travelling, her bows could well have penetrated the hold and created something of a potential cornfield in the Thames Estuary.

The super glanced at me, stressing his urgency to get the *Albert* away virtually immediately, with me sailing as chief officer. He interrupted my obvious protest stating quite bluntly that the superintendents were well aware my experience aboard dry-cargo coasters was nil, but they wanted me to sail anyway, being conscious that my extensive deep-sea experience on large dry-cargo ships would more than adequately equip me to sail as Mate of a coastal vessel, and that both Master and the other officer aboard were eager to fill gaps in my knowledge. At that point he stopped, having effectively plugged my only line of defence, but also for breath. I noticed also how the corporate appeal had crept suddenly back into the conversation, perhaps in realisation that the personal approach was unlikely to cut very far into this particular ice block.

I sat there reflecting. A confusion of thoughts raced across my mind – and I was most certainly not a happy nautical bunny. To allow myself further thinking time, I sipped coffee and munched absent-mindedly at more than my fair share of the biscuits. My first thought was to ponder who on earth would want china clay so urgently, reflecting it could hardly constitute the lifeblood of any nation, let alone the Dutch. Strangely enough, I had few doubts about my ability to do the job reflecting, quite rightly, that the navigation would be largely familiar, and that the cargo work should be fairly straightforward. The ship-handling during watches should also present no problems. Deep-sea chaps spent much of their time in coastal waters, even if they did not enter such shallow-draught ports as their smaller-capacity cousins. I had been very happy on supertankers, after all I had yearned for that class of ship for years before my appointment, and did not want to leave them. So I could hardly admit enthusiasm, but the thought entered my mind that by sailing on the coast I could see Sue more frequently than if deep-sea service remained my lot. It seemed my resolve to 'be tough' was waning as these musings led to a slight warming towards the idea. Visions of numerous cosy weekends at home wining and dining with all the delights of matrimonial bliss passed contentedly across my mind. It was undoubtedly this factor more than company (and certainly not group) loyalty which led to my decision to accept the offer. The super positively glowed as I 'spread a little happiness', leaving me to ponder where I might have experienced that sensation before.

'So you'll be off, then?' He posed, breaking my train of thought.

I rallied, came back to earth, and found myself phoning Sue telling her of this latest link in that unknown chain of events constituting seafaring; advising my approximate time of arrival, and asking if she could have a meal ready. While I was busily engaged on the phone, the secretary came in with travelling details and a train warrant. I almost changed my mind at this point, for her return was far too quick and the super had clearly had everything made out in my name – before I even came to the office earlier that morning. I filed away a few more 'superintendenancy tricks'. There was need for me to be philosophical about this turn of events. They were far from my making and choice, and so it was in a sort of a whirl that I made tracks for the station working out how much time was available for packing, eating a meal and then setting off again. In the excitement of the moment, I had quite forgotten to enquire what passed for uniform necessarily worn by the chief officer of a medium-sized coaster.

The 930 grt mv Nascence *was a typical light-air draught dry-cargo coaster of her day that plied around the UK coast, continental and middle-trade ports carrying a varied assortment of mini-bulk cargoes (Courtesy A. Duncan).*

Sue took the news with accustomed aplomb. She was clearly resigned to the idea that my leave was coming to an end, and a change of ship and trade held, for her, nowhere near the portent of potential concern it had for me. And so, at 1500 that same day, I was settled comfortably into the window seat of a Cornish Riviera Express rushing from Paddington to St Austell, the nearest stopping station to Par. I took a taxi to the ship, arriving by the gangway before, it seemed, I had time to sort out myself and my gear in the back. My first impression as we rounded into the jetty, above which the correctly loaded ship (I was quick to notice) sat gently rolling on the rising tide port side to, was surprisingly favourable. It struck me that the dock area seem to be inordinately bright, and as I stepped onto the quay I saw this was caused by a thick film of dust which I took (correctly as it happened) to be china clay. *Prince Albert* was longer than I had anticipated, and reflected overside deck and bright moon and

146

jetty lights in her clean fresh paint. This at least indicated a well-maintained hull and spoke positively for the remainder of the ship. Lugging my clay-washed gear across the correctly adjusted gangway to the top of a nearby companionway, I dumped it inside and took stock of my surroundings. In the alleyway lights, the shiny-blue lino and white-painted bulkheads again showed evidence of recent attention. The Master's cabin was across the alleyway on my left-hand side, while immediately to my left as I entered on the port side was the engineer's cabin. This looked forward across the main-deck, next to a short companionway which I assumed led to a combined wheelhouse and chart-room. The remaining officers and all crew were obviously berthed below. The time was just after 0130 and merely fourteen hours since my hurried departure from the Kremlin. The Master's door was open with the curtain drawn across the entrance and I could hear the faint sounds of a popular music station coming quietly from the radio. Responding to my knock on his outer bulkhead, a quietly firm voice invited me to enter.

'Good evening, Captain. My name is Jonathan Caridia and I've been appointed to your ship as the Mate,' I formally introduced myself. An intelligent, suntanned face made an appraising, square-on eye-contact, which I returned equally directly. His immediate smile emphasised a wreath of either weather or humour lines; I thought time would decide which. I judged him to be about my own age – and very firmly in control of the situation.

'Am I glad to see you, Jon. I was just wondering if you were going to make it before we sailed to an anchorage, so releasing the berth,' came the spontaneous response, which was at least promising. 'My name is Bob Aitken. I'll just phone the agents and let our engineer know you're aboard and we can sail once the pilot's here. That'll not take too long as we ordered him on stand-by immediately the Kremlin told us you were on your way.'

With that, he shot out of the cabin, leaving me to my own devices. I was glad to hear that even in the coastal trades the familiar name for head office was universally bandied around. It was quietly reassuring. Attracted by the faint sound of Tammy Wynette's *Stand by Your Man*, I grabbed my holdall and went below, passing the unlocked chief officer's cabin on the port-side athwartship alleyway opposite another cabin leading aft, and dumped my holdalls on the lino surround of the carpet until I could dust off the bottoms. The starboard side, I presumed, held the second mate's cabin and another cabin for the crew. The engine-room was sandwiched in between the two main alleyways. I then wandered out and followed the music to its source, which turned out to be aft of the cabins in a combined mess-room and lounge. Entering, I saw a well-built female, probably in her early twenties, sitting on the settee wearing a none-too-clean boiler suit, with crossed legs and paint-encrusted army boots reposing on a coffee table. She had heavy lines across her forehead and around her lips and was rolling a cigarette, with a not too clean pint mug of what looked like very strong tea, and one-inch-thick slices of heavily buttered marmalade toast by her side. I paused and tried (probably unsuccessfully) to hide my shocked surprise at the sight of this apparition. She glanced in my direction listening intently as I advised my recent joining and appointment to the ship as Mate. Giving a watery smile in repsonse, she introduced herself as Maggie Kendall, the second mate, although I detected what appeared to be a look of guarded reflection crossing her features. Going through the process of mutual summing-up, I informed her that the Old Man had left to rake up the pilot and chief and that it seemed we could soon be sailing. At least my remark filled what was obviously an awkward pause. At that moment we heard the Master clumping down the companionway and, attracted by the sound of our voices, he joined us in the mess-room.

'Right. That's all arranged. There's been a slight delay with the pilot, who will now be here at 0230 so we'll be able to leave immediately with the start of the tidal ebb. I've seen the engineer and see you've met each other. Maggie, you might as well continue relaxing for a while and then get the lads organised from about 0215, please. Jon here will go forward and you can go aft for me.'

He turned and left Maggie to get on with her smoke and what passed for supper and, motioning me to follow, glanced with some amusement at my expression. He pointed out that the layout of the cabin on the starboard side was as I assumed, with the crew sharing a two-berthed cabin on that side also, and the galley aft of that – equivalent to where the mess was on our side of the ship. Entering his cabin, he motioned for me to sit and referring to Maggie, spoke of her efficiency as a second mate – which was, after all, the main requirement. She had served with a leading coastal and middle-trade company who had been amongst the first to acccept female navigating cadets on small ships and had risen to uncertificated third mate. Maggie had just three months previously passed her Mate (Home Trade) certificate of competency (which was why she had not been promoted chief officer) and was eager to sit for coastal Master's once she had accrued requisite sea-time. He added that, appearances notwithstanding she might admittedly look a bit ferocious, but was in fact a 'bloody good second mate' who put the fear of the gods up his crew and didn't care either what she said – or how she expressed it to them. He concluded that once she had more sea-time under her belt, she would certainly be promoted chief officer. This last comment was added partially defensively although there was no real need for that. Certainly I had never met a female mate before, especially one of such initial engaging personality, and I supposed something of my bewilderment and a thousand other questions must have continued across my face.

Bob interrupted further thoughts by suggesting he take my discharge book, sight and enter details of my certificate, and sign me onto ship's Articles. He also poured us both a large whisky and soda and suggested we have a chat before sailing. On the way (completely devoid of irony) he told me about my predecessor's severe alcohol problems to the extent that, as Master, he had been 'forced to sack the chap two days earlier' for being, as he put it, 'totally unreliable, even by coasting standards, which are, in all honesty, more than a bit laid back.' Coming alongside had been a nightmare, in the face of a strong crosswind and light ship so, in the end he had to go forward him-self and leave the pilot in charge alone on the bridge, apart from a hand at the wheel.

He confirmed also that Captain Hillier had advised my sea-time to date had been completely deep-sea aboard considerably larger ships than coasters, particularly my last 300,000 sdwt supertanker, which was confirmed by glancing through my discharge book. He told me bluntly that life aboard regular dry-cargo coasters would be totally 'out of the run of my experiences so far'. He was not too sure about the VLCC experience, but thought my time on dry-cargo vessels would 'come in extremely handy.' About my ability to do a Mate's job professionally both at sea and on deck he had no doubts whatsoever, but otherwise the way of life was completely different. My thoughts were racing wildly as I signed Articles and, returning to my seat on his settee took another sip of my drink. I waited then for exactly what might come next. He looked at me quizzically as he swigged from his glass:

'Look, Jon. There is something I have to say. Not all ex-deep-sea blokes find coasting to their taste. You state the group's intention is for you to do one tour of only two or three months but, even during this period, you may need to make some changes in your outlook.' He concluded, 'I've been deep-sea as a cadet and third mate myself, with the South American Saint Line, some years ago now, admittedly, and before I decided to leave foreign-going and took Home Trade Master's, after Second Mate's. Many of the company's Skippers flatly refuse to carry ex-deep-sea officers because they find them superior and difficult. I'm better equipped than many of our older coastal Skippers, most of whom have been promoted from motor and even sailing barges, to appreciate the differences. I had to change my ways considerably when starting as second mate on coasters.' He paused before continuing, 'I had even more problems before my promotion to Master, recommended by the directors and super, was ratified.' He looked at me while I attempted unravelling what he might have meant. After all, it seemed to me if the company wanted him promoted Master then I could not see what the hell this had to do with any of their other captains. I did not pursue this thought, but left him to continue in the hope that inspiration and a few more answers might be forthcoming.

'It's up to you how you react to the life. For a start, Jon, there are no stewards here to wait on you hand and foot, as you've probably been accustomed to, especially from what I have heard about the hotels that seem to float the world on ships with Asian catering crews. You'll also have to supervise the crowd from the sharp end by rolling up your sleeves and actually doing deck work alongside them. There's another thing you will find is different. We all use Christian names and have meals together sharing the same mess. The grub is cooked by one of the lads on a daily rota basis. Anyway, Maggie and I'll help you settle in – so don't hesitate to ask us for anything you want to know.'

On going below to stow away my gear, my thoughts were very much my own. In almost a daze, I was surprised to find my cabin large, well equipped and comfortable, with a roomy shower cubicle attached forward. 'Why the bloody hell couldn't they have left me on my VLCCs?' I pondered, full of self-pity, locking my certificate and wallet in a small desk drawer, and packing away a bundle of shirts and, yes, now rather more fearful of an unknown future that I did not want anyway. 'Good job I had the sense to bring my boiler suits,' I reflected, casting my mind back to 'our Maggie.' 'If that's the second mate, I dread to think what the rest of the crowd are going to be like,' was my next rueful reflection. 'Well, I've signed on now, so will have to stay and face things. The Old Man, or Bob, as I suppose he should be called, was right about one thing, my outlook is certainly going to have a damn riotous shake-up! It's a good job I've always considered myself reasonably flexible and open, so far as seafaring is concerned, and able to see things from a wider horizon.'

When my cabin and bags were squared off, I returned to the mess-room to meet the crew. Additional to Master, Mate, second mate and engineer, the coaster carried two deck-hands-cum-general-purpose ratings, comprising a qualified able seaman (AB), an ordinary seaman (OS), plus a ship's deck-boy. The lads stood around scratching and yawning while adjusting to 'turning to' for stand-by following arrival of the pilot. We had two cadets on board – something I found a complete novelty – because deck cadets carried on coasters was something of a deep-sea mystery. But then, it was only recently that I had heard of female officers, for most of those chosen when the scheme was introduced some years previously had dropped by the wayside. In fact in my limited experience, Maggie was the only girl of whom I had heard who had successfully completed her time. The youngsters were pleasant enough: Toby had about eight months' sea-time and the other, Oliver, had served with London and Chatham for about two-and-a-half years. The younger cadet was additional to the normal complement of crew, while the elder replaced the ordinary seaman. The carriage of the former as spare hand was something not only of a rarity but a considerable bonus and, apparently, was done to give him extra sea-time and experience before appointment as OS aboard another vessel. It certainly proved true even if the company were light on (or indeed, desperate for) navigating officers, they possessed an abundance of deck-hands.

'They've a bit of experience at least, and the AB and older lad look quite useful,' I thought as we shook hands and exchanged casual pleasantries. A first-trip deck boy named Ricky, was lounging by the jalousie looking a little lost. I found that he had joined the ship earlier the same day, after serving at sea for just three days aboard one of the smaller 200 grt coastal motor barges. It proved how desperate were the company to get this hooker off the berth. The ship's able seaman, Jim, was a sharp-featured man of about fifty, so far as I could judge. The AB and Ricky shared a cabin abaft the second mate's, while the two cadets were berthed aft of my own cabin. All accommodation was self-contained complete with shower and, like much accommodation on even these small ships nowadays could easily be adapted to carry female personnel. This must have been similarly the case with General Steam Navigation Company, enabling Maggie to complete her time, which meant that she served probably only on the newer vessels, and not some of the older tubs I knew this company owned. I felt her very strong personality and character must have been extant even when she was just sixteen, and guessed her four-year deck service must have been quite demanding. It seemed no wonder that she was 'as tough as old boots' with little trace of 'female femininity', as I termed it.

Clean linen was distributed weekly by the duty cook-cum-steward on the appropriate day and was collected and sent to laundries ashore. Each person made up his (or her) own bunk including the Master. One of the duties of the boy was to clean the four single en suite officers' cabins. The food was prepared and served to all by the duty cadet or rating. None of the crew were on a regular salary, including the Master and engineer, but worked on a percentage share basis of the value of the cargo according to the rank or rating held on board. Maggie explained later that earnings over a year were never known until it had ended, after which it was 'too late to argue'. Each April, officers and crew simply 'looked back, considering it had been either a good year, an indifferent year or a bad one.'

It seemed, on average, that they were quite well paid, but did not earn as much as crews engaged in regular deep-sea trading, especially (as I was to discover) in terms of the hours they put in each voyage. They did about four months as a tour of duty, with one month off, although officers received an additional two weeks between voyages. The turn-round between crews therefore tended towards officers and rat-ings working intermittently for overlapping periods throughout the year. Crews in general tended to remain with the same ship, although many variations occurred. As I was doing only a short tour, until (hopefully) I could be relieved and return deep-sea to my supertankers, I retained a salary at permanent deep-sea VLCC chief officers' rate which, I suspected, was considerably more than the Master's – although I prudently kept quiet such 'a thought for the day'.

I certainly felt more relaxed, having met this cheerfully uncomplicated bunch and, by the time the pilot came on board and we went to stand-by, was positively determined to make the most of my sojourn. My initial impression on leaving for the main-deck was how small and compact was the forecastle, and miniscule the gear, compared with my very recent experiences of vast roominess aboard cargo ships and especially my VLCC.

Waiting for the pilot to board after talking to Bob, I popped off to the forecastle head and helped the lads single up, after which I watched idly the comings and goings of shipping in this small port. Bob had told me that it was amazingly busy for its size. There were thirteen loading berths, with two centre places generally reserved for maximum 4.5-metre-draught vessels (like ours) around 1,300 grt and over 200 feet in length, although the average size ranged between 200 grt barges and around 500–800 grt coasters of all nationalities. The port had been constructed in the 1830s to cater for the tin and copper mine trades. Nowadays, there were about 1,500 shipping movements, with any number being moved on each high tide, and around 800,000 tons of cargo handled each year, 90 per cent of which consisted of varying grades of china clay. A coaster of our capacity could be loaded when things were going well and a 'proper job' could be done, in an optimum time of four hours, although this was apparently rarely achieved.

I was on stand-by for leaving left Par *en route* for the Dutch coast at around 0300 hours, after a few delays by the pilot, who had experienced difficulty finding a taxi at St Austell and had to wait for one to appear. We were also delayed slightly by waiting for the agent who had to clear the ship and collect the Department of Industry's copy of our ship's Articles for depositing with the Shipping Master's office later that day. Bob was not particularly phased by these delays, but merely accepted them as a matter of course. As a result, we hit the tidal set into the maximum drift and shot out of Par like a proverbial 'cork from the bottle' with about two metres under-keel clearance. There were no problems with the stand-by forward, but I kept the deck boy well out of the way, suggesting he watched to see what was happening around him. I certainly had neither time nor inclination to start training him at this particular moment, and did not wish to launch either of our new careers with an accident.

Once I had seen away the pilot, I was on bridge watch. Oliver, the elder cadet was assigned to the wheelhouse with me – a luxury, as I soon found out, that was never repeated, or at least not officially. I guessed he had been placed, not to 'keep an eye on me', but to allow a gentle breaking into 'the coast' when questions might arise concerning the unfamiliarity of gear and routines. Certainly, the navigation gear was impressive. It was all very modern and, wonder of wonders for a coaster, great was my joy upon discovering a Sperry SR1200 gyrocompass with wing repeaters, of a similar pattern found on many larger ships. The steering was governed by the familiar Decca Arkas 450 system – a smaller version and earlier model than the 750, with which I had been accustomed. The radar was a Raytheon 20XR, with which

I was not familiar, although the controls were conventional. The dimensions of the ship were 72.3 metres overall with a beam of 11.3 metres and a moulded depth of 4.21 metres. The ship would have virtually fitted lengthways thwartship across the VLCC's beam, which was a sobering thought. She was fitted with two hatches, each 17.9 metres by 7.9 metres served by universal Magregor steel hatch covers. The vessel's cruising speed was 10·5 knots on laden draught 3.4 metres.

I had been informed while on stand-by forward with Jim, the experienced AB who had served on older types of all classes of coastal vessels, that she had steel tank tops instead of the gouged, work-worn wooden slats that were 'a real sod to clean, especially between, say, mixed cargoes, and the like'. I reflected for a moment and then deduced that this was the reason why the newer vessels were so versatile. I agreed that it would have been a real sod of a job dislodging coal dust and preparing, for instance, to load a grain cargo, or even china clay. It also accounted for the fact that most older coasters were restricted to one specific trade. Replacing the ship statistics card, I turned my attention from reverie towards the cadet:

'Right, young man. How much navigation and bridge experience have you?' I enquired, putting a ring of authority into my voice.

'Well, I've done both with various captains over the last two or so years, sir, but not a great deal. I was not at nautical school before coming away to sea, but have attended Newcastle since for short seamanship and bridge navigation courses.'

I detected a note of anxiety in his response.

'OK. You're a navigating cadet, so let's start cadeting, as it were. Use whatever means you like to put a fix on the chart for me.'

I carried on keeping the lookout, but offering a discreet eye on the way in which he set about the task. There were a number of useful headlands around, and Portland Bill was flashing happily off the beam at 14.2 miles, so he acted reasonably quickly. He took radar ranges and visual bearings and then (I was pleased to see) looked again at the radar to see how his dot on the chart tallied with the land around us on the port side. He then reported he had a position which he thought was accurate for the time when it was taken – quickly adding the latter to the chart before I could pick him up for failing to do so. We exchanged a quick tacit smile, which broke the ice and enabled us both to become more relaxed in each other's company. I told him that in future he should plot a Decca fix after his previous visual and radar bearings, reminding him of the Regulation to ascertain the ship's position by all available means, but commended him for his competence and efficiency so far.

Looking over his shoulder, I could not believe my eyes. There was nothing wrong with Oliver's fix, but I was completely staggered to notice there was no course line drawn onto the chart and, as I glanced around the chart table, saw no sign of a voyage plan. Telling him to move over and keep lookout, I rummaged in the chart-folio drawer and eventually grabbed the short-scale chart for the immediate passage area and, with a few deft strokes, constructed a series of course lines and transferred these to the large-scale immediate-use chart. The boy stood by with a look of astonishment on his face. The idea of professionally executed practical chart work aboard these hookers was clearly outside his experience. I then left him to fix our position every half-hour.

About two hours into the trip, I noticed we were being set to the north of our course line. I supervised an alteration of course for another coaster we were overtaking and, once happily back on track, asked him if he thought his navigation fixes indicated anything remotely odd occurring to the ship. He took another fix and compared this with previous ones and identified correctly a strong set and drift of the current which, without a course line would not have been quite so apparent. He cast an enquiring look in my direction, and I nodded my pleased confimation that he was indeed correct and suggested he did something about it, leaving him to determine precisely what. He checked the tidal information on the chart, compared this with his previous two positions and paused before plotting his tidal triangle. He was clearly confused over something, so I went over and asked him what he thought he should do. It soon became apparent that his confusion was between the two tidal conditions known as 'course to make good' and 'course made good'. Once we had sorted that out, I reminded him which one to choose and why, and then supervised his triangulation to put the matter right. Then, convinced he had done the set correctly, I left him to go to the gyro and apply the estimated three degrees set. I saw him apply this correctly, which left us steering 089 degrees (G) course.

Once shunted onto the right course, as it were, he clearly knew the theory of what to do, but was sadly lacking in confidence. I asked him about his studies and he assured me he was following a correspondence course through the same nautical college that he had attended for his theoretical training. This was the standard practice, for all navigation had to be learnt initially by what was becoming popularly known as 'distance-learning'. I suggested that if he felt it might be useful, then I was always on hand to assist and advise him with both the academic and professional aspects of his training. He brightened considerably and was all for going below and grabbing his latest work immediately. Suggesting, with a quiet smile, that it might be more appropriate to leave this until we were off watch below, I motioned for him to continue navigating the ship. With renewed confidence, his plotting and further alterations of course increased in proficiency, so I left him to work out position fixes and assess collision avoidances, with corrections updated for the inevitable set and drift, over the remainder of the watch. My surreptitious eye, while apparently focussed on the radar and lookout, rarely strayed too far from his efforts.

As Oliver relaxed, I learnt more about his past. He had served aboard smaller coasters in the company and had gained lifeboat and ordinary seaman's qualifications, as well as his Electronic Navaids and Radar Observer certificates. He expected promotion to the equivalent of AB shortly. He was fairly certain that the company would make him uncertificated third mate for the final year of his cadetship prior to sitting Mate's Home Trade exams, if not (hopefully) before.

Maggie relieved me after a six-hour watch when the crew started to surface on deck around 0900 and, handing over, I pointed out the chart work and suggested she might like to continue the process initiated by accurately plotting the ship's position and endeavouring to keep her on track. In the face of her astonishment I stood down Oliver, completed my log-book entries and went below for a well-earned breakfast.

Once below, I had to admit feeling none too well. The lively motion of this light, narrow coaster made me slightly seasick so, working along the lines of experienced principle, I took just a lightly boiled egg (which came as hard as a bullet) along with equally lightly buttered toast, and washed this down with half a mug of tea. Delicate bone china cups and saucers appearing with milk jug and sugar basin on a silver tray were now clearly things of the past, although I had done without them quite well on ships in the group other than Ellerton's. Recognising my predicament and, as there was little to do with the crew painting quietly on deck, Bob suggested I got my head down until lunchtime at 1300.

Painting the main-deck was a perennial task aboard all classes of ship to prevent rusting, and to keep the smart appearance of the ship that was the desire of all responsible chief officers (Courtesy BP plc).

When I returned to the saloon around four hours later, feeling much better, it was obvious the Skipper was angry. It was not so much what he said, but the way he looked. In fact, he did not say anything, but just grunted in greeting as I sat next to him, joining the others at the communal table for lunch. The atmosphere could be cut with a knife. Pete, the engineer on the side opposite me, just smiled as I sat. I had not met him before as 'he was playing down below with his rubber bands in his domain' after the pilot came on board earlier that day and had turned in immediately after stand-down. The air of gloom remained over the table until Bob, merely grunting again, got up and left to relieve Maggie in the wheelhouse for her meal break. I assumed while he had pottered around in the wheelhouse during a morning visit that he had seen my efforts at organising his navigational practices and was not feeling very happy with me. As it happened, I could not have hit further from the truth. Pete explained:

'He was doing rounds this morning and found Ricky, our new deck boy, being seasick in the soup.' He ventured this with an infectious grin.

I took that one on the chin without comment, but my thoughts were very much my own!

'Obviously – made him ditch the lot, and then stood over him as he remade some new. Heaven only knows what would have happened if he hadn't caught him – the mind boggles – or, at least, mine does!' he added pensively – voicing my own reflections.

I asked where the malcreant might be at that moment, receiving the reply he was washing up in the galley, not fancying lunch for some reason. I did query whether or not it had been quite wise putting such an inexperienced youngster in the galley first day out and, after a pause, enquired whose responsibility it was to work the duty roster. I might have guessed. Pete looked me directly in the eye, explaining that it was my job but that Maggie had sorted out something 'knowing you had the watch and was new.' He added that Bob had asked Jim, the AB to keep an eye on Ricky until the latter found his sea legs. It would not be too onerous a task seeing, to the chagrin of the senior rating, they shared the same cabin.

I took the challenge on the chin, advising I would have a word with Maggie later, but could let her continue, meanwhile, with this particular job as I was due to be on the vessel for only about two or three months. Testing the waters of my new trade a little more, and mindful of the OS drinking in every word along with his coffee, I changed the subject by suggesting that Bob might have already mentioned this, but apparently not: the Skipper's comment had merely been along the lines of 'thank goodness, now we can sail' with nothing further being mentioned. I continued the line of conversation:

'Well. I'm certainly not booked for anything longer than when they find another Mate to relieve me here. In fact, Captain Anson, Master of the *Viscount Gwendoline*, told me when I spoke to him just before leaving home, that if they hadn't found him a new second mate by the time she sailed, I'll probably fly out to Las Palmas to join the outward-bound VLCC.'

'Hmmm. Why Las Palmas, Jon? That's not an oil port, surely?'

'No, but it's reasonably cheap most of the time for bunkers. These large hookers take one hell of a lot of fuel. In fact, it works out as the biggest single running cost.' I volunteered.

'They're sure as hell short of officers in every company within the group – deck as well as engineers,' Pete ventured, going off on a different tack.

'Can't be too short of ratings, anyway,' Toby offered tentatively, adding: 'otherwise they would not have put Ricky as an extra hand here.'

'Better hurry up and get in your sea-time for a ticket then,' came Pete's immediate response, adding to me as a sideline. 'I reckon, they'll promote Oliver to uncertificated second or third mate before too long, depending on the size of the vessel,' he added for my information.

'Well, from what limited amount I saw on the bridge last night, he could be ready for it perhaps sooner than later.'

I suddenly realised that I had been speaking aloud thoughts that, although complimentary, should not have been voiced. After all, it was not really any of my business and, anyway, would probably have been better said only to the Skipper. Pete glanced across at the cadet and smiled:

'Yes, he's a good lad. Has always worked sensibly when he's been below with me, as well as what Bob has said about him.'

I realised that I need not have worried too much. On coasters, thoughts came and were spoken. There was none of the division which existed between officers and ratings that was so predominant deep-sea. Sharing Christian names with cadets, as well as the Master, was certainly something of a novelty!

I spent a couple of hours early afternoon checking ship's Arrangement, Capacity and various other plans, sorting out my duties, and getting to know better both ship and crew. I also took the opportunity to chat individually with the cadets and inspect their cadet journals which, on first appearances, I was pleased to note, appeared promising. Toby was a quietly spoken chap about seventeen years old. He had joined the company directly from his secondary high school in his home-town, Harwich. Pensively, and looking at me very directly, he paused, leaving me wondering what was coming next. He began by asking me about my own background as cadet and officer and suddenly the direction of his thoughts became clearer. This was reinforced when he asked me how he might leave the coast and apply for deep-sea trading. He apparently had a yearning for 'wider horizons' but was not quite sure how to set about this. He was reluctant to ask Bob or any of the others in case they thought he was becoming fed up with them and life on the coast, or even aboard. I told him we could discuss this later and that I would respect his confidence. In essence, I wanted to sound him out a little more before deciding whether I should become involved by offering more practical suggestions.

Further discussion was terminated by the appearance of Oliver asking if I would relieve Bob on the bridge. Maggie was running the crew. It was just after 1700 hours when I entered the wheelhouse. There seemed to be no fixed system of watch times while under way. As I had already discovered, the duty mate did a somewhat elastic four- to six-hour stint and then sent for his or her relief. The conventional 4–8, 8–12, and 12–4 sequence of this coaster's larger cousins seemed to go completely 'by the board.' Although not a matter of any real significance, it was strange to relieve the watch at odd hours, but was clearly one of the areas in which I would have to 'change my views'. Hearing the wheelhouse jalousie opening, Bob smiled up from his crossword puzzle and related the events concerning Ricky. It was clear he was not enamoured of this particular young lad.

I noticed there were no position fixes on the new chart in use so asked him where we were. He pointed a grubby finger which more or less covered about two miles of English Channel on the small-scale chart he had out on the table, reasonably close to my still-inserted course lines from the previous night, after which he made a mark with a very blunt chart-room pencil that frankly could have put the ship anywhere within a half-mile probability circle:

'Right, she's roughly there – and all yours. Steering 105 degrees True and Gyro. That bugger over there on the starboard side needs an eye kept on her. You might have to open up for her later in your watch, judging by the angle she's making. Only just a crossing vessel and about the same speed, although she just might be very slightly faster than us. In fact, she will almost certainly still be there, but a bit closer when you want Maggie to relieve you, or when she decides to come up. Anyway, you can use your own judgement about that – you've got enough experience. Everything else is OK. So, if you've no questions, I'll be away.'

Glancing in the direction Bob indicated, I saw the British-owned 'yellow peril' slowly crossing us at an oblique angle very slightly forward of the beam, confirmed I had the watch and would call him only if necessary. I received a very blank look in return, and with a taciturn grunt my esteemed Skipper left to get his head down. It was quickly becoming quite apparent that coastal navigation and relieving the watch were very much *laissez-faire* in practice, principle, philosophy and attitude.

Neither of us mentioned the question of chart work, but it struck me as quite astonishing that neither Bob nor Maggie put course lines on the chart, but merely 'popped in a position dot' as the spirit moved them, and with little accuracy. It seemed that navigation on all coasters was done largely by buoy-hopping using that stalwart of my happy cadet days called *Brown's Nautical Almanac*. This august publication had pages devoted to coastal passages and distances. I noticed on moving the filthy dirty and well dog-eared copy to the side of the chart-room table that it was open to the relevant page covering our passage. *Brown's* had the added advantage of giving these prudent coastal mariners the compass courses to steer between the buoys. It accounted also for the fact that the gyro, with its true course to steer, was largely ignored (regardless of error) and the magnetic compass still made the major source of navigation, with corrections lifted more-or-less piecemeal from the ship's deviation card. Putting a gyrocompass on this hooker was like feeding proverbial navigational pearls to swine. I began to understand again why Oliver had been so amazed at my meticulous insistence on 'proper navigation' the previous evening. The practice was something completely outside his experience.

My own views were abundantly plain: I would continue to perform the precision chart work, which was second nature, so immediately set about obtaining an accurate fix after setting up the Decca Navigator. A course line (after sharpening the pencil of course, and resurrecting my previously sharp one from the wheelhouse window box) was then corrected and transferred to the appropriate large-scale chart. I then amused myself devising a passage plan, using small- and large-scale charts covering the remainder of the trip, which I inserted in the Mate's rough log-book. Opening the drawers below the chart table, I noticed that charts were just thrown in completely at random (as I had discovered the previous night) with no apparent order or method just as they were finished with. Pencil marks had not been cleaned away from previous fixes and they were torn, dog-eared and decorated with a welter of tea mug stains. All were uncorrected and most were out of date by up to ten years or more, and resided on an assortment of chart-folio covers. With hardly any shipping around, I spent the rest of the watch between keeping a lookout and navigation putting the house into some sort of order, not least by completing an up-to-date and accurate chart indent for the areas in which the vessel normally traded, and requisitioning a set of local *Admiralty Pilots*. I left the remainder of the chart-sorting until a later watch, but felt this was probably the most that could be done initially to mark my sojourn in the coastal trades.

Watching the ship's head careering round 105 degrees (T) on the auto-pilot I was struck by her yawing. A quick guestimate placed this around one degree. Accustomed to gyro compasses steering to an accuracy of within one-quarter of a degree – especially in the calm sea, with low swell and light airs through which we were steaming – there had to be an explanation for this apparent phenomena. I opened the casing and glanced around the settings only to discover our latitude was placed some ten degrees south of the Equator. A quick adjustment to 50 degrees North and the ship immediately behaved herself, leaving a wake astern looking more like a course line and less like a maze of spaghetti.

Keeping a journal that was shown to the chief officer regularly every week, throughout the entire four-year apprenticeship or cadetship, was a requirement of all trainee deck officers serving with reputable companies. The entries covered a very wide brief which included items considered to be of interest in furthering learning (Courtesy BP plc).

Maggie came up with a mug of tea around 1900 to give me a meal relief. She was clearly impressed by the tidy and neatly laid out chart table and glanced askance at the completed yellow order forms awaiting the Skipper's signature. I enquired if she had any ideas concerning deck-store remains on board, only to receive an adenoidal grunt to the effect that 'the previous Mate, Charlie, had looked after all that'. From what I had learnt about 'our Charlie', nothing would have surprised me, so I decided this would be my next target, once I had deduced the jobs of painting and maintenance which were required. I also told her I would take over the crew rota for duty cook. She remained very subdued on the bridge after my return from a well-cooked and plentiful supper and had, I noticed, put a position with time on the chart covering the half-hour fix that had become due during my meal break. Placing this very definitely under the heading of progress, I enquired about her experiences at sea, which caused a slight thawing in her attitude. She confirmed what Bob had told me and I sensed our Maggie was really quite serious about her chosen profession. She seemed to have received considerable encouragement from the Kremlin in advancement towards her courses. She was aware of traditional methods of watch-keeping so far as chart work was concerned from her GSNC coastal and middle-trading around the Mediterranean and North Sea experiences, and seemed happy with the idea of doing the job properly. It seemed also that a showdown between Bob and myself was inevitable over a range of issues, but I remained adamant that whatever else might go, I would not budge from performing correct chart work.

The wheelhouse was very much the social centre of the ship while at sea, for shortly afterwards we were joined by the cadets and deck-hands who, fresh from deck work and a good supper, were clearly quite at home squatting below the wheelhouse windows and prattling away happily, totally unperturbed. Oliver sidled discreetly over to the chart table clearing hoping for an invite, so I suggested 'if he wished' he could do some *ex-officio* navigation, as well as asking him what he thought about the seamanlike antics of the 'yellow peril' still off to starboard. Bob came up a couple of hours later to 'see how things were' just as the lads went below to watch a western on the tele. Oliver looked very guiltily in his direction, but I told him to continue with plotting his latest fix, after which I suggested he went below to 'catch up with the adventures on the range'. I had already arranged with Maggie for her to come back and relieve me at midnight, which left the Skipper and I alone.

I sensed this was a prelude to my own *Gunfight at the OK Corral* (although I hoped not). He went over to the chart table, while I kept a lookout and prepared to cope with the fallout from what could well prove a nuclear explosion. There was a lull while he rustled around the papers obviously taking in the correct-scale chart with its up-to-date position fixes, accompanied by soothing sounds from gyro and regularly rotating Decca wheels. He glanced towards me while leaving the chart table and I watched his expressionless face, attempting to deduce some intimation of mood. I took and held a very deep breath, until suddenly, he spoke:

'Well, I did wonder if your presence indicated some 'big-ship' stuff, and now I know. Aboard all coasters, not only our company but virtually all ships of this class, we have sailed the waters around the UK nearly all of our working lives and know where we are at a glance. This is one of the reasons, as I mentioned, why most of my fellow captains do not take too kindly to you ex-deep-sea blokes. You've got me by the 'short and curlies' really, I suppose. If I don't do the chart work and even sign the indents, and we have an incident, then I and London and Chatham will undoubtedly be liable – so, you will see I've already done the latter and we'll send them off from our next UK port. Fair enough, I suppose, Jon, but not really necessary and in my opinion a complete waste of money. Still I am not paying for it, although I don't know what the Kremlin are going to say. I notice young Ollie is now working for you, and expect you've already worked out a programme for the lads regarding maintenance on deck? And I notice the ship is actually steering a direct course. What did you do to achieve that? I've always accepted her yawing, without questioning this too much, as merely an indiosyncracy and, as I told you, coasting generally has a far more casual approach to seafaring than you have been used to.'

He paused and I came in explaining about my proposed work list, and the corrected Decca Navigator, and gyro setting. I mentioned also the importance of a navigation procedure that was 'perhaps a little more formal, especially with cadets on board who needed examination preparation', and so I had introduced an informal training programme for Oliver. Taking this particular bull by its potentially sharp horns, I also told him that we had a second mate who was clearly happy doing her job more efficiently, as well as preparing for her Master's Home Trade ticket. Bob smiled his rueful grin and agreed to humour me by also 'popping on a dot' occasionally. I did suggest, while the iron was still hot, that Maggie in furthering her experience as second mate undertook chart ordering and corrections, which was received with an incoherent adenoidal grunt, but no further comment.

It was 0630 a day or so later when Toby gave me a shake and said that Bob wanted me in the wheelhouse. My esteemed Skipper smiled as I entered and, in one sharp outburst, thrust a steaming mug of coffee in my hand, said we were approaching the Maas Centre pilotage station from where we would enter the New Waterway, and would I take the watch for the passage with the pilot through Rotterdam to our berth in Dordrecht. He wanted to get his head down briefly having been on duty since relieving Maggie. I was quite taken aback as my previous experiences usually meant that the Old Man stood to with the pilot but, after all, it was his ship. Still, having won the battle (if not quite the war) concerning navigational practices at sea, I was not too concerned. I called the port authorities on the VHF radio and cleared the ship inwards, and then slightly eased the vessel's speed as we approached the pilot cutter. He bounded on board quite happily and we settled to what for me was an interesting passage. I gave a rueful smile as we passed Europoort and I caught sight of two impressive supertankers: the 250,000 sdwt *Esso Northumbria* and the similar-capacity *King Haakon VII*. Apparently, we had passed another two VLCC's awaiting berths and pilots in the outer anchorage, but Bob felt it inappropriate to break my beauty sleep by informing me – I was glad to hear. There was not much I could say to this – after all, he knew where my shipping heart really lay, although

Rotterdam's Europoort and oil berths were specifically designed to handle very large supertankers such as the 250,000 sdwt Esso Northumbria and King Haakon VII (Courtesy Captain 'Tinker' Taylor).

I had purposely not 'gone on too much about these ships', but shut up and merely answered any questions as these had been posed.

It took us about 3¼ hours before we approached the conglomeration of channels leading to the jetty in Dordrecht where we were booked to berth. I sent Oliver to call Bob with a cup of tea, having already suggested to Toby, our duty cook for the day, that he provide my breakfast on the bridge, along with an extra meal for the pilot. Thus when Bob appeared, yawning and scratching indelicately, I was fed and watered and ready to rally the troops; to send Maggie aft (complete with boiler suit and boots), and then go forward for stand-by. Oliver came from below to take his trick at the helm.

The lads were already hard at work on the forecastle by the time I had told Bob what had been done and meandered along there. I put the senior cadet on the windlass-cum-winch and prepared to help the others who were engaged in passing ropes out of the forecastle locker onto the main-deck area. I was glad to see Toby had the wire back-spring already out, so changed my mind, left them to their digging, as it were, and laid this out for instant use. As Ricky's training was my largely my responsibility, I told him to reeve the spring loosely round the bitts and back over the outside of our rail, ready to pass to whoever was going to jump ashore. While keeping a very close eye on how he did it, I reflected coasters were very much a 'DIY job' having been used to, if not a posse, at least a couple of shore-side gangs to handle hawsers on bigger ships. There was not much point voicing views which were frankly irrelevant. The lads with me, not unnaturally, understood little other than coasting. I kept silent, putting the submission of such thoughts under my own heading of 'personal progress'. The AB apparently always went aft with the second mate aboard these ships, two being sufficient to cope with the requisite tasks.

While I was musing happily, I saw the inevitable occur 'right before my very eyes' as the old music-hall comedians (perhaps appropriately enough) used to say. Ricky, totally disregarding my instructions, was also quite happy as he passed the wire spring over the rail top, completely bypassing the bitts. I stepped in quickly:

'Ricky, dear boy. What did I tell you to do with that spring? No, not what I'd like to tell you to do with it, son, but what I did tell you? Was it not something about passing it loosely round the bitts before turning it up against the outside of the lower rail? Think about what you are doing – like where do you want the wire to end up, and how it is likely to get there!'

He pause and shot me an engaging smile before sorting out his spring as indicated.

'Sorry, Jon. I forgot,' he added disarmingly.

'Look, Ricky. If you don't wake your bloody ideas up soon, I think the Skipper will boot you off this hooker, you know. You're not flavour of the month at the moment. Good job your mum probably loves you because you may well find yourself returning to her quicker than either of you thought!'

The rest of the stand-by went smoothly enough and we were soon brought up alongside the jetty. It was still a novel experience for me to take over the windlass and land Ricky onto the quay to take the spring forward before he raced aft to accept that from Maggie, and then rushed forward to complete my moorings…and then raced aft…and then back to the forecastle head. I felt a distinct learning curve was being undertaken and, of course, hoped that Ricky also was finding one of his own.

After standing-down the lads, I rejoined Bob in the wheelhouse to find out when the agent was due, or if he had received radio instructions from the Kremlin regarding our next cargo and destination. The agent would not be visiting, which dashed my hopes of letters from Sue and any forwarded mail, as ships this size did not have agents other than in major regularly visited UK ports, such as Par. Another learning curve. All mail would be sent from London to the next major port of call where there was an agent. This apparently was a system which generally worked very reliably. Any crew changes that occurred at these minor ports were entered on the Master's copy of the Articles and then made up with the second copy deposited at 'central station' Par.

After breakfast, the sun came out, the wind dropped and Bob informed me that cargo would not be worked that day as it was a Dutch bank holiday. To the unmitigated delight of the crew, I told them over a pot of tea in the mess-room that we would be turning to immediately afterwards for a number of painting jobs. Bob smiled his agreement (not that I had included him in my rota) as I delegated Maggie to take Oliver and Toby for accommodation cleaning and then funnel painting where necessary, while I took Jim and Ricky to start touching up the railings port and starboard – fore and aft – so making a substantial start to my maintenance programme. Bob surprised me by stating that he would join in and help with the railings.

We had been under way and were well advanced with the job when Ricky fell over his feet and kicked over the paint tin. The remainder of us stood there momentarily transfixed in horror watching white railing paint flow liberally along the green main-deck. Bob and I shouted a variety of curses and lamentations and brought down our wrath to bear onto his head so effectively that he ran along the main-deck into his cabin and locked the door. I left Bob to sort him out and, grabbing Maggie and the cadets, we joined the other crew mopping up the mess and making desperate efforts to prevent too much disappearing over the side. It was, of course, inevitable. Looking over the ill-fated railings, we could see a few white streaks flowing gently down the black hull and into the water. There was little we could do to stop it. Bundles of cotton waste, rags, cloths and saw dust were sprinkled without regard to supply or cost. In fact, we used our entire stock. We simply had to clean up the hull before the harbour service launches made their duty run, saw the evidence emanting from our incident and reported us, resulting in a very hefty fine on the ship. We lowered the jollyboat and, with Bob and the cadets looking after our hull, the rest of us set about cleaning the main-deck. Not a lot of paint had run into the dock, not that there was much we could do about it, anyway. Luckily, it was quick-drying and Bob managed to black-paint over the relevant white-splashed parts of our hull reasonably quickly, hiding at least most of the evidence. We saw the tide taking our little trails of white paint further away from the vessel. Bob told me bluntly that if we were fined, he would sign off Ricky from the ship the moment we touched the next UK port, recommending to the company that he be dismissed. As it happened, we got away with that incident for nothing was heard from the harbour authorities. It took a hell of a time to tidy up the ship, though, much of which was left to Ricky under the various supervision of all officers.

It seemed, from radio-telephone instructions, that we were to shift ship once the china clay was discharged, and go to another berth to load a full cargo of duff coal from the Frans Swarttouw coal jetty, Botlek, near Rotterdam, bound for Yelland power station, close to Barnstaple. The coal apparently had been imported by bulk carrier from Australia, of all places, leaving me to cast a very odd thought to the demise of our own coal industry. Bob broke into my reverie by explaining this would be 'easier in one sense for, were we to load grain after coal the holds would have to be cleaned extremely thoroughly'. He reverted to humour by saying the task would then have to be 'a proper job' as the Cornish loaders in Par put it, thus offering me a cross-fertilising reassuring memory of the Second Officer on the *Earl of Bath*, from my cadet days, so very much in the distant past; 'another country', in fact. He also advised there was no agent in Yelland, but that the next port after that, wherever it might be, could produce mail.

He stated, this time without any trace of humour, that a couple of problems would make life interesting. There were no refinements at the particular coasting jetty to which we had been assigned. The ship had to be lined up to a fixed loading crane which meant warping her backwards and forwards along the jetty as each hatch was partially finished, which was a 'bit fiddly', although there was nothing we could do about this. It was a situation that occurred fairly regularly in the coastal trades. It meant, of course,that an officer and two hands would be required on stand-by to warp her backwards and forwards as each part of our hatches was partially loaded. A further difficulty would be assessing how much cargo had been taken on board. There was no alternative method of tallying the amount of coal received other than using ship's capacity tables. Again this was not a completely rare situation aboard this class of vessel. Both came as unforeseen surprises to me, helping me appreciate comments from Bob regarding essential differences in operating practice between coasting and deep-sea ships – this time on cargo practices. There were no problems with either so far as I was concerned. I would take the former as it occurred, while the latter was familiar from foreign-going service, where reference to capacity tables, checking against recorded draught marks, had also been taken regularly in my stride.

We could not berth so close to the famous Botlek stores without paying them a visit, particularly as, in response to a phone call, they sent a minibus to collect us, which would then return us to the ship afterwards. We were not restricted in quantity and loaded the ship and our cabins to the gunwales with 'goodies' at much-reduced prices compared to those in the UK. I bought also a range of working clothes for already my boiler suits, much abused from tanker days, were wearing very thin and closing the last light of their days.

We arrived without incident at Yelland power station near Barnstaple following an uneventful two-day trip in perfect weather with calm seas, bathed in hot sunshine, enabling much deck work to be done. There was little bridge work for 'our Ollie' on that voyage. The fifty-minute pilotage was a straightforward run and we ran the ship alongside the jetty where, once both the pilot and tide fully ebbed, she sat fair and firm upon a sandbank with no traces of either the River Taw or sea for many miles. I had been on watch for the rounding of Land's End and revelled in watching down all my old favourites on the radar and checking these while plotting the ship's position against our chart: Lizard Point, Tater du light, Runnel Stone buoy, Gwynepp Head, Sennen Cove, The Longships light, Pendeen, Gurnards and St Agnes headlands were all 'grist to my nautical (and perhaps romantic) mill', for they were all such magnificently resounding names. Bob was working on deck with Maggie and all the crew busily engaged on the forecastle head and forward stores in a full-scale chipping and painting job I had set them. It was quite a good feeling watching them working with a will under Bob's direction, while I stood happily in the wheelhouse navigating the ship without any hint of guilt at not joining them.

Of course, Ricky 'did a Ricky', as we were coming to catalogue this young man's already endless series of incident-cum-accidents. Bob set him the task of knocking off the clips securing the hatch covers before our arrival. This entailed hitting these fair and square with a heavy 16 lb, or 8 kilo hammer. Bob repaired to the wheelhouse, bringing me a cup of tea and smoking contentedly, leaving the residue of work for Maggie to supervise. The ship was moving easily in a calm-to-moderate south-westerly Force 3–4 sea and swell, with brilliant summer sunshine and we chatted idly watching Ricky swinging his hammer and systematically working his way through the clips. Suddenly his enthusiasm overtook his common sense (yet again) for, with an enthusiastic swing, he missed the next clip and we watched horrified as the weight of the hammer continued its momentum and passage out of his hands to describe a

In many places the Cornish coast was bleak and barren, but it was also bedevilled with outcrops of rocks and dangerous currents, which meant that bridge watch-keeping had to be performed carefully and conscientiously (Author's Collection).

delightful parabola as it disappeared dramatically over the side. Only a slight 'plop' and the faintest hint of ruffled water indicated that it was no more. The boy stood there while the cogs ticked over painfully as he assessed what had occurred, until he was roused by a shout from Bob. The Master dived out of the wheelhouse, down the short companionway to the main-deck giving vent to his feelings with quite one of the most sustained and continuous bursts of foul language I had heard for a long time. Ricky stood there petrified while Bob climbed onto the hatch with murder in his eyes. The boy sudenly became galvanised into action and they chased each other round the main-deck, with Ricky, of course, romping through the recently painted area leaving a trail of delicate little green footprints everywhere. Bob was far less agile than the boy and in the end returned breathless to the wheelhouse still bandying around threats and assorted colourful adjectives.

From the time Bob had left me, I could do little more than fall about, paralysed with unrestrained laughter. Maggie had seen what was happening and along with the crew she also was convulsed and, while the lads went below out of range of Bob's anger, she came into the wheelhouse to share the scene with me. It was with considerable effort that we composed ourselves and straightened our faces for Bob's return. Still fuming, he relieved me to go on deck and grab Ricky with the first priority of getting the boy to take off his shoes, stopping his *avant garde* art display spreading further over our foredeck and throughout the accommodation block. Ricky was quite white with shock, but this moderated my own exasperation only mildly for it was my job now to repair the damage. I handed him a slightly smaller verison of the ill-fated hammer which, because of its lesser weight, required much more effort to release the dogs. I made it quite clear that it was now Ricky's job to undo and make fast the hatch clips regardless of whatever time of the day or night this duty was required, even if it meant turning him to in the middle of his sleep. I then rallied the crew and with paint remover, pots and brushes renovated the main-deck.

I took advantage of our high-and-dry condition alongside to put the lads overside cleaning some marine growths from our hull. Bob joined in enthusiastically as a member of crew and scraped away as if his life depended on it. The task was not that drastic, but removal of weeks of accumulated acorn and a lesser growth of gooseneck barnacles (along, of course, with that ubiquitous fur-like micro-organism known as good old fashioned slime) that had accumulated since the vessel's last 'grounding', certainly helped add an extra portion of a knot to increasing the ship's speed. It was then a case of applying a coating of quick-drying anti-fouling and anti-corrosive the next day, which caused the remaining poisoned growths to disappear into the sea. Very recently, the entire Ellerton Group fleet had been issued with new anti-toxics that included an alternative to the previously tin-based paints, as part of a new and growing international policy designed to 'make the seas greener', something with which all thinking mariners wholeheartedly concurred. It was while the whole lot of us were busily engaged in this task that we heard a hailing from the main-deck.

Glancing up, we saw a uniformed figure looking down requesting our presence back on board. Bob was just about to ask questions along the lines of 'who the hell are you and why should we?' when the figure announced they were customs officers making a surprise call to check our bond. It was certain that we each went through what the medical fraternity would call 'palpitations psychosomatic with shock' as we thought of our recent purchases in Botlek and other places, none of which had been declared on the Customs Form C142 that we had handed to the pilot along with our free pratique request (or health clearance coming from abroad). Alas, we were all well over the limits of our official issues. Two of the gentlemen awaited us as we followed Bob's lead clambering up the ladder onto deck. Our small group of dockers were watching events with unaccustomed anticipatory joy for, after all, any variation to the boring norm was welcomed, especially when there was the added glee of safely witnessing someone else's misfortune. The officers turned over the ship to such an extent that a customs van had to be called to collect the confiscated loot of beer, assorted spirits and thousands of cigarettes, pipe tobacco (which Bob loved) and over two hundred cigars ('present for my father, sir'). As an official van was not readily available they chartered one from a local plumber that bore the self-painted slogan on its side panels 'Employ us to clear away your blockages and smells.' In point of fact, the smell definitely remained even if the blockage to the country's revenue was well and truly removed. That, of course, was largely academic so far as we were concerned. A senior customs officer was called to debate the way forward. Potentially the situation was very serious and we were wondering if a court case would ensue with a subsequent delay to the ship. Bribery was not even an option, and we were sufficiently quick to appreciate Maggie shoving a paint-encrusted hand firmly over Ricky's mouth so preventing another 'Rickyism' before it had time to be pondered, let alone uttered, and so preventing us all being invited to attend a court appearance with added charges.

Eventually, the senior man decided that if we each paid a fine against an official receipt and accepted the consfication of the goods, the matter could as he phrased it, 'be dealt with summarily.' The fine allotted to each of us was twice the value of the goods confiscated. Frankly, from my deep-sea days witnessing the capture of other mariners who had fallen foul of this particular aspect of the law, we were dealt with really quite fairly, although it was not an immediate thought that I bandied around during the post-mortem over lunch. My share virtually wiped out my wages for the past month, and I got off comparatively lightly to some of the lads. It would be true to say that a sea of long faces accumulated over the mess table along with the Irish stew, so kindly cooked by an equally financially reduced Oliver.

Ricky's (it had to be) next *faux pas* occurred while we were storing ship in Barnstaple with sufficient food to get us round to Par, where we would again take all main-deck, engine-room and catering stores (including another 8 kilo hammer) plus my navigational charts and publications, I was pleased to be advised. I never asked Bob's opinion. I took Ricky to the nearest supermarket and set him the task of navigating the trolley – something I thought even he could do without incident. Oh, how much I underestimated his ingenuity. While I was concentrating on finding the food and deducing how much to purchase, Ricky, leaning on the trolley, jerked it forward so that the lower wheelbase caught the back of my right shoe, splitting the seam and leaving me in my stockinged foot. Instinctively, I turned round and in the loudest possible voice called him the delightful name by which he was now commonly referred to by all on board, supported by a few choice equally spontaneous expletives. After all, my response was in the manner of the sea. The words reverberated round the supermarket and bounced along the aisles to settle cosily upon the shelves. All nearby, mainly female shoppers, turned and looked at me with undisguised horror. However acceptable my little love message may have been at sea, it was clearly not appreciated ashore. I tried to bury myself in the floor, but with no avail. Ricky collapsed with laughter over the trolley, at least gaining some measure of the disapproval dished out to me. It was in an atmosphere of chilly silence that we continued our shopping expedition. Even at the check-out there was little respite, for we were treated like Martian aliens by the good folk of Barnstaple – not surprisingly really, I supposed. Even while waiting for the taxi, looks of unbridled animosity bounded our way. As a shopping expedition, it could hardly appear under the heading of an unmitigated success. It seemed our stay in this delightful region was not appreciated either by officialdom, ourselves, or the local residents. It was clearly time to leave.

We finished discharging almost completely forty-eight hours after arrival. Bob had phoned the Kremlin to be told that a full cargo of assorted stones had been found for us in Newlyn. So we would not be calling at Par for mail, china clay or stores. I stood down Maggie to prepare a voyage plan and charts, while my job was to rally the lads and supervise hatch-cleaning in readiness for their loading. This was not the major task it would have been had our next cargo been grain or even china clay, because all that required was a thorough wash-down and sweep-up. Bob joined in the fun, but not without stating his continued displeasure at what he referred to as my 'deep-sea ways' by telling me he was doing the work with us that Maggie should have been doing. I noticed, however, that he did not overrule my actions, and contendedly (I don't think) joined in the fun. We took the pilot on board and sailed just before 2000 hours, but by the time I relieved the watch at 2300, we were pitching moderately to violently in a rough sea and heavy north-westerly swell. It seemed the seas did not take too kindly to a ship of this size in ballast. I remained on watch for the passage past Tintagel Head to Pendeen light once more, and a few hours later we took the pilot and entered the small port of Newlyn. One we were safely alongside and with hatches opened ready for loading, I suggested Oliver talk me through the process that had brought us alongside, as he witnessed this from the windlass, thus preparing him to do the job, intially under supervision, but eventually on his own. Obviously, with the lack of sufficient hands I could not let him actually do the latter, but at least he could follow the reasoning more closely behind what had already happened. I also got him to talk me through a proposed departure procedure, based on hypothetical suggestions from the pilot and orders from Bob. Watching his earnest young face strained with concentration, there was almost yet another sense of *déjà vu* when I thought back to my own early days. It was all 'grist to the training mill', as I recalled one of my officers saying to me when I was a cadet under supervision while doing the same operation on stand-by aboard larger deep-sea vessels.

Above: Deck cadets worked with the chief officer on a range of duties including checking the forecastle head store-rooms and rope lockers (Courtesy BP plc).

Left: When alongside or at anchor in calm waters the opportunity of doing essential over-the-side painting was rarely missed (Courtesy Captain Peter Adams).

It seemed that our cargo consisted of stones for use in cement and ballast, plus 400 tons of facing stones destined for Deptford for use in a major London building project currently under construction. We only just fitted alongside the jetty at Newlyn, which added extra piquancy to my recent instruction session with Oliver. Our run ashore was not particularly spectacular for there was little to see or do, although we all made very short work of some of the most delightful fish and chips I had ever tasted, bought from a quayside chippy. Neither the batter nor the chips were greasy, while the fish melted in the mouth. It was worth calling in for that alone. We also popped into the local supermarket and stored ship for a two-week trip. I took Toby along on this occasion. The only diversion available was the interest our arrival attracted from tourists to this holiday resort, but even that was short-lived once we commenced loading, as the deputy harbourmaster, in the interests of safety, posted a series of white-lettered on red background 'Keep out' notices along our portion of the jetty. It took just four hours for loading. We had arrived at 1415 hours and commenced loading within thirty minutes, completing my loading plan with 710 tonnes in number two and 630 in number one. The various parcels of stones were sectioned off in the hatches by extended polythene sheeting. The pilot boarded at 1940 and we were off the berth at first ebb by 2000 hours.

I spent the next forty minutes with the cadets battening down and preparing the vessel for sea before going to the wheelhouse to relieve Bob. It was very busy for the first two hours on both navigation and collision avoidance with the usual run of trawlers, pleasurecraft and assorted fishing vessels associated with this part of the Channel. Everyone behaved themselves by conforming to international regulations but a few wide swings to starboard were necessary as some of the minor boats crossed our bows alarmingly closely. Oliver joined me for most of the watch, doing the navigation and collision avoidance. Surprisingly, Maggie came up after five hours to relieve me following a smooth watch with decreasing visibilty and the vessel moving easily in calm seas with light airs. She seemed subdued for some reason, but thawed a little without expressing her thoughts or feelings as we chatted and shared a pot of coffee.

It was a different story when I popped up to relieve Bob so he could go for breakfast. The vessel was proceeding off Portland Bill in dense fog. After he had left, the fog did not join him, for seriously reduced visibility persisted throughout my watch, leaving me on continuous radar obserservations and plotting of ubiquitous vessels, most of which I assumed were fishing, apart from a couple of coasters a few miles each side. We had a slight problem. The radar worked only on the six-mile range, when ideally the two- and even one-and-a-half-mile ranges would have been far more useful with the frequent close-quarter situations experienced. How often had I advocated to deep-sea cadets the importance of using a range commensurate with both conditions of visibility and circumstances, and here was I going against the very dicta in which I had been brought up to believe and, even more importantly, to trust. After all, I would never have dreamed of using only a six-mile operational range on a coaster for working purposes, with occasional moves to twelve miles, gaining an idea of developing situations. Every time I switched to below six miles, the PPI disappeared completely from the screen leaving merely a black expanse of space. Both the Old Man and I fiddled about with the thing enthusiastically, but our efforts to produce any kind of positive response proved fruitless. He suggested Oliver should come to the wheelhouse for lookout duties, which was welcomed by me as much as for the extra pair of eyes and extra training it would offer the boy.

By the time St Catherine's Point was bearing 041 degrees (T) x 7.7 miles, four hours later, the situation had, if anything, worsened. I could not even see the forecastle head from the wheelhouse. Bob was, of course, aware of the conditions and popped up occasionally, but there was little for him to do other than to chat about 'all and nothing' while leaving me to get on with things. We had passed the stage of fencing with each other and worked together quite well, although I had to accept his taciturn nature for what it was and realise after reflection that it was equally difficult for him to accept me as, to all intents and purposes, still a deep-sea Mate. Over the past few weeks, experience had given me much insight into the significance of his remarks at Par when I joined the ship.

It was around 0200 when I was called again to take over the watch with heavy cloud, dull and foggy. Noting we had Dungeness light just abaft the beam, and that visibility had improved to around a mile, I grabbed the coffee from Maggie, confirmed I had the watch once she had handed over, and noted her making the requisite entries in the log-book before scurrying gratefully below after a quick 'good night'. I was quite happy with things for the leg of the trip before me – the approaches to and from, with the passage in the Dover Strait, were amongst my favourite stretches of water. The wheelhouse held its customary darkened condition to protect night vision and, once Maggie had left was lonesome without seeming lonely. In fact, I welcomed being up here on my own and relished the various responsibilities associated with navigational watch-keeping, particularly during night-time. There was always a sense of the unknown on opening the wheelhouse accommodation door, for no watch-keeper was ever sure exactly what conditions and situation he/she would find. In a strange way, things seemed different from similar watches held during daytime or in good visibilty. I kept the wheelhouse doors slightly open to permit a flow of fresh air. This removed the otherwise stuffy atmosphere so conducive in the central heating to a dangerous nodding off and slackening of attention. I often found it necessary after an extensive period on watch to moisten my eyes and step onto the bridge wing, letting my face droop over the dodger in order to freshen up. As watches in the coastal trade were inevitably prolonged, I found an increase in the frequency of these occasions, as well as popping into the bridge 'heads' for a refreshing face wash. Music playing softly from the radio helped to keep me awake and added a flavour of reality to something of an unreal world.

This particular summer night was not too cold, and the sound from a regular swishing of the sea coming through the open doors contrasted with the irregular clicking of our gyrocompass as it corrected slight variations to our course. These were subconscious noises, reassuring and vaguely comforting, yet immediately noticeable were the gyro to cease functioning. Another background contribution came from our VHF radio tuned to channel sixteen, largely ignored, but drawing suddenly focussed attention when a navigational warning was broadcast from local coastguards, or at the mention of our own ship's name. It seemed that all watch-keepers 'listened without hearing' until attention was attracted. An ethereal contribution to watch-keeping at night came from the subdued noise and weird elongated shadows cast around the large wheelhouse as these were reflected from our uscreened radar.

As time came to fix the ship's position, I moved to the chart table behind the small screen and adjusted the angle lamp allowing its dim light to help me change charts from BA2451 to BA1892. I altered course forty minutes or so later to pass Dover Harbour abeam by one mile. Visibility remained the same but, as we passed one-and-a-half miles off the blurred bulk of Folkestone cliffs before passing the harbour, we met a strong tidal set making it necessary to allow two degrees to maintain the true compass course of 062 degrees (G). It was then that we encountered a decisive build-up of shipping, centred around the Dover Harbour area. This was not a situation requiring Bob to be called to the wheelhouse, for I had quickly learnt that navigating officers in the coastal trades sorted out their own problems, unless circumstances clearly required the Master to be present. Such a situation would perhaps occur while encountering shipping during any approach to a berthing port or harbour, when the Captain would reasonably expect to be called. As it happened, I was quite happy with the way things were developing here, and felt all was well, remained under my control, and could be managed. It was shortly afterwards that the ship crossing from starboard that I had been plotting had closed to under one-mile distance, with a ferry leaving the eastern harbour entrance. There were also two ships that we were rapidly overtaking, and a number of coasters on various courses inside the traffic separation zones and cutting towards our general direction. Even though our speed was a modest six knots, it seemed logical to slow down to three knots and allow the other ships to sort themselves out. I watched through the swirling fog their navigation lights vanishing into the night, and noticed they disappeared from view visually through binoculars at around three-quarters of a mile distance, confirming the restricted range of visibility deduced from the six-mile range now permanently fixed on our radar. It was some fifteen minutes later that I built up speed before we lost complete steerage way, so we passed at one mile distance either side of our vessel both the harbour, and South Goodwin's welcoming sweeping light. A quick alteration to 014 degrees True and Gyro; a change to chart BA1828 and we cleared the Dover Patrol memorial by five-cables distance. The passage reminded me of time aboard our training ketch and a comfortingly spectral glimpse occurred in my mind's eye of LBB (or that 'little bearded b****d'), as we cadets all 'affectionately' referred to the Skipper of the *Stenwood Navigator*.

The inland passage up the Downs was very busy with coastal traffic, requiring a number of alterations of course for collision avoidance. I had to keep a close eye on the set and drift for we passed quite closely to the Goodwin Sands. With Deal Pier, just over one mile distance, course was set to 008 degrees (T&G), but it was only ten minutes later that careful plotting revealed we were meeting a strong tidal stream setting us onto the sands. The vessel responded immediately to my alteration of eight degrees to port leaving us to pass safely the South Brake buoy by two cables. The remainder of the watch passed without problems, and by the time we were approaching the Princes Channel, I called Bob to take over the watch and see his vessel into the Thames bound for Deptford Wharf.

This watch was quite one of the busiest I ever experienced aboard the good ship *Prince Albert*, with continuous navigation checks and alterations of course for collision avoidance in reduced visibilty. My verdict on going below for a well-earned rest was one of quiet satisfaction. Quiet because only I knew what had happened. No one else. I was the only person alive who was aware of the assessments necessary in collision situations on this passage, and instinctively by 'knowing within my knower' (as I once termed it) the instant necessary to alter course, and by how much. It was similarly very much a singular act to have fixed the ship's position on this run, having studied the tidal influences and made correct allowances, then watching to see how these developed. These things collectively made navigational watch-keeping at night so interesting, important and worthwhile. I could not express how I really felt about my job, even to Sue, for these were things people who had never done the job could not even begin to understand – things of necessity outside their experience. I could not find a similar parallel of comparison among shore professions but I did know, as I settled down for a read from my beloved Kipling before dropping off to sleep, I would not have changed places with anyone. That day had also been my birthday.

There was really inadequate time for sleep. I had been relieved by Bob around 0630 and less than five hours later was woken up to stand-by forward. Once we had made fast alongside and I had both hatches open with discharge commenced, Bob suddenly appeared on deck and announced that if I wanted to, I 'could stand down for a bit of local leave'. I needed no second telling. There was no time to phone faithful Sue, so I just appeared on the doorstep of our Canterbury home to her total astonishment, for an overnight 'quickie'. I reflected, as we snuggled up on the settee watching a video, well fed and definitely wined, that this was the first time I had been home since joining the coaster two months previously. So much for my optimistic thoughts that being on the coast would allow more time 'with my beloved'.

Navigation and watch-keeping during the hours of darkness were generally quieter periods than doing the same work in daylight hours when the wheelhouse was often invaded by a range of officers passing through engaged on essential duties (Courtesy BP plc).

Bob's thundercloud face met me as I reported back on board at 1000 hours next day. It seemed he was not angry with me, but with the port and pilotage authorities who insisted that we carried a pilot to Gravesend. He was particularly livid because, on reporting in as we cleared the pilot station inward bound, he had been allowed to see the ship into Deptford on his own. My own face also recorded displeasure for there was no relief for me, nor any news of one. I had left home too early to contact the Kremlin, but Bob had done so on my behalf. Anyway, after I had calmed down and supervised the crew closing hatches and preparing the vessel for sea (with Ricky happily engaged on his special 'clip job'), I stood down Maggie to prepare her passage plan and charts for the run to Rotterdam. There was then little to be done but wait for the pilot. We took on board some deck and catering stores and Bob arranged for a local representative/technician to give our radar some first aid. I had no idea, even afterwards, what had caused the problem, although Bob murmured something vaguely about 'weak contacts'. Anyway, following maintenance, repair and servicing, the thing worked on all ranges, but we checked very thoroughly before letting the guy leave the ship.

We had a crew change while I was away. Jim, our able seaman had been sent on compassionate leave due to the illness of his mother. We took in exchange an AB

Usually marine radar sets were perfectly reliable, but often defects would occur for which there was no obviously apparent reason, which required considerable attention from either the ship's officers or from technicians called in at the next port (Courtesy BP plc).

who had been deep-sea for many years and was on his first coastal ship. He was also extremely disgruntled and spent the entire first day among the crew moaning about 'the easy time officers enjoy and how their jobs aboard coasters are so much of a doddle'. The first we as Master and mates knew that something was amiss was when our engineer reported to Bob on the bridge shortly following my return on board that he had overheard some alarming comments being made and how after lunch, 'the new guy was spreading seeds of discontent'. Apparently he felt he ought to have joined the ship as an officer, and had taken an AB's job only to help out the company. The latter at least sounded reassuringly familiar, but the former was not quite so clear. Bob told us on hearing this news that, from this chap's discharge book, he had been promoted from AB to uncertificated third mate 'to make up the numbers' aboard a tramp ship for a eight-day period crossing the south Atlantic before his last leave. This hardly made him a Master Mariner, but the mere fact that he had accepted his post aboard our vessel and not stood out for a mate's job spoke volumes about the company's idea of his true status. He would not have been given the job anyway, Bob assured me, on the evidence of just five days' deep-sea bridge experience. For my part, I sincerely hoped not, but frankly nothing would have surprised me. We debated what would be the best way forward as neither Bob,

Maggie nor I had not encountered this problem before. I mentioned sailing with an uncertificated third mate on two occasions which had resulted in the Old Man of each ship getting rid of the guy, but had also heard positive stories of some 'uncert officers' who were competent, experienced and reliable – purely within that junior rank.

My first encounter with him was telling him to organise the cadets and ordinary seaman to stow away a brand new mooring wire we had received last time in Par which had been resting quietly and inoffensively in the forecastle stores. To do this effectively, it was necessary to rig a turntable and unreave the wire along the main-deck, working with the lay, and then restow this devoid of kinks. Bob and I watched his progress from the wheelhouse window and were suitably impressed by the manner in which he organised the lads in setting about the task, and did a first-class job. He was clearly a very competent AB but, as Bob remarked, 'So he bloody well should be after all his years on deck.' There was no answer to that.

Walking towards the stores, I encountered him and complimented him on a job well done. I then set him the task of teaching the lads where necessary to splice eyes into a couple of new mooring warps. This also he started satisfactorily enough and then had to stop as lunch was announced and we afterwards prepared the ship for sea. The pilot finally arrived at 1320 hours and we departed five minutes later. Bob let me take the ship from Gravesend round to the Isle of Grain where we were to take bunkers. It was a busy period caused mainly by our vessel being hampered during frequent overtaking situations and having to keep within the narrow dredged channel on a falling tide, with numerous vessels inward bound preventing us coming over too far to port in the main channel. It proved an interesting situation, because attention to the heavy density of traffic was compounded by the presence of Bob and Maggie lounging in customary fashion in the wheelhouse and chatting away 'ten to the dozen'. I managed to keep cool, but only relaxed inwardly once we had cleared Number Six Sea Reach buoy and edged away from the main stream of traffic to round the Isle of Grain. Our AB continued his work on deck of wire splicing over the two hours it took to pump on board fifty tons of fuel oil and depart for the continent. Again my inspection indicated he had made an excellent and professional job, but both Maggie and Bob could not help overhearing the comments he made as asides about officers. He really seemed to have a chip on his shoulder, which, frankly, was not our fault or an area in which we could do anything constructive to resolve. Or, at least, so we thought. It was Bob who offered us a solution. Why not, he suggested, put him on watch once we had cleared the Thames entrance and there was very little shipping about and leave him to navigate us towards Rotterdam. I must confess to an initial feeling of horror, but the more I thought about this and seeing something of a twinkle in both his and Maggie's eyes, went along with the idea, upon gaining Bob's approval that the AB would call me before we hit the main shipping lanes off the North Hinder light-vessel.

I went to the wheelhouse just as we should have been approaching the North Hinder. I had not really slept at all, for I had fallen only into a light doze so it was only a couple or so hours later that I made my way into the wheelhouse. Even in the gloom, I could make out the perspiring face of Frank, our AB, which told its own sorry tale and, as he turned to me with such an abject expression, I found myself feeling just a little sorry for the guy. He had absolutely no idea of the ship's position or even remotely where we were other than we were still somewhere in the south North Sea, which, I supposed, was something! The radar was out of tune and set on an ineffective 12 mile range. The Decca navigator was unsynchronised: and I knew that Maggie had kindly set this up to help him before she left the wheelhouse. The ship was actually heading for the West Hinder light and approaching the port of Antwerp. I formally relieved him of the watch and made him stand and observe as I put the house back into order. First I showed him the tidal diamonds on the chart and then the *Dover Tide Tables*, then picked the *Tidal Atlas* from the bookshelf and, explaining to him how to find the correct page, pointed out the seriousness of completely neglecting the set and drift of the current. In the Dover Strait for the time we were on passage, and because we were crossing the flow of the current west–east, this had caused the vessel to be carried considerably southwards. I then retuned and altered the radar to the three-mile range, set up the Decca Chain to 'E/MP Holland' and fixed our position. From there, I drew a new course line and with a bold alteration of helm headed us towards the North Hinder light. I then increased the radar to a local working six-mile range, ideal for these shipping conditions. The tidal set and drift was still adverse, but weaker now and acting fore and aft instead of athwartships. This combined procedure enabled the vessel to join the traffic separation zones (TSZ) at a gentle angle and to merge into the general traffic flow. There was the inevitable build-up of shipping as we joined, but this mostly conformed to the regulations and behaved itself. There was little more for me to say, especially when he mentally collapsed and admitted that perhaps there was a lot more to doing the mate's job on a coaster than he had realised. He admitted his original complacency had occurred simply through ignorance. Acting as a third mate on a deep-sea ship engaged on a broad ocean crossing, he said, was far easier than the hectic professional watch-keeping necessary for any ship in coastal waters. His deep-sea Master had kept more than a close eye on him at all times for both navigation and collision avoidance. I told him bluntly that he had impressed Bob, Maggie and myself as a first-class AB, which was how we wanted to employ him on our ship, and that everyone had considerable respect for his ability. This he was able to accept and went below a considerably subdued, shaken and different man. I did not tell him though that he was far more competent than I at splicing and general rope and wire work.

The remainder of the watch resulted in a steady period on both navigation and collision avoidance with the usual run of fishing boats cutting across at all angles with or without rhyme and reason, regardless of separation or any other kind of zones. I reported to Bob when I called him on our approach to the Maas pilot, if the AB had not lost too much face over the incident and decided to stay, then he would be an asset to the ship and indeed the company. Bob's highly unorthodox methods had proved a point in an affair unprecedented and in its way quite bizarre. It is pleasing to report that we had no further problems with Frank.

A loud banging on my door followed by Bob's quiet 'Jon, will you come onto the bridge, please?' broke into my rest at 0200 in the morning, after less than two hours' sleep. He had been having problems with the engine. Pete had been turned to some time previously and was now below in a fume-laden atmosphere trying to find the cause. I arrived in the wheelhouse to discover the ship sailing at reduced speed as we encountered yet another thick fog bank and a complete electrical failure with everything switched off: radar, gyro, radio and Decca navigator, and our junior cadet steering manually by standard compass. I knew something was wrong because there was no cabin lighting, apart from a dim alleyway glow from our emergency battery source. The wheelhouse lights were also on emergency battery power so the boy could see to steer. Apparently, the binnacle light had just blown – one minute it was working, the next minute it had died – I knew the feeling. The vessel was doing about three or four knots heading into an increasing south-westerly wind, currently about Force 3–4. We had no idea where we were other than vaguely off the Dutch coast, which was quite worrying, for the ship was down to the mean marks of 3 metres 31 with a full load of 1,350 tonnes of animal bones. This apparently bizarre cargo was bound for Rochester, where it would be offloaded into a warehouse and then taken by lorry to a factory in Queenborough for use as the basis of powerful wood glue. We were too deep-draughted to enter the jetty at this port and, for some reason never explained, the nearer and more logical Sheerness could (or would) not take us. I had soon found after commencing my cadetship, many light years ago now, that logic and the sea are not always consistently happy bedfellows.

Suddenly, Toby called out that he thought he saw something 'off the starboard side'. Bob and I immediately focussed there, and through the swirling mist and opaque visibility, thought we could see the outline of a cardinal buoy. I immediately told Toby to swing her hard over to starboard and then check her swing before straightening out to head for the thing. It was imperative that we knew where we were, although I did express the passing hope that the buoy had not broken her mooring chain and was drifting off station – something which had not been unknown. My comment earned a well-deserved glare from Bob and he muttered, 'I think we've got enough to think or even worry about – anyway, that's all we would want.' Toby was now on course heading for the buoy, and Bob was leaning over the chart with parallel rules and pencil at the ready.

'What does it say? What is it called?' he shouted, his voice raised with concern.

'No idea at the moment. The visibilty is too dense to read it, even with binoculars,' I replied. After a few minutes, he asked again.

'Jon, what is it called? What does it say?'

'Sorry, Bob – I still cannot read the damn thing. Give me a chance.'

'Is the name any clearer now?' he enquired within a few more moments.

'Yes. Yes. I've got it now I think,' came my urgent response, caught up, despite myself, in the urgency of Bob's excitement.

'Well, what is it? What does it say – what does it say?'

'Yes. I can see it now. It says…it says… "Wet Paint",' I replied.

The two of us fell about laughing. The humour in my laconic comment had broken the tension of the moment to such an extent that we were still chuckling as we closed it. Bob had to grab the wheel quickly from Toby, who was creased across the helm with laughter, to prevent us hitting the thing.

The immediate panic was over. We plotted our position on the chart, finding we were just north of the Fairy Banks, well to the south of where we even suspected. We looked at each other, amazed yet again at the power of the tidal set in the Dover Strait. I suggested it might be the water surge from the southern North Sea, to the English Channel in the south, which created a force similar to that experienced in the Straits of Gibraltar. Bob agreed, and mentioned it was no wonder our AB had been so unnerved. It was probably a sign of the tension but, wonder of wonders, I could not help smiling quietly as I watched Bob, working deftly with parallel rule and pencil, carefully constructing a course line cutting at right angles across the separation zones, leading us north of Ramsgate for the Thames Estuary. He then went below, leaving me to it.

It was another two hours before the engineer sorted out his rubber bands and electrical jingles below. The first I knew we were back into action was when the wheelhouse and gyro lights flickered, went out, glowed with a little more enthusiasm, only to go out once more. Ten minutes later they again came on again, flickered, and then decided to behave by steadying, and then glowing brightly. Pete popped into the wheelhouse filthy dirty, covered in perspiration and clearly feeling the effects of fumes. He was very tired and yawned widely as he reported the engines were back into action and everything was functioning normally. He shot below before I could ask any questions regarding causes, embarrassing or otherwise, but merely left me to my own deliberations and thoughts, and making my appropriate entry in the rough log-book.

My first task was to switch off the wheelhouse and accommodation emergency lights and get the gyro, radar and Decca back into action. I tested the radio and called Sheerness port control to let them know we were still in the land of the living; that 'Yes, we were still bound for Rochester and they could expect us, but we would definitely be later than planned,' although it was hoped our revised estimated time of arrival was reasonably accurate. Then onto the Decca, but this was hopelessly unstable and totally useless with the electronic beams caught up in the various atmospheric layers. It would have to wait for the stability of daylight before we could expect it to settle and obtain any sense out of the thing. The radar came on without problem, so at least we could gain an approximation of our position until the UK coast came into the six-mile range. Then to the gyro. I had called Ricky to relieve Toby and do a trick on the helm. 'Doing', of course, being the operative word. I had, over the preceeding weeks, called him to the wheelhouse and given him some tuition, trying to raise his standard to that required for his steering certificate. It was proving hard work because of his limited concentration span. I had to speak quite sharply to him to stop him lounging against the wheel, from which position he could not even steer, let alone see the compass. Our course since he had relieved the cadet had been erratic to put things mildly. It reminded me of my own steering – approximately in these waters as a cadet on our pre-sea training voyage. I still shuddered a little at the thoughts of those days when I had fallen well and truly foul of the Skipper of that illustrious craft. I am afraid these feelings did not mitigate my own towards Ricky. Still, I was determined he should persevere and eventually master one of the skills essential still, even for today's modern seaman.

I called Maggie to relieve me just as we approached the Shivering Sand Towers off Herne Bay. It had been a long watch. I felt quite tired and needed a short rest before going to stand-by for arrival at Rochester. I wrote up the log, told Maggie we had been reported in to Garrison Point, and that she should call Bob after rounding the Medway Bell buoy. This would give him ample time to come to, have a shower and pot of coffee before coming on watch to see his ship inwards. I then went below for a short read, a very short read as it happened, because I had hardly opened my poetry book before I fell into a deep sleep.

There was no relieving chief officer for me in Rochester and not even a sign of one. So, at 2200 hours, two days later we were on passage in the Dover Strait heading for Rouen. The ship was pitching and rolling violently at times as we headed directly into the teeth of a Force 10 gusting 11 south-easterly storm. Even before coming on watch, I guessed things up top were pretty lively by the motion experienced below and had felt the almost physical bang as the propeller regularly cleared the water. We were sailing in ballast from Rochester, after bunkering in Grain and taking fifty tons of diesel at a rate of four tons per hour, which did a little to stabilise the ship. I had been called by Bob to take the watch at 0100 hours, after two complete power failures at 2200 and midnight due to severe buffeting from the storm. We had been forced to reduce from our cruising speed of around ten knots down to three once again, just sufficient to maintain steerage way. He had switched off the radar because, with such a low-sited aerial the thing was useless in these heavy seas. Oliver was on the helm steering manually by the standard compass because the gyro had been well and truly thrown. The lads stood up to our unaccustomed motion remarkably well, although Ricky was violently sick, to the disgust of the new AB who shared their cabin, and had elected to sleep temporarily on the settee in the smoke-room.

As we were feeling pretty peckish, probably the result of nervous energy, I popped below and made a pot of tea and a couple of thick slices of cheese on toast for us both. Oliver was good as a quartermaster and it was safe to leave him also as lookout, after all I was not in Outer Mongolia, just below in the galley for twenty minutes. I did a quick check anyway before leaving the wheelhouse, satisfying myself it was safe to leave him. There was not a heavy density of shipping as we crossed the traffic zones; other vessels clearly having more sense than us. The Decca always came in very strongly on the 5B/MP Chain and by the time we closed La Basseurelle light-vessel at two miles distance, I had altered course to close the inshore area off the French coast. As I allowed what to me seemed a necessary but phenomenal twelve degrees set and drift, and munched away at the cheese and toast, the thought crossed my mind that this was the first time in my nautical career I had actually made the supper for a cadet! It was a rueful reflection on the way things had changed, including my perception of life. I had gone below to make supper automatically, without giving any thoughts to role reversal. Coasting was indeed different to deep-sea trading. At around 0430 hours I popped below to the lounge and called the AB to relieve Oliver for a trick at the wheel. The boy had performed sterling duty there, but I felt it was time to give him a spell. Within a few minutes Frank appeared so, giving him a cup of coffee (another role reversal), I stood down Oliver for a well-deserved rest.

It was 0500 hours before we picked up the loom of the Pointe d'Ailly light at some twenty-two miles distance, and I changed to the Decca 1B/MP South-West British Chain. This also was very reliable and it proved a comfort to have an accurate position on the chart while the ship continued pitching and rolling heavily. We still were taking green seas over the main-deck up to the hatch covers, with heavy spraying across the wheelhouse windows, necessitating keeping the Kent screens in continuous motion. It was lethal out on deck with water swishing against the wheelhouse doors, so there was a lot to be said for internal companionways in such weather. Even though the vessel was keeping well to her course line the AB reported she was becoming increasingly hard to steer, requiring considerably more helm than seemed usual, even in these appalling weather conditions. I had meanwhile been trying to sort out the gyro, seeing if this could be steadied sufficiently reliably to go over to automatic steering, but to no avail. The master gyro in the wheelhouse against which the steering repeater worked was whizzing round like a top. It was obvious we could not rely on that for some time yet. I took the helm myself to get the feel of the ship and endeavour to understand what Frank was saying. He was quite correct, not that I underestimated his opinion – on the contrary, I valued his expertise. She was a cow to steer, causing me to think through what might be an explanation. In this sea, it was impossible to make an accurate personal asessment of how the ship was sitting in the water, but I began to wonder whether she might be considerably down by the head, possibly caused by an ingress of water up forward somewhere. I knew the steel hatch covers were completely water-tight and reliable. I had seen a photograph of a ship in a listed condition where the sea had washed completely over the deck, but the cargo had remained dry with McGregor's invention, so I had every confidence in the hatch integrity. The only logical thing left for me to think of was that the severe weather had broken our quick-drying cement wash, always placed over the spurling pipe when such conditions were forecast, leading from below the windlass to the chain locker. Maggie had supervised this covering of the plate effectively sealing it – under moderate conditions at least. If the cement had been broken, this would have allowed the sea to enter the chain locker and would account for the sluggishness in steering. If I was correct, there was nothing we could do to improve things even if the weather moderated sufficiently for us to make an inspection.

At 0600 Bob came into the wheelhouse quite unexpectedly. He said that, although he was asleep quite deeply, he had felt an alteration in the motion of the ship and so decided to investigate. I looked at him with renewed respect, stated I had similar thoughts and told him about our sluggish steering, explaining my reasons. It was his turn to look at me anew, for such a situation was exceptionally rare deep-sea. In fact, I had only experienced it once before, even though encountering phenomenal weather conditions in typhoons and hurricanes. It was from that moment a different and deeper relationship seemed to blossom between us. We both knew we could never be bosom buddies, but each felt confident in the other's professionalism. He agreed completely, both in diagnosis and immediate situation, and stated there was little to be done until either the weather settled or we were in the calmer waters of the River Seine.

I came to quite naturally from a refreshing sleep and, after lunch, went into the wheelhouse. We were rapidly approaching Rouen jetty, where we would lower the two masts and radar scanner before making the river passage under pilotage to

Small vessels were inevitably prone to adverse effects of severe weather when they would plunge directly into green seas forward – with spraying extending to the wheelhouse… (Author's Collection).

…and experience a maelstrom of confused and very rough water along the foredeck, which caused severe stresses to the hull and often resulted in taking water through the spurling pipe into the chain locker forward (Courtesy Mike Jackson).

Bonnières. Both Bob and I congratulated ourselves on actually being proved correct 'for a change', as he put the situation. Sharing the watches with Maggie had left him free to investigate forward once we were in the calmer waters of Le Havre approaches. The ship was well down by the head, the cement wash had been washed away completely and he could actually see the water sloshing up from the spurling pipe. We estimated we must have taken at least eight tonnes, which left us with a flooded cable locker. Then came the good news. There was no pump fitted to the locker and the only way to get the water out was by forming a bucket chain involving all hands and manhandling the stuff out through the forecastle-head entrance and over the side. We estimated this would take something to the order of eight to ten hours: a joy and a delight. He looked at me and grinned before telling me that once we had cleared the jetty I could organise the crew upfront and 'have a stab at putting the sea back into the river', as it were. The job had to be done, and there was little more for me to say. As it was, Bob was proved correct. It was a sod of a job. To give him due, he relieved Maggie and I in turns to have a break standing by the pilot in the wheelhouse and got stuck in. By the time we had berthed in the first lock at Amprevilles and passed through this thirty minutes later, we had at least made some impression. By the time we passed the second La Garenne lock, we could actually see even greater improvement, and by the time we were alongside in Bonnieres, some eight hours later, there was just a little mopping up to be done. Needless to say, once we were alongside we locked up the ship and all made off to the nearest bar, where we stayed until thrown out in the early hours of the following morning. It was, of course, in the jocular manner of coasting, and filled 'beyond our load lines' with a delicate French wine indelicately drunk, that I made my joke: 'If Ricky were to fall into the river, would he necessarily be insane?' I could not have picked a more susceptible target, for although it took a while before the penny dropped with the subject, Bob mentioned that if he did not wake up his ideas, he would be in a thicker substance than the Seine. Once back on board, there was no poetry reading for me that night.

We loaded 1,210 tonnes of grain consistent with my cargo plan, taking 580 tonnes in number one hatch and 630 in number two, leaving with a mean draught of 3 metres 35. I had made certain the grain was stowed well below the beams and covered the entire lower surface of the hold. We had the regulatory percentage of bagged grain to give more stability and received notice that we were bound for Silloth, on the north-west coast of England, near the Scottish border, for discharge.

We dropped the pilot off at Le Havre without incident, and the ensuing passage proved uneventful with typically busy watches for the three of us on navigation and collision avoidance. We were overtaken crossing the main shipping lanes by P&O's liner *Oriana*, which passed us in a blaze of lights with the nameplate brilliantly showing off the name. On a passing nautical whim, I picked up the Aldis and flashed her, asking 'What ship are you?' Bob creased with dry laughter as repeated flashing evoked absolutely no response from the watch-keepers on board this illustrious vessel. They obviously appreciated mild sarcasm for what it was, but so much for the brotherhood of the sea.

Oliver often popped up for bridge tuition and experience after finishing his deck or cooking duties and seemed to be taking to the job like, appropriately enough, the proverbial 'duck to water'. Bob was well pleased with him. The weather was kind for a change and I was able to proceed well with my planned maintenance programme. I even managed to pass Toby and, wonder of wonders, Ricky, through their steering certificates. Toby was no problem and, after a few more hours' instruction by basically leaving the lad to sort himself out, this correct approach with Ricky seemed to work. For suddenly, at the end of another hour's frustrating session, things 'suddenly clicked into place' and he found his expertise. It was difficult to keep him off the wheel after that for he was for ever begging to be allowed to 'have another bash to keep my hand in.' My own personal view was that in the absence of any educational qualifications, this modest certificate was the first achievement of his young life, and I quietly rejoiced for him. I think Bob also felt the same way because although neither of us mentioned our thoughts, he signed Ricky's certificate with a flourish and made a formal presentation to him after lunch that day by putting it on the mess-room tray, surrounded by four lit candles. It was a delightfully momentous and light-hearted occasion, and we all agreed that perhaps – just perhaps – there 'might be some light at the end of this very long, dark tunnel'. We then sat back and, with typical cynicism born of long experience, waited for Ricky to do the next thing wrong! Sadly, it was not too long before fate and Ricky hit the jackpot, for two days later he dropped the tea tray complete with teapot, mugs and milk jug bound for the four of us in the wheelhouse, smashing the lot. Pete had joined us for the break and had already opened the door in expectation when Ricky tripped over the step coaming. I left Ricky to do the mopping up, while Bob mopped up 'our lad' once more.

We waited at anchor eight cables off Workington south jetty with two shackles in the water on the starboard anchor. The final stages of the passage when I was on watch were extremely and surprisingly busy. I had clearly but for some reason temporarily forgotten that the ubiquitous fishing fleet in any waters was precisely that, for I was kept on my toes with numerous course alterations. The navigation was pretty straightforward with a number of interesting bold course alterations clearing such delightful names as Douglas, Maughold, and St Bees Heads. I called Oliver to the wheelhouse once more and allowed him to try his hand at collision avoidance, with equally surprisingly encouraging results. I also tested his more intimate knowledge of the Regulations by asking him a gentle series of questions relating to lights, sound signals and shapes. He did well, apart from a lack of knowledge about the finer points, all of which I felt would come with time and experience.

Once at anchor, we lay quietly in calm seas with light airs and the vessel holding firmly to the hook. It was 0500 hours when the pilot boarded and we berthed alongside the grain jetty port side to. By 0800 we had commenced cargo and the gangs worked continuously and well, so that by end of working day around 1700 we had only thirty tonnes remaining. I was quite happy because once I had sorted out a working job for two of our lads to keep them happily engaged, the remainder of us left for a day on various pursuits in Carlisle. The next day being Sunday, no cargo was worked, so in the afternoon we took advantage of a gloriously hot sunny day to lock the ship and go swimming and 'grabbing some bronzy' on Silloth beach. We completed a relaxing day with a cinema visit and fish-and-chip supper. Such is life for crews on the coast, but this was a rare occasion.

It rained heavily during the night. This continued throughout Monday morning preventing the working of cargo. I let the other two lads go ashore for the day and do their own paddling around Carlisle in the rain, and took advantage of the delay to take the remaining two crew and, somewhat ironically, thoroughly wash number one hatch. The rain suddenly stopped and at 1600 hours we managed to complete discharge and, by 2015 were off the berth and heading again for Par. Bob stood down Ricky to cook the evening meal and with the other two lads back on board earlier than expected. They had been, not surprisingly, largely washed out of town by 'La Deluge', as the French would say.

The pilot related to us the adventures of a small coaster a few weeks previously, which had us all rolling around with laughter. It seemed that the Master of this ill-fated vessel had gone home for the weekend leaving his chief officer in charge of the ship. This erstwhile adventurer had led his lads with untold enthusiasm into a gigantic booze-up throughout Saturday and Sunday leaving them with more than thick heads on the Monday morning – yet again to the entertainment of another group of dockers. This was fine so far as it went, but the harbourmaster then had to call them to shift ship to another jetty at right angles and across the harbour to their present berth, making way for another vessel. The move across the dock was impossible to perform purely by warping the ship along the quay, as we had done in Rotterdam and indeed occasionally elsewhere, and so the engines had to be engaged. This took a while to perform, but the subsequent ship handling under the influence of considerable quantities of alcohol was as efficient as could reasonably be expected. In the opinion of the pilot who told us of the incident, the Mate was not up to the job, even had he been sober. He ordered his second mate to let go everything fore and aft without holding on to any spring wires, resulting in the ship, as she swung off, crashing her stern onto the jetty. The bang and the expensive sound of plates hitting concrete resounded around the wharf, bringing office workers and assorted passers-by rushing to the scene, all agog to know what was happening. The Mate then rang for half-ahead and turned the wheel to starboard intending to come alongside port side to. The ship swung obediently to helm and engines, but he failed to bring her up in time and she hit the far end of the quay with another resounding crash and additional dents to plating and paintwork, up forward this time for variety. He then put the engines slow astern to take the way off the ship, but put the wheel the wrong way over, leaving the bows to bounce back onto the quay. By this time the second mate had managed to put a couple of the lads ashore with warps, the eyes of which they managed to pop quickly over bollards, leaving the second mate to make them fast on the winch drum forward, before racing aft to do likewise with the stern of the ship. All of these actions were carried out while befuddled with drink, leaving the onlookers amazed, creased with laughter, and clearly wondering whether or not Nelson might be turning in his grave. It was an appalling exhibition of seamanship. The ship looked as if it had been involved in a collison, with dented and split plates and besmirched paintwork. The Master, when he returned, could not believe his eyes and, as the pilot remarked, his language was appalling and accompanied by a host of uncontrollable actions. A surveyor had to be called before the harbourmaster would allow the ship to sail in what he regarded (rightly) as 'an unseaworthy state'. The denting of the plates had extended towards the waterline and looked as if water ingress in any kind of seaway would have occurred. The Captain had no option but to contact the company head office informing them of events and await the attendance of both surveyor and marine superintendent. She lay on the berth for a further four days before survey, and the subsequent insistence that local welding and numerous cement boxes had to be made good. The bill to the company for harbour dues, professional fees and work was considerable. The pilot, when he eventually took her out to go north into dry-dock for more permanent repairs, stated that it was with an entirely different crew from that with which she arrived. And so ensued another salty saga of capers on the coast.

We arrived alongside Par in time for the August Bank Holiday. It did not take the sight of a totally empty jetty with its raft of derelict ships to inform us there was clearly going to be no cargo worked over the holiday. The last official break in Cornwall was clearly to be taken very seriously and with wholehearted enthusiasm. Once alongside, Bob went ashore to check with the local agent the date when gangs had next been booked. I was on deck deciding to scrape and silver-paint the underside of our hatch covers and saw Bob leaving the office. Even at that distance, I could see he wore a very broad smile. Leaping enthusiastically back on board, he called all hands to the lounge and explained that no gangs would be working for five days, due to the addition of a local holiday. Dishing out mail like a liberal Lord Bounty and still smiling broadly, he suggested we lock up the ship and all shove off for an extended leave. There was an immediate flurry of packing and checking of train timetables. It seemed there was a London train expected to stop at Par in just over one hour. With little time to waste, I threw a random assortment of gear into my holdall and hurried back on deck, joining Bob as he locked the wheelhouse. We raced after the others as they hot-footed it to the railway station the other side of town.

Sue and I tentatively discussed our future plans over a meal and bottle of wine that developed into another bottle, and continued into the early hours of next morning. We were both quite open as, well-oiled, we discussed whether or not I wished to remain in the merchant navy. I loved the challenges of navigation and collision avoidance and thought these were being handled quite competently, but remained uncertain about the rest of seafaring as a permanent way of life. We discussed the vagueness of my on-going thoughts on leaving the sea at some stage in the future, currently undecided, and coming ashore, but were not at all clear what the future should be. I was able to tell her how an idea that was possibly worth developing had been growing in my mind. I explained the enjoyment of teaching deep-sea cadets and, recently on the coaster, Oliver and Toby, who aspired to officer status, and I had wondered increasingly whether or not there might be any mileage in my studying to be a schoolmaster. She encouraged my thoughts, agreeing that my conversation recently had been focussed more on remaining ashore and that she was not surprised about the possible idea of teaching. She could foresee few difficulties about finances, as her job in the surgery was permanent and as a senior nurse her salary was sufficient to cope with a course, especially as I would be entitled to claim a generous grant with even more liberal mature-student allowance from the local educational authority.

It was in this uncertain, but slightly shifting mood that our long weekend continued. No decisions had been made as neither of us felt the time was really right, but undoubtedly a few seeds had been sown.

6

MAKING FAST

The remainder of our holiday was all I had anticipated, and more, so it was something of a wrench for me to rejoin the ship at Par and report back on board. I had phoned both captains at the Kremlin suggesting my relief was perhaps a little overdue, only to be advised there was no one immediately available to send to the ship. I was promised that as soon as they had a chief officer off leave, or even new to the company, they would send him out to us at whatever port, or even anchorage, the ship happened to be.

Two gangs made their appearance aboard each of the nine moored ships, so before long the jetties on all three arms were a hive of industry as a variety of medium-sized coasters loaded their ubiquitous and inevitable cargoes of china clay. Our ship joined in the fun and while I opened the hatches, the agent came aboard to confirm we were again bound for Dordrecht.

We often relaxed in the saloon after meals. It was an ideal meeting place for all hands and, as an extension of the lounge, became a natural haunt for social chatting and drinking, particularly when alongside with little or no cargo worked, or delays swinging off the hook awaiting a berth. Anchor watches on this class of vessel were casual, to put things mildly. Anchorages were well known to Masters and mates from constant usage while serving with this or other ships in the fleet and were picked particularly for their good holding ground, with little chance of dragging, and permitting ample swinging space between other ships. With considerable deck work regularly taking place when the weather permitted, there was generally little need for formal watches to be kept, other than at night, when the duty officer occasionally roused himself to pop onto the bridge and see what was happening. During the day outside of meal-times everyone accumulated in the wheelhouse, making this another social centre of the vessel. There was always a deck officer on the bridge on all occasions when at sea, and most times on duty somewhere while in port. It was during these relaxed and very casual occasions that conversation turned inevitably to other company ships, including details of the antics of their crews.

191

Bob told us, creasing with laughter at the memory, of a 'peculiar diversionary to cargo work', as I later termed the incident, which befell the *Prince Arthur*, another of the company's coasters. This illustrious vessel apparently had been discharging grain alongside the jetty of a famous Suffolk flour mill one hot summer's day a couple of years previously. Following the usual meeting of all hands in the local public house for an extended lunch break, something of the order of four hours, they returned on board more than a 'little in the arms of Bacchus', for they were each absolutely plastered. They had also recently stocked up with considerable quantities of booze from Wilhelmshaven, their previous port of loading. Even though he knew the Master and crew involved, Bob remained uncertain to this day exactly how the incident had developed.

Slowly meandering around the two hatches listening idly to the soporific swish of grain disappearing into the elevator, the local dockers suddenly became aware that a full-scale water fight had developed amongst the crew. Their hilarity increased as stark-naked men from the Captain to deck boy ejected suddenly from below decks. Modest water-squirts from soft plastic bottles had quickly generated into buckets of water, which within minutes gave way to the rigging of jetty and ship's fire hoses. It seemed wholsesale warfare commenced. The rumpus created broke the afternoon silence and soon a batch of lady secretaries were watching with interest ranging from genuine to mock horror and sustained excitement as five nude men shrieked and frolicked around the jetty, drenching each other, showing every indication of complete abandon and total happiness. The sight was, of course, compounded by delightfully expressive language as the mariners shouted their glee at targets well hit prior to capitulation, or vocal laments from the extinguished, until new strategies could be devised. The heat haze was far from effective in distorting the cameo. Even before an impasse could develop, one of the office managers phoned the police. A duty patrol car duly arrived and the two officers were met by the astounding sight. In fact, they were met by more than an unusual spectacle for that sober part of the good county. As they emerged from their car, the nearest constable was hit full-square in the chest by a jet of water from a powful hose that shot him over the edge of the quay to submerge into a rapidly rising tide. In the midst of the hiatus that followed, the other constable, leaning full-length over the jetty attempting to catch his colleague's flailing arms, was hit fairly behind the ears by an ill-thrown lifebelt cast in his direction by one of the still-befuddled crew. Amidst the chaos that ensued, a docker managed to throw the by-now very soggy police officer a rope enabling him to be dragged up, swearing and cursing, onto the quay. Looking at his still-slightly concussed mate, he wallowed over to the car and radioed for back-up, reporting that a comparatively innocent situation had gone more than slightly out of control.

It must have been all of ten minutes before sirens were heard smashing their piercing howls into mid-afternoon heat and a van and further posse of police made their dramatic entrance around the office buildings and warehouse. By this time workers were hanging out of the windows, dockers were rolling around creased with uncontrollable laughter, and even the crew began to realise that factions other than their own were now involved in what had started as an innocent post-luncheon jape. It took no time at all for order to be re-established by the simple expedient of the crew being taken below to dress before they were herded into the van and driven out of sight, presumably to the 'local nick'.

The agent had been informed of events by the police, who suggested he arrange for someone to attend the vessel so, upon arrival, he decided to remain *in situ* to protect the open wheelhouse and accommodation from theft. He also used the local office phone to notify the London and Chatham Shipping Company, only to be informed that the managing director of the flour mill had already been in touch offering his graphic and somewhat irrate description of events. The company advised the agent either to lock the vessel and leave, dropping off the keys at the police station, or to remain where he was for the returning crew and to keep the Kremlin informed of developments. Inevitably, it was some hours before the lads returned on board sober, suitably chastened and full of remorse. They had been arrested and charged with a range of offences including indecency, assault of police officers, disturbance of the peace, with a few other *ad hoc* items popped into the proverbial pot to carry their own weight. Their case was due up before a special sitting of magistrates the next day, and meanwhile they had been let out on surety of bail, courtesy of the long-suffering agent. London and Chatham were far from amused. The directors instructed that the resulting fines imposed upon all hands be covered by the agent and subsequently deducted from the pay-off due to each man. The Master was dismissed, but went away with another leading large coaster company after agreeing, with tongue somewhat in cheek, to conform to more sober behaviour. Other than that, the team was split across other vessels in the fleet so that eventually a new crew emerged to carry *Prince Arthur* into newer and, hopefully, freshly sober pastures. Inevitably, the story went over the ether like proverbial wildfire. Officers gleefully related it by VHF radio and in conversation until, with inevitable embellishments, it passed into seafaring annals. A more sober circular emanated from the Kremlin advising crews to be mindful of their behaviour when alongside all jetties and wharfs.

It was also over lunch a week or two later, as we awaited cargo in Antwerp, that Bob regaled us, to great hilarity, with a report of the antics over the previous festive season of another of the company's coasters. Around noon on Christmas Day, the antiquidated *Prince Roland* made fast to a buoy in Gravesend's small-ship anchorage about three cables offshore. She had arrived with a mixed cargo in both holds from

Until regulations were revised, deck cadets were required, for examination purposes, to be proficient in transmitting and receiving Morse code by Aldis lamp at the rate of five words per minute (P&O Lines).

When off watch below there were a number of interesting pursuits which passed away leisure hours and allowed a solitary hobby to be followed that made a change from the usually busy social life that was led by most cadets (BP plc).

continental ports and awaited a berth alongside Denton jetty presently taken by a British and Dutch coaster, with the other wharf space serving a small German vessel. It seemed that none of the ships had managed to beat pre-Christmas discharge and would now be alongside until early in the New Year.

Once secure to buoys fore and aft, the all-Scots crew lowered the longboat and shot off ashore to investigate the delights of Gravesend. All eating places were firmly booked for the festive day so with nothing other than a light bar snack to serve as traditional Christmas dinner the crew returned on board far from pleased with their excursion ashore. They were not too perturbed; Christmas was not really their celebration, for they eagerly awaited Hogmanay. Their last port of call had been Rotterdam, and in the way of all seamen internationally calling at this port they had availed themselves of a seasonal top-up of dry goods from the famous Botlek stores, together with locally purchased spirits and assorted booze. Mindful of the legal requirements of Customs and Excise, they had duly completed their C142 and lodged this with the local office, who had granted them also free pratique. The customs officials, however, were unaware of the extra alcohol, which had most certainly not been declared and was stashed on the ship away from any casually prying eyes of authority. With cases and bottles stowed in the paint lockers, under spare warps and lashings in the forecastle store and secreted away in engine-room, galley and cabins, there was sufficient drink aboard to supply one of the local hostelries for a week. They had stocked also with adequate supplies of food, including some seasonal delicacies that would normally grace only the tables of perhaps more exalted families. For, amongst the traditional meats, vegetables and puddings, the ship's fridge and freezer were chock-a-block with samples of game birds, paté, ripe Dutch, German and French cheeses, plus a few jars of exotic deserts stacked in the galley lockers, including delicate jars of cherries in brandy.

As with the exploits of many coastal vessels and their crews, Bob declared that a certain haze still shrouds the exact course of developments. It was during the fifth day into the New Year that the company head office in London received a telephone call from one of their shippers initially enquiring politely, and then with increased agitation, why their goods despatched aboard *Prince Roland,* and expected in their warehouse shortly after Christmas, had not arrived. The directors and superintendents of London and Chatham suddenly realised they had somehow lost one of the company's ships. It was known that she had reported in and was somewhere in the Thames, but nothing had subsequently been heard either from the Master or port authorities regarding her movements. A phone call to the recently established Thames Navigation Service confirmed she had arrived on Christmas Day and was still moored to buoys in the small-ship anchorage. The service confirmed also that there were occasional sightings of crew-members, indicating that there was certainly someone aboard. They offered to send their harbour service patrol launch to investigate and report back. This was duly accepted and later the same day the shipping company received a phone call saying that no one had been seen on board, but the ship was in a sorry state externally with loose warps and fluttering canvas that had not been battened down, after its coming adrift during the strong winds experienced over the previous days. Certainly noises from a radio or other source of entertainment had been overheard, although there had been no visual responses to their hailing. The boat's crew had no authority to board the coaster.

Once this call had been received, with some concern, the company sent their marine superintendent to Gravesend and, taking out a mooring boat, he boarded their ship. The sight that met his eyes was unprecedented. The entire crew were drunk and it seemed had been in that state for many days previously. The accommodation was in an appalling condition with empty bottles strewn around all cabins, while the galley and mess looked as if they had been hit by a bomb. He had tried to get some sense out of the Master and Mate, but they were both in a stupor, not knowing, as he reported, 'if they were aboard a ship or the Royal Scot'. The engineer was near-comatose, with the other two men totally befuddled with drink. He broke all the alcohol bottles he could find, pouring their contents down the galley and cabin sinks and then left the ship, admitting there was little more presently he could do. Reporting back to London, the company arranged for another crew to board the ship a few days later to relieve the current members. The original lads were eventually paid off and dismissed, and the costs incurred for cleaning the vessel deducted from their pay-offs with, it might be added, the 'voluntary approval' of the crew. Once more, with only recent deep-sea experiences as a base for my seafaring, I was left to marvel at the antics in which my coastal colleagues became embroiled. The incidents confirmed yet again that Bob was correct: while both deep-sea and coastal vessels operated in the merchant navy, there were many differences between the two methods of service.

While alongside Southampton, where we had delivered a cargo of steel reinforcing rods from Bonnières, on the River Seine, for use in ferro-concrete, Bob, in the process of a cursory deck inspection just before lunch, stepped off the engine coaming, a distance of around two feet, landed awkwardly, and collapsed on deck. Picking himself up, he experienced a shooting pain up his right leg that made it impossible for any weight to be placed on the ankle. It was apparent that walking would be totally out of the question. I was called by Frank to assist him, with considerable difficulty to the wheelhouse, where Bob, in between gasping for breath, told me to call an ambulance from the local hospital for 'a check-up and a bit of plaster of Paris'. The ambulance crew immediately placed him on a stretcher, carried him over the side of the ship, into the 'blood wagon' and drove away, with our good Captain inside, alternately groaning and cursing. The entire incident took less than forty-five minutes, leaving half-painted anchor cable and its markings, and his ex-crew in something of a state of shock, with an unexpected lunch topic.

All eyes turned in my direction as I entered the saloon, took my usual place around the table and told Frank to bring my meal. The atmosphere was virtually tangible, and the seat where Bob normally sat seemed to scream its emptiness. They were clearly waiting for me to suggest a way forward. As the AB placed a steaming hot plate of food before me, I explained that Captain Hillier had been advised by courtesy of the dock-office phone. He had told me to keep him informed of hospital reports regarding Bob's progress, especially when he might be expected to return on board, and meanwhile to take charge of the ship and await developments. This information was received in silence, giving me opportunity to consolidate a novel situation. I advised that until further news was received we would work the normal routines of completing the cable, internal accommodation cleaning and overside painting while continuing discharge of our steel rods.

The incident provided a new experience. For the first time since serving at sea I found myself, however nominally, in charge of a ship for more than a previously agreed few hours. We all went ashore that evening for a 'jar or two' in the nearest dockside public house, where the topic of conversation centred inevitably around Bob's accident and what might happen next. Oliver asked me outright if I thought Captain Hillier would promote me to command, but I hedged over this by stating 'it was pretty unlikely'. I felt confident and able to accept the situation as it developed but later, in the quietness of my cabin, focussed my mind considerably on my own future.

For the first time ever, I seriously considered the challenge of command. There were few problems in accepting the unexpressed certainty in the reactions of those aboard and the natural way they had looked to me for leadership. I felt confident in situations of navigation and collision avoidance, cargo handling, ship maintenance, officer and crew control, and shipmaster business. The last was regarded as comparatively simple, and in any area of doubt I knew where to ask, and would be happy to do so. There were few doubts in my mind that if the company wanted me to assume command, then I would be capable of this. There were two exceptions, immediately outside my control, which created uncertainty. I was all too well aware of being very much 'the new kid on the block' in coastal trading and was certain from casual chats with Bob that promotion from chief officer to Master aboard these ships, either from within the company or 'external visitors' (like me), was jealously guarded. As a mark, I supposed, of our deepening closeness, he had let me into a company 'secret' only a few days previously. It appeared there was very much a 'command club' amongst existing Skippers, and that appointments were open to discussion from within this exalted body, and not necessarily made entirely in agreement with the wishes of either directors or superintendents. It seemed very much a bizarre matter of 'democratic discussion'. Of the rights or wrongs in this, there was little importance or relevance – it was the existing situation, and Bob had been trying to tell me, were I to remain with the company hoping for command, then that was fine, but I would need to not exactly 'ingratiate' myself with existing Masters, but certainly 'win their approval'. In this comment I read many implications, most of which told me I would have to conform to their (what I regarded as) *laissez faire* ideas regarding many shipboard practices, which was something my own professionalism would not permit me to do. My meticulous approach to navigation stood as a case example, particularly the way this had been accepted since I came on board, where passage plans and correct use of up-to-date small- and large-scale charts was now the norm. I sensed that Bob was certainly not in total approval of the 'Skipper's club' even as a member, and knew I would never win this case before the 'unofficial Court of Masters'.

That, as it happened, was largely academic, for I was aware also of another factor, possessing more personal import. Commanding these vessels was very different to being Master aboard their larger cousins. While on the latter, whenever they approached port other than for anchorage, the law dictated that a pilot should be taken in an advisory capacity, the Captain always remaining in charge of all aspects concerning his ship. There were nevertheless countless situations that arose which demanded he handle his vessel in restricted as well as wider waters. I had seen ample evidence of this and had enjoyed opportunity of manoeuvring vessels, generally while in or approaching a port, such as anchorages and pilotage operations, under the judicial eye of the Master. In essence, I knew within myself, the most important place for recognition, that a much longer period of service as chief officer was needed before this aspect of the job could be done with the necessary competence (and confidence), even aboard coasters. All the time a vessel was at sea and during river passages, things were fine, but I doubted my ability to manoeuvre the vessel safely within the confines of harbour, especially where this might involve difficult berth-shifting. The last thing I wanted was to experience the ignominy of circumstances that had occurred to the ill-fated coaster in Silloth. I needed more practical experience with close-water ship handling across the range of conditions likely to be experienced when in command of a ship. I would also need to take my Master's certificate, either foreign-going or home trade/coastal, which was a decision that attracted its own set of unique implications.

The crux of the matter resolved around whether or not I wished to remain at sea for the remainder of my life. For some years now, this growing sense of unease had not been confronted directly. I had merely played with thoughts, although this last leave I had, of course, discussed the situation with Sue. I felt a gradual awareness that part of me was becoming slightly bored with the limitations and parochial nature of seafaring. There was a sense that there must be more to life than carrying crude oil, diverse general cargo or china clay around the world: that life must surely incorporate something more substantial than this. It proved a rather scary notion because, were it to be developed, it would present profound repercussions for my future. This was probably why I had in the past refused to look further ahead than the current voyage and immediate family situation.

There were another couple of factors to be put into the equation for, since becoming a deep-sea second and chief officer, I had found an unexpected enjoyment in the teaching side of my duties and (very occasionally) had wondered if there might be any mileage in examining this idea further. It seemed providential that it was only three or four weeks previously that this had been discussed however vaguely with Sue. Meeting the young cadet Colin Ashby aboard the *Earl of Nottingham* some years previously had awakened a deepening love of English literature that was now a real delight. There was nothing I enjoyed better, after being on watch and prior to snuggling down for sleep, than to dip into the ever increasing library of poetry anthologies, classical novels and dramatic works that were now, as a matter of course, carried away to sea. In fact, this library had recently superseded navigational books (apart from my *Norie's Nautical Tables* with its additional copious handwritten notes) and I worked in the hope that any further tomes required might reside in the library aboard whatever ship I happened to be serving. Coasters did not carry libraries but fortunately my nautical tables had proved sufficient. Since those two realisations, further random thoughts had led me to wonder if there might 'one day' be an opportunity of combining the two interests into a full-time career change. I could not teach navigation, seamanship and allied nautical subjects because I did not possess Master's, but I felt there might just be some mileage in teaching literature, if I could initally talk an unsuspecting university into accepting me as a mature student, and perhaps follow this with a teacher training certificate.

My present situation of being in nominal charge of the vessel invited me to look facts firmly in their metaphoric face and consider what I really wanted to do with the remainder of my life. With the initial decision made, I resolved to discuss things more deeply with Sue during my next leave, test her opinion, and see what developed from there.

Phoning the hospital next day and speaking to the ward sister where Bob was billeted brought little satisfaction, and no answers. I told Maggie I was going to the hospital that afternoon to see Bob for myself. I reminded her that she knew what was involved in my maintenance programme, and that I would leave her to supervise this and the lads in my absence.

Navigational watch-keeping was always taken seriously aboard most ships with the bridge team of officer-of-the-watch, cadet and quartermaster working together with intense concentration on the task in hand (BP plc).

Bob was in a foul mood when I approached his bedside. It seemed that he had torn a ligament in his leg and required lengthy bed-rest, putting him ashore and out of action for an estimated four to six months, depending upon how seriously he acted on advice to rest. He most certainly would not be returning on board and I should pack his gear, have this sent to the hospital so it could be driven home when he was discharged and, by the way, notify the Kremlin of events. I liked the order of his priorities and, on the way back to the ship called in at the agents' and phoned Captain Hillier, informing latest developments regarding both his Skipper, and discharge of the cargo. The latter would take probably another day but I ascertained from the harbourmaster that we could remain on the berth for a further day or possibly two until the next ship was due. The good Captain Hillier stated he had already put another Master 'on stand-by' and would now hasten his departure for the ship. This was certainly acceptable so far as I was concerned, particularly in the light of my recent reflections. He advised also that he would keep my direct boss, Captain Henshaw, in the picture.

Captain Phil Appleton joined late the next day, having travelled from his home town, Manchester, in time to cart Bob's gear to the hospital in a taxi for he and Bob 'to enjoy a chat about matters maritime'. This was my first introduction to 'the marine club' for, although I did not expect to go with him, I was not invited to anyway, but spent my time preparing and singling up the ship for sea, ready for his return. Phil was an elderly man whom I assessed to be in his mid-seventies, and clearly brought out of retirement for this one-off job, in a manner similar to my own introduction of being shanghaied. I reported to his cabin after Maggie had told me in an urgent stage whisper (for some reason) that he had repaired on board. It was not a fortuitous introduction for, glancing through the curtain of his open door while giving the customary knock, I saw him looking through our collective discharge books. The pack of light-blue-covered booklets was unmistakable. He hastily stuffed them into a drawer as I entered and I found myself fixed by a pair of rheumy blue eyes. He opened his mouth to speak, but before he could do so, was racked by a thick, chesty cough that made him wheeze and blow like a pair of very old bellows. I detected a chill response to my welcome of him on board. Clearly in all innocence I had said the wrong thing, for he was a plainly a relic of what is perhaps euphemistically known as the 'old coastal school'. I sensed his instant dislike of me as he introduced himself. I soon learnt that he not only disliked me as a personality, but also disapproved of my ways, disagreed with my seafaring background, my methods and delegation of the crew, and probably resented my age. Other than these mere irrelevancies affecting relationships between a Captain and his chief officer, we got along fine. He was plainly one of Bob's anti-deep-sea men, and a staunchly paid-up founder-member of the 'Masters' Club'.

Phil brought orders with him: not surprisingly, we were to return to Par in ballast and load a further cargo of china clay for Dordrecht. I wondered what on earth they did with the stuff out there – they certainly seemed to use a considerable amount of it. Phil gave a very direct glance as his acknowledgement of my formal, 'All crew are on board and the ship is in all respects properly ballasted and ready for sea, Captain,' and with the local pilot, radar and Decca correctly tuned and impatient to depart, he simply sent us to stations so that, within thirty minutes, by 1100 hours, we had dropped the pilot, cleared the Needles and steadied on our estimated eighteen-hour passage to Par.

I spent the day supervising the lads cleaning the hatches thoroughly and the accommodation, before standing myself down around 1630 hours for a rest and sleep. I reported to Phil, but other than receiving an adenoidal grunt, which I assumed to be of approval, there was no more positive a response. I did ascertain from him, however, that I would take over the watch from him 'around 0500 hours or so', which was fine. It was something of a surprise, therefore, when I was given a call at midnight by Maggie. She had given Phil a shake but he had not responded, and she had sent Ricky down to call him, but he had ignored the boy, who had come away. Maggie explained that after I had stood down, Ricky and Phil had 'exchanged words', although she was not sure why or what it was about, as Ricky had shot below like the proverbial 'cork evicted from a gaseous bottle' as she entered the wheel-house, and Phil had not commented further. It appeared also that he disapproved strongly of female officers, for he handed over the watch and left clear orders that the meticulous chart work to which she had now become accustomed was 'fussily unnecessary'. There was no answer to that but, as she lingered sharing a pot of cof-fee as we approached Portland Bill light, she made clear her intention of contacting London office advising she was not prepared to sail further with Phil and conse-quently required relieving in Par. The fact that she referred to the Kremlin by its correct title was sufficient indication of her agitated state of mind. I explained that the idea of female officers was still a novelty to many existing Masters deep-sea, let alone coastal, and that she could not reasonably expect a Captain of Phil's years to accept changes easily in this area. I doubt if either of us were convinced and, while I concentrated on altering course for a trawler that suddenly shot across our bows from port she must have left the wheelhouse for, turning round to continue our con-versation, I found no sign of her. I must say that seeds had already been planted in my mind also to sign off and leave the ship in Par, whether or not the company had a relief for me. Sailing the ship would then become very much their problem, for I also could always recognise a 'hiding to nothing' when I saw one.

The rest of the watch passed without incident. My first task was to reinstate chart work. I grabbed the small-scale and larger-scale charts from the drawer, made a quick passage plan, and dutifully popped my dots onto the large-scale BA2454. There was a fair amount of shipping crossing from all angles, but the vessel moved easily in a calm sea with low swell and light airs. At 0445 I phoned Phil to come and relieve me on watch. I must confess feeling a certain sadistic delight as I dialled his number, but this soon developed into slight concern as there was no answer. I thought he was probably a deep sleeper. I had to give Ricky a shake with, I must admit, an even more sadistic glee, as he was duty cook for the day. He appeared fifteen minutes later along with the first trace of sunrise and a welcome pot of tea, rubbing sleep out of his eyes and yawning widely. I told him that before returning to the galley and preparing the day's vegetables and meal, I wanted him while in transit to call the Master and advise him it was time for his watch.

He was back in a few moments stating that he had not been able to rouse Phil. He had opened the jalousie and seen the Captain lying on his settee, not in his bunk. The alarm bells rang very mildly, but hesitatingly clearly. I popped down myself, leaving him to keep a lookout. This was a perfectly safe action for there were no immediate ships within two miles even though a build-up of fishing vessels and coasters was imminent, and I would be off the bridge for only a few minutes. The boy was quite correct. Phil was indeed lying on his settee. I did not need my St John's Ambulance first-aid certificate or any other diploma to tell me that he was dead. Crossing the cabin and glancing down at his waxy, staring eyes, I noticed his hands crossed over his chest. I recoiled after my first touch of his wrist while I felt for a pulse. There was no feel of any movement, just the touch of cold, clammy skin. I stood there while a myriad of thoughts turned somersaults within my mind. I pondered what to do next and was tempted to close those open, unseeing eyes. I could not bring myself to do so, but taking the stethoscope from the medical locker in his cabin, sounded those parts of his chest I could reach with the thing listening intently for anything, even if I was not quite sure what. There was nothing. I put a small hand-mirror from the kit across his mouth, but there was no misting. Steeling myself, I touched his left jugular vein, but again there was no response.

Taking Phil's keys from the table, I locked the door and returned to the wheel-house. Ricky was looking at me with a strange expression that altered into shock as he caught sight of my face. He told me that I returned to the wheelhouse looking as white as a ghost and, with a typical Rickyism continued, 'like death warmed up.'

'Well done, son,' I said. 'That's all I needed.'

The unexpected had happened. Even though I had not wanted command of a ship, this was precisely what had happened. I reflected how glibly people talk about the vagaries of fate.

What to do next? Absent-mindedly, I altered course to starboard for the first of our end-on coasters in good time giving him opportunity to see that I had noticed him and taken some action, even of the correct sort. My movements were really in auto-drive and it must be realised I was not quite myself. It was typical of the deliberations of people who move about in a state of shock. Then, I gradually came to. I did not discuss with Ricky what had happened, for there was certainly nothing he could do. Instead I instructed him that, while *en route* once more for his galley, that he should knock on Maggie's cabin door and ask her to relieve me on watch. I felt not so much the personal need to share events with someone, for more practically, I wanted her to take over on the bridge. This would leave me free to think about things and then to act.

I think Maggie's wary look as she came into the wheelhouse was sufficient warning that she had 'sussed there just might be something amiss', as they say, appropriately enough, in Cornwall, confirming what Ricky had told her. There was no point in mincing words so I mentioned what I suspected and that I required her to take over the watch. She gave me a cautious look, venturing the question of what I was going to do. By this time, my 'conscious me' had taken over, enabling a course of action to clarify. Taking Phil's keys from my pocket once more, I re-entered the Master's cabin and, other than giving him a fleeting glance in the vague hope that he had somehow mysteriously come-to, I opened the ship's safe. There was no miraculous awakening of the dead on this occasion, leaving me to take the office register from the drawer and relock both safe and cabin.

Returning to the wheelhouse, I phoned the private number of Captain Hillier that was lodged with every Captain in the coastal fleet for use in dire emergencies. I felt this incident fell firmly into that category. Maggie listened with half an ear as I had told him the circumstances, gave him the exact position of the ship, and asked directions. It was confirmed that I was to take temporary charge, not command, and navigate her into Plymouth, which was by now about eighty miles distance, or at least eight hours steaming, taking into consideration a fairly strong adverse tidal set for much of the way. The Captain would contact Plymouth and arrange for a pilot boat to meet us once I had made VHF contact with them during our final stages of approach. There we would be boarded and the pilot would bring us alongside 'a quiet jetty somewhere'. Captain Hillier would also contact Phil's wife and arrange for police, doctor and an ambulance to be on stand-by. The police would have to attend, as Phil's death had to be reported initally as suspicious. There was little more for me to do, other than to inform the remainder of the crew over the breakfast table. The news was greeted as I expected, with varying degrees of astonishment, alarm, confusion and incomprehension. It was with some relief that I left them happily discussing things and went back into the wheelhouse to give Maggie her meal relief. I spent the remainder of our time before arrival Plymouth on watch. As it was a clear, fine day, I turned to the entire crew under Maggie's supervision engaging them on a marathon of chipping and painting designed as much to keep them occupied as continuing my planned programme of shipboard maintenance.

A VHF contact with Plymouth pilots as we closed the port resulted in the launch approaching as we entered the pilot area in the Hoe. He boarded along with a doctor and uniformed police sergeant. Phil's wife, Doreen, was presumably still travelling by train from home. As we had arrived from a UK port, no inward clearing was necessary, so formalities were kept to the minimum. I admitted to Maggie that the Kremlin did not waste much time once they decided on a course of action, and then opened the Master's cabin, stood back for the doctor and sergeant to enter, and left them to it. I thought ahead to when Doreen arrived. I would doubtless feel some diffidence speaking to her for I could hardly tell her that her late lamented husband had set the entire complement against him since his arrival on board. But, while the officials were in the cabin, I composed a few hopefully consoling statements that, when the time came, would probably develop into obscure sympathetic grunting noises. Other than getting Ricky to bring a tray of tea to the Master's cabin for everyone, with instructions not to drop it, there was little I could do. Anyway, my place was back in the wheelhouse with the pilot as I had told Maggie to continue with preparing moorings for arrival alongside and to leave the painting until later. The doctor finally came to the wheelhouse and informed us that his preliminary investigations indicated Phil had possibly died from a massive heart-attack, but there would have to be a post-mortem before a death certificate could be signed. The police sergeant suggested firmly that we all remained with the ship, although local shore leave was permissible. Meanwhile I arranged for doctor and police to sign my entry in the ship's official log-book, folded my arms and, in the absence of Captain Hillier, deliberated my immediate future.

By this time, we were approaching a jetty where I could see discreetly parked an undertaker's van which would take Phil's earthly remains to the mortuary for the autopsy. I went forward, telling Maggie to take charge aft as normal, leaving the pilot safely to his own devices, with Oliver on the helm. I handled the windlass myself as I had a clear view of the quay from the forecastle head. Once we were in position and made fast fore and aft, Maggie had the gangway rigged and we left the final disposal of Phil to the undertaker's crew. There was a distinct sense of relief once the doctor, police and the Master's body had gone ashore. A welcome sight shortly afterwards was Captain Hillier, who had made a marathon drive from London, as well as a locally appointed agent who came with a batch of mail that the super brought with him from the office and handed over for safe-keeping. I was very surprised that in the heat of the moment he had thought of doing this. It was a very good move that served as a tonic for everyone, including me, although I had little time to read mine. Glancing through the six envelopes before putting them into my pocket, I noticed two letters from Sue and one from the Inland Revenue: trust those gents to catch up with me.

I was then asked to come into the Master's cabin, where our super asked me bluntly to let him know what I wanted to do. He made it quite clear that the company wanted me to remain with them and not return to the wider Ellerton Group, but this would be as chief officer until I had sufficient wider experience to take command. He suggested were that to happen, I would need eventually to take a Master Home Trade Certificate of Competency, although we both guessed there would be few problems passing this, in the light of my Mate's Foreign-Going certificate and considerable subsequent experience. Having 'heard him out' I explained my misgivings about navigational procedures experienced on the company's coasters, and about the 'Masters' Club'. Surprisingly, he gave me a very direct look (where had I experienced these before, I asked myself rhetorically) and stated that the directors had been pressing recently for a tightening of standards on navigational practices (plus 'quite a few other things') within the fleet and that my approach as reported by Bob was precisely what they wished to beome their norm. It seemed that a spate of recent accidents, not only with London and Chatham but in other coastal companies, had attracted the attention of major authoritative shipping organisations and a spate of regulatory measures were about to emerge from the official pipeline. It looked as if the 'maritime writing was on the wall' where almost criminally lackadaisical procedures prevailed within certain elements of the coastal trades.

The remarks made at my early interview with him and Captain Henshaw four months previously suddenly clicked into place. At that time, he was reluctant to say too much, not because the issue was particularly thorny (which it was), but because without the experience of even a short voyage I simply would not understand the situation. It seemed London and Chatham were not the only coastal company requiring an official 'shake-up'. I had often, while deep-sea in coastal waters, experienced some bizarre actions from coasters of certain companies, such as unmanned wheelhouses and a sudden crossing of our bows without warning, and had wondered at the time what the hell might be happening aboard them, and then dismissed this as being none of my concern. I even knew personally (having seen the paper Discharge certificate of one such young officer) that one coastal company regularly took senior cadets from a nautical college as uncertificated third mates for short coastal trips. So far as the so-called Masters' Club was concerned, the directors and he were well aware of their influences and had placed these under a review designed to curb such unofficial powers. Having little to lose, I expressed my cynicism on the latter, only to see his brows tighten as he advised that those Skippers who were not prepared ultimately to conform would be asked to resign. It seemed that things were about to be shaken up all round, making the future career structure sound very rosy. I was still not entirely convinced, wondering from where the company would recruit the necessary men and women, especially in the light of my own relief, and then rapidly dismissed these thoughts also as 'none of my concern'. I did acquaint him of the unrest Phil's appointment had caused, and told him bluntly that I at least had been ready to walk off the ship in Par, regardless of consequences, being quite simply not prepared to put up with this kind of arrogant nonsense from anyone, even, or especially, from the Master of a ship.

So far as my own future was concerned, I advised the Captain that I wanted to talk this through with Sue. He stated his disappointment at my decision, but asked if I was prepared to take the ship round to Par and then stand by for her loading. I had no problems with this. It seemed a new Master, a Second Officer and an engineer would join the ship there, but they still saw no hope of a chief officer coming off leave, even though he had approached one or two who were in the middle of their period ashore. He asked me about Oliver as the company were 'thinking about promoting him uncertificated third mate aboard one of their larger 3,500 ton mid-sea traders, where he could continue to gain experience under supervision'. I was delighted to report that I felt he would be reasonably competent to do the job to any Master's satisfaction, providing an eye was kept on him until he had more experience. Certainly, his enthusiasm, interest and readiness to learn and gain qualifications proposed quite a rosy future for this young man. It seemed that Bob also had given him very positive reports. The other lads would also be relieved to go on leave and, it seemed, in the light of Phil's demise a completely new crew were to be appointed. I supposed that was one way to 'settle a ghost', or even the memory of one. He also asked my views about each of the other crew-members. I mentioned the AB incident of a few weeks previously, attracting a rueful smile and the affirmation that 'it *is* useful if navigating officers a-navigating do actually know what they are doing', and agreed that Frank should remain with the company and be posted to another ship as AB. I related Ricky's various adventures, which caused him to smile and frown simultaneously, but he agreed with my suggestion that, following a period of leave, the boy be given a further chance aboard another vessel, but preferably not the same one as Frank. In this way they could both enjoy completely fresh starts.

Captain Hillier accepted my invitation to join us for lunch, after which he advised the lads about future events. His news was taken with due aplomb and I instructed the agent to order a pilot as soon as possible and then gave shore leave all round for four hours, knowing it would take all of that to rustle one up. I felt a new mood was required and a run in the delightful city of Plymouth might help towards achieving this. After all the paint work and ship maintenance would, like the poor, always be with us. It was in the middle of these machinations that Phil's wife arrived. I was delighted to leave her to Captain Hillier to sort out and it was with considerable relief that I saw them both down the gangway. Once the crew had departed, I remained aboard to get my head down for a light snooze on the settee in the Master's cabin, which kept me close to the gangway, and in less than ten minutes *Prince Albert* looked like the *Marie Celeste*.

It was a mere couple of hours steaming to Par, once we dropped the pilot and I straightened the ship to clear Rame Head, and then set course for Gribben Head and the anchorage. We had to wait two days for a berth, giving the company at least some time to organise their crew change. Captain Hillier and I kept each other up to date with latest news by radio telephone, not that there was a great deal for us to exchange. He advised that Bob was home by now with wife and family where he was taking very badly to his imposed rest, but was 'trying to behave himself'. Bob had also completely reaffirmed my opinion about Oliver's promotion, and with Ricky remaining with the company. I kept the crew busy with cleaning and painting routines and allowed the lads to swim over the side near the lowered pilot ladder, and for Maggie to lower our working boat for a sail round the harbour with the cadets and Ricky. The latter had settled very well to our routines now and managed to lose at least a little of his 'two left hands and two right feet' syndrome.

Our new Captain came out with the pilot mid-afternoon of the third day. This was his first ship with the company and he had been appointed without recourse to the Masters' Club, so it looked as if the board were adamant in their resolve to clip the wings of this nautical anachronism. I welcomed them on board, told Ricky to take the Master's bag and stow it away in his cabin, and then went forward to prepare for coming alongside. This was without incident and while putting ashore the final head rope saw the gang heading for our vessel to commence loading yet another cargo of china clay. I left Maggie to square off fore and aft, discussed my loading plan with the dockers under the interested eye and ear of the Captain, saw them under way and then reported at long last to the mess-room to discuss my adventures with the Master as he chatted to the agent over a pot of tea.

He glanced up as I entered and, giving me an openly direct smile, finished his sentence. He then stood up, poured me a mug of tea and introduced himself as Trevor Rashleigh from Mevagissey, just down the coast. The agent bid us farewell and left us to get on with things. Trevor suggested we went to his cabin, where we could continue chatting as he stowed away his gear. I assessed him to be in his mid-forties, tall, deeply tanned and possessing the broad but pleasantly soft burr of a Cornish accent. He told me he had transferred from another large coasting company only four days previously, having been interviewed by the directors while Captain Hillier had been with us. Apart from his cadetship with Elder Dempster, he had served the remainder of his sea career in coastal tankers and had been in command for fifteen years. The reason he left his previous employers was due to an irresolvable dispute concerning seniority pay and pension rights. He did not go into further details and I certainly did not ask. He told me also that our cargo was bound this time for Dublin.

Our conversation was broken by the sound of laughter and chatting and then the distinct sound of heavy foot-falls up our gangway. The noise broke my reverie and I popped out to see what was happening, only to run literally into two men jostling to be first up the gangway. I always applauded enthusiasm. As the first came on deck he stated they were replacements for our crew. The cause of the merriment arose from their recognition of Oliver, our senior cadet, with whom they had served previously. I went on deck to stand down our AB and Oliver, and then met a third man, who was chatting quietly to Maggie on deck. It transpired he was the relieving second mate. So, in the midst of great rejoicing, she also joined the two men in going below to pack gear. Meanwhile, Toby, Ricky and I cast longing looks along the quay for our reliefs… It was not so much that Ricky was desperate to go, but having prepared mentally for departure, he basically wished now to do precisely that. I was, of course, resigned to staying aboard until, like the Ancient Mariner, I drifted into old age and infirmity.

I said farewell to the three as they trooped down the gangway en route for Par railway station, where the agent advised them (with a familiar refrain) that the last stopping train for the day was due in around an hour's time. The alternative would have been to travel by taxi (at company expense) to St Austell, where virtually all trains bound for London Paddington called. I was quite sorry to see them go, and wished all three the customary good wishes for their futures. The AB had settled with us extremely well following his 'bridge shock' off Antwerp, while Oliver was full of excitement about travelling to Sunderland, where he would join his ship as third mate. Sacrificing leave seemed to him a small price to pay for the chance to 'spread his nautical wings' upon promotion. He thanked me profusely for the help and encouragement I had given him, which was quietly pleasing, and told me he was aware how much he owed to Bob and me for his step up to acting officer rank. Maggie was to go for two months' leave and then stand by for reappointment as second mate. I felt able to trust Ricky to look after the linen issues and collection, and to cook the evening meal. Meanwhile, I wandered out on deck to see how the loading was progressing. There was little for me to do in this port, for the dockers here were experts in loading ships correctly. 'And so they bloody well ought to be,' I reflected, seeing that china clay was the only cargo this port handled, apart from limited general goods. We had to close the hatches quickly just before knocking-off time in the face of a very threatening raincloud. This cargo was notorious when it was wet, for it became very dangerous. It was some weeks now since I had stepped into a patch forward off number one hatch that had become wetted and left by a small overflow of water from a badly run hose left to dry after being used in washing down. I had slipped badly and grazed my shin on our deck electrical pipes. My comments to Oliver, who had badly stowed the thing, raised both eyebrows and smiles from the docker who overheard them. The wound, although shallow, was still painful and open, and Bob had told me it would take a long time to heal, due to the lack of tissue under the skin. It seemed he was correct. By the time I had closed both hatches and adjourned to the wheelhouse to write up the log-book, it was raining heavily through the last rays of the setting sun. The rainbow that followed shortly afterwards, spreading across Par bay, was spectacularly romantic, although I was more interested in being notified by Ricky that our meal was ready.

There was considerable laughter when I joined the others in the mess-room. A range of joking and teasing was taking place with, it seemed, Ricky being the butt of some humour. I guessed immediately that he had made his mark with the new crew by doing a typical 'Rickyism' and watched him mopping up some spilled gravy from the deck and collecting together assorted-sized pieces of what had been the jug we used. It seemed my meal, at least, was to be taken devoid of extra nourishment.

About 2200 hours, over the sound of a classical Mozart cassette I had popped into the mess player, I thought footsteps up top could be heard walking, it seemed, with some hesitation. I was the only person on board, for Trevor had gone home for the night while the remaining lads had adjourned to one (or more) of the local pubs for the evening. I had not joined them, feeling that with some reliefs due, someone ought to remain on board instead of us locking up the vessel according to our normal custom when we all decided to go ashore. Discussing this with the Master led to his clear approval, and I was quite happy to read quietly and catch up on some correspondence. I had already phoned Sue from the dock office and enjoyed a lengthy chat, advising her I would phone again in the morning when my relief had (or, as seemed possible, had not) made his appearance. Slightly irritated, and moving myself from the entrancing delicacy of the slow movement in a piano concerto, I laid aside the *Four Quartets* of T. S. Eliot and popped up the companionway to see a very young lad standing and knocking tentatively on the Master's cabin door. He was clearly wondering what to do next. Even by looking, I could tell we were now blessed with a new deck boy. I introduced myself and encouraged him below, setting him up with linen on the spare bunk in the ex-cadet's cabin for the night. It crossed my mind that Ricky would not be in much of a fit state to assist after boozing and dining under the dubiously favourable influence of our lads. Larry would probably stay there, as Toby had been our extra hand and Bob had decided the two cadets should berth together. This meant that Frank had then to share his two-berth cabin with the deck boy, but now as it seemed unlikely we would have two cadets (or even one), the AB could continue enjoying the cabin to himself. Toby (and, of course, I) still awaited our reliefs.

The deck boy was new to seafaring and had been recruited from Ellerton's Liverpool office and sent to the ship via the Kremlin in London. He had no pre-sea training but impressed as a reasonably intelligent youngster who, if he took to the life, might fare quite well. We spent the evening, after I had made him some supper, generally chatting until the lads came back on board, each clearly the worse for wear. Although they were rowdy, until they decided to settle in their cabins, the evening passed quite amicably, and I turned in at last to spend a quiet and uneventful night.

Inevitably, salty tales of the sea continued to enliven our after-meal conversations and although these centred around debacles of varied and often hilarious natures concerning the coastal trades, Trevor regaled us with a variety of stories from his cadetship days aboard 'ED' ships. One particulary vivid tale concerned a voyage when they had loaded a cargo consisting of slings of cut timber into a couple of 'tween decks from some 'Godforsaken port stuck one hundred miles or more up a West African river', as he termed the setting. The chief officer, as the ship approached Liverpool was routinely checking all holds via the inspection hatches that led down to the 'tween decks. As he threw open the hatch cover, the duty mate and Trevor, as duty cadet, saw him throw over his leg to descend but suddenly stormed out of the hatch like 'a genie out of a bottle'. He was white-faced on entering the wheelhouse where the second mate enquired interestingly what had occurred to reduce the chief officer to a clearly shocked condition. It seemed that, as the Mate shone his torch down looking for the hatch ladder, he saw a movement which momentarily brought him up in his tracks with wonder. Shining the torch more directly down past his foot, he suddenly realised that this 'tween deck at least was covered by a variety of snakes, which had seemingly been spirited away, snoozing in the cargo, only to be awakened in the heat of the hold. This accounted for his rapid exit and shocked features. The Old Man radioed ahead to Liverpool and the ship was diverted to an anchorage just off the Bar light-vessel pilot station to await a fumigation party from ashore. They duly arrived and did their stuff, with the officers watching safely from the wheelhouse windows, and soon declared the holds safe to enter. The bonus paid to the dockers to discharge the cargo and sort out the bodies of the snakes would have apparently paid off the national debt for a year.

He also related what had happened while serving aboard the delightfully named *Oti* as they were leaving my favourite Royal Group of docks in London. Apparently, as they entered the lock leading to the Thames, the telegraph jammed at half-ahead, to the consternation of the pilot, Old Man and officer on the bridge. A calm but rapid rush of movement led to a quick VHF message to the after tug, and a rapid phone call to the engine-room, just managing to bring up the vessel before too much damage was done.

Cargo was completed by mid-day and as no sign of my relief had appeared, Trevor phoned the Kremlin to confirm my worst fears that Captains Henshaw and Hillier would like me to remain with the ship. Fine. I had already relieved the second mate on deck for him to pop into the wheelhouse and prepare a voyage plan and charts: actions, it was pleasing to see, Trevor acccepted quite happily as a norm. Alan, the second mate with his Mate (Home Trade) certificate, was surprised but quite happy

Above: The crew covered a range of deck duties under the eye of the second mate or bosun, including holystoning a rail in preparation for varnishing... (Athel Line).

Above right: ...and renewing the splice in a wire... (Ministry of Defence).

Right: ...while pointing out a navigational point of interest and instructing the deck cadet to take an accurate bearing (BP plc).

to continue my insistence on correct chart work so it seemed that another of 'Hillier's birds had come home to roost'. The only other crew changes occurred around mid-morning when the engineer's relief reported on board with a surprising amount of gear. Trevor also received orders that Toby was at last to be sent home on leave without a relief. Trevor was quite happy to keep an eye on things aboard, allowing me to pop ashore, do some shopping and phone Sue. I returned in time for lunch, over which the Master informed us that the pilot was due around 1600 hours and we would then be departing Par. He mentioned to Alan and myself that he preferred his navigating officers to follow traditional patterns and do regular four-hourly watches, even if our erratic patterns of trading would not always permit the traditional 12–4 plus routines. This was an action which met with our unreserved approval. I recalled our previous conversation earlier in the trip with Toby about going foreign as a deck cadet but, chatting to him in Plymouth, he seemed more contented with remaining on the coast, and so the matter had been dropped.

Trevor and Alan shared the first watches leaving me to supervise the crew on deck until we cleared Dodman Point, when the weather began a rapid deterioration. By the time I came on watch, with the ship on course to round the Lizard and set course for Longships light, the wind had increased to a north-westerly Force 6–7 with rough seas and moderate swell. Being low in the water helped our stability considerably but we still took occasional seas over the bows with constant spraying down the starboard side. Trevor told me, with a rueful smile, that our new deck boy was hopelessly seasick. By the time Pendeen was abeam, we were rolling heavily in a short, steep sea and occasional rain squalls. Something was wrong with the Decca, for its fixes were placing us a phenomenal two to three miles astern of our radar and visual fixes. This was unusual because the Decca was normally reliable and completely trustworthy in the whole UK region. I assumed the instability was caused once more by the inconsistency of the sky waves. The shipping was considerable with, at one time a heavy preponderance of around fifty fishing vessels heading in all directions and crossing from all angles as they (presumably) chased after shoals of cod, or mackerel or something. With the occasional coaster, it proved a very hectic watch and I was not sorry to pop down and call Alan after my stipulated four hours' duty.

There was no relief awaiting me in Dublin, but I eagerly expected to be off the ship in Liverpool. Trevor was hugely sympathetic but obviously required me on board, particularly with my dry-cargo ship experience. We eventually sailed with a full general cargo, including three hundred cases of bottled Guinness, bound for Liverpool, which was a comparatively short passage and was accomplished without delays or problems. All three of the crowd, including our innocent deck boy, went wild ashore upon our arrival overnight, resulting in thick heads the next day and, we suspected, a loss of Larry's innocence. The remainder of us went for a quiet drink, returning on board in time for me to enjoy a late-night read and restful sleep. The next day we commenced loading drums of caustic soda and assorted chemicals for Belfast. I was blandly informed by the Kremlin that there was no chief officer available to relieve me and asked would I mind taking the ship down to Belfast, please. Once more I let off steam to poor old Trevor, after which tantrums I calmed down and once again accepted the inevitable.

In the absence of any deck crew for breakfast, all officers turned to and completed what little deck work was necessary, while Alan prepared lunch. The lads returned on board around 1100 hours very much the worse for wear. There was not a great deal we could do other than for me tell the AB to take over cooking for the day and allow the other two to stand down and recover. Trevor treated the incident with more resigned humour than anger, but a certain glint in his eye led the lads to understand that, 'if they valued their jobs, there had better not be any more reoccurrences of this nonsense', as he put it. He was clearly accustomed to the 'extravagances of the coast', as I termed it, but was also made of sterner stuff than his crew. We made a fresh start the next day with all hands turned to in readiness for departure.

Once clear of the Bar light-vessel with the vessel pitching and rolling easily, we set course for the Calf of Man lighthouse, south of the Isle of Man, from where we would continue a north-westerly course towards South Rock light-vessel, meet the traffic separation zones and steer for Belfast. The wind meanwhile had freshened from the south-west and, within a couple of hours, had increased to Gale Force 7, gusting 8. Larry again took to his bunk with severe seasickness and we did not see much of him for the remainder of the passage. By midnight we were forced to decrease speed to around three knots as we headed into a full Storm Force 10 that lasted until we crossed the Irish Sea for South Rock, by which time the weather had moderated considerably, although we rolled heavily in the residual swell. As we sailed up the Irish coast towards Mew Island, our weather and the ship signed yet another peace treaty. Soon, it was almost like a mild-mannered summer-cum-autumn day. Even Larry made his appearance for breakfast, showing some interest in what was happening around him. He admitted openly that he had been extremely scared during the storm's worst excesses and was not sure if he wanted to remain at sea. We took this in silence for a while until Trevor suggested he give things a little longer before making decisions that he might one day come to regret. I told him that my own stomach 'still had its moments' and, although I was now no longer physically sick, I often felt quite queasy. Admittedly, he enlivened a little at this news. I decided not to put him cooking that day but to give him some steering instruction for variety and to keep his mind occupied, and then turn him to cleaning our accommodation alleyways and paintwork. Trevor and I discussed things later, and agreed that he might 'go one way or the other' regarding his future at sea, but ultimately there was little we could do other than encourage him to stay if that what was he really wished to do, or sign him off if he did not.

From 1100 to 1400 the next day, while at anchorage off Belfast pilot area, we pumped about four tonnes of water from the chain locker while I meditated on the poor quality of concrete and cheekily put in a stores indent for a powerful portable pump. To my surprise, Trevor signed this, putting it with the official mail for onward transmission to the Kremlin. Larry had recovered more or less completely, with the ship a few hours at anchor, but he simply had no clue about cooking or anything else remotely domestic, so I had to turn him to with the AB for instruction, which meant that we were two men light on deck instead of one. It was then that the bonus of having Toby as a spare hand really came home to me. We came alongside starboard side to Albert Quay for bunkering as our fuel tanks were desperately low, and waited instructions to shift ship later and commence discharging cargo. It was a restless night, for the movement of other ships berthing fore and aft spread over the sleeping time created strong surges that set our ship straining against her moorings. On one occasion, I slipped on some clothes and went on deck to ascertain all was well, only to bump into Trevor, who had turned to with the same idea in mind. We exchanged a few caustic sentences and then settled for thirty minutes, sharing a pot of tea in the wheelhouse (which he made in the democractic way of coastal service) chatting about 'everything and nothing' nautically, including our past careers. Eventually, we both became drowsy and stood down, until, of course, another ship came alongside aft.

By the following mid-day, there was still no sign of either life or the agent, so Trevor phoned the local office to find out what was happening, especially regarding my relief. It seemed that a number of token strikes amongst the dockers were in danger of developing into a major one and the port was virtually at a stand-still. Talks were, it seemed, continuing in an endeavour to break the deadlock. I turned the second mate to, telling him to sort out 'M' notices to mariners, Decca modifications and to start making some headway into the mountain of chart corrections that had accumulated, restricting each to the areas in which we were most likely to sail. It was quite a long job, for charts and folios each required minor attention. Meanwhile, I turned to the lads completing Larry's work of soogeeing all cabins and accommodation, hoovering throughout and embarking on a general make and mend. Once that was completed my plans were for us to complete mopping up the forecastle-head store area, and then to oil and grease shackles, windlass and winch and all hatch wheels and chains. By now I was well accustomed to turning to and leading the lads by example and was equally used to the Master and second mate chipping in. On larger coastal tankers, Trevor informed me, the second mate was the working boss of the crew and performed the duties of a bosun on a large deep-sea ship, but I was quite happy to keep an overall eye on all things associated with crew management. There remained a stony silence from the Kremlin regarding my relief. It seemed that either there was no spare chief officer 'rooting around the old corral' as I put the situation, or there was one, but he was not heading in my direction. I had been on articles for five months now and was definitely ready for leave.

The dispute developed into a full-blown strike, so Trevor suggested I might like to use the local shuttle to Gatwick Airport and pop off home for a few days. He had my telephone number to give me a recall in the event of any emergency. I was not at all reluctant to hand over the reins and, after a quick phone to Sue, paid my airfare, caught the train to Canterbury on arrival at Gatwick, and was home in time to take us both out to a local Indian restaurant for a solid wining and dining.

A couple of days later we settled for a serious talk about the future, continuing our discussion of the previous leave. The difference between the two occasions was decidedly marked. In the light of events and thoughts evoked during the two brief times in charge of a ship, my mind was considerably closer to making positive decisions. There was no doubt at all now that I did not want to sit my Master's certificate, neither Foreign-Going nor Home Trade; nor did I wish to remain permanently at sea. Tentative research in the local public library confirmed the best way forward would be to sit for a full-time university degree and then go for post-graduate teacher training on a programme that would take a proposed four years. This way into the profession would, I believed, make me better equipped as a schoolmaster than would doing a straightforward teacher training certificate course of three years' duration. The next revelation to Sue, as it was to transpire, was that I would not teach maths and physics, the logical subjects for a navigating officer, but develop my deepening love of literature by, as I confirmed, 'trying to talk an unsuspecting university into taking me as a mature student on a Single Honours English degree course'. I thought if a 'career change', as the pundits ashore determined the jargon, was going to be attempted then I might as well do the training and course I wanted. The hurdle was to gain acceptance. My intermittent studies, spread over only five months while at sea through the National Extension College of Cambridge and passing, albeit of a low D-grade at Advanced level GCE in English Literature would, under the circumstances in which the course was followed, at least indicate 'good academic intent', and I had proved the ability to sustain consistent and advanced study since the age of sixteen years by taking professional maritime qualifications. I knew the system of applying through the universities application registry, having obtained the necessary handbook and information. The problem was that I had no idea how to set about choosing the 'right university', so this would have to be 'boxed and coxed' as I went along.

Meanwhile, we agreed, it would be best for me to continue at sea and, with all these thoughts floating around our minds, I telephoned Captain Henshaw as my immediate boss, requesting an interview at short notice the next day before rejoining the coaster. To say the good Captain was surprised is putting things mildly; in fact he informed me later that he had thought initially I had walked off the ship and was coming in to resign. A quick phone call to Trevor had scotched that idea. I hastily explained about my local leave and apologised for giving him such short notice. He was his usual cheerful self and, once he had sorted out his thoughts as we chatted, he shifted a few casual office engagements around in his diary, arranging for me to see him at 1000 hours next morning.

It was decision time with a vengeance. Captain Henshaw expressed what I felt were genuine regrets that the sea and I would be parting at some stage in the future and discussed my plans about when this time might be. I told him about putting in a mature student application to a number of (yet unchosen) universities, but that I had no idea what (if anything) would result. He told me to keep him informed and return to Belfast, rejoining *Prince Albert* the next day. She was bound for Par once more, but immediately upon arrival I would definitely be relieved (even if he had to come out and do so himself!) and I should go home immediately. If I were happy to do so, I could then fly out to Las Palmas and rejoin my outward-bound supertanker. Captain Anson was still in command and I would rejoin as first officer, continuing to do second mate's duties, as clearly a chief officer would already have been appointed. Glancing at me ruefully, he explained that this course of action had arisen by the necessity for a Mate aboard that large tanker. It also meant liquidation of my accrued leave from the coaster voyage. In other words, nearly three months' additional salary would be credited to my bank account. The choice was mine – something, it seemed, I could regard as 'Hobson's nautical'. Needless to say, I accepted.

Five days later found me on a plane heading not for Las Palmas but to Capetown, and being whisked out to the ship by helicopter along with stores, films and a first-trip engineering cadet. I had indeed joined the outward-bound VLCC, as I thought might happen the day I signed on the coaster. It was simply that in between there was a six-month delay and just over two complete supertanker trips without me! Such was the delight of the coastal trade. I had to confess the prolonged tour had proved quite an experience and, yes, while I may well have contributed something constructive during my brief time on board, I had learned and gained considerably more. This included greater levels of professional flexibility, reciprocating firmly tolerant patience and, not least, more about the foibles of human nature.

While I felt still considerable peace and relief over my decision to leave the sea and apply for full-time education, initial reflections 'on things' gave a distinct sense of *déjà vu* – of having travelled a similar path previously. Echoes of novelist L. P. Hartley's 'foreign country' stirred in my distant memory, recalling my feelings and thoughts as I had set off to Keddleston Navigation School at the age of sixteen many 'light years' ago. Once more I was treading into an unknown entirely of my own making but, on this occasion, my slight concerns centred on whether I could cope with academic demands from university-level study, combined with questions regarding acceptance for undergraduate, let alone post-graduate teacher training and entry into that profession. Strangely enough, the thought of being turned down at any hurdle was not over-worrying for, were this to occur I felt that disappointment could be put behind me: I would remain at sea, make a renewed and determined effort to go for Master's and work towards ultimate command aboard my supertankers.

Once I had confronted these fears, I spent more spare time researching and contacting a range of traditional universities. Very unusually, on a subsequent voyage the berthing authorities had taken us alongside Milford Haven refinery, even though there was insufficient capacity in the tanks to take all of our oil in one go and we had to lie quietly alongside our jetty without working cargo. The chief officer and I split the 24 hour duty officer period. He went ashore overnight and I had the daylight hours from after breakfast until 1800. I spent my time in nearby Tenby, completing the UCAS application form in their public library, posting this to the tutor supervising my correspondence course in English literature, who was my only academic referee, and then celebrating with a slap-up luncheon, schooner of sherry and bottle of wine in the local Berni Inn.

My university interview was conveniently slotted into a later leave. It proved unexpectedly gruelling and grilling, reminding me of my initial appearance before Ellerton Shipping's selection board. A hostility in delivery accompanied the first question: 'What is the connection between navigation and English literature?' that left me a little bemused for a few seconds but rallying, I almost instinctively threw back the first stanza of Kipling's poem *Sestina of the Tramp Royal*, explaining the relevant connective evidence. This led to mention of cadet Colin Ashby on the *Earl of Nottingham* and the dramatically concentrating effect he had contributed to my previously unguided range of reading. The senior of the two lecturers paused and then fired: 'Yes, but why literature rather than the more obvious choices for a navigating officer of maths and physics?' I continued by stating that my love of literature and desire to teach this was greater than my feelings towards reading for three years and then teaching maths and science. This seemed to be well received and the remainder of an hour was spent discussing in depth my opinions of poetry (particularly), and the plots and characters in plays and novels which had given so much pleasure during my off-duty reading. As I spoke, this love for language and an opportunity of discussing literature with what soon became sympathetically warmer and understanding ears overcame my initial nervousness and helped me relax. My performance could not have been too barren. I was told before leaving that something of this attraction towards, feeling and enthusiasm for *studying* literature had 'come across strongly' and the lecturers felt my analytical reasoning faculty would benefit from enhanced study. Subsequently, they offered me a place on their Single Honours English course commencing the following October. I left the interview at Lampeter feeling as if I had been put through a 'mental mincing machine', but accompanied by a decisive sense of contented achievement. The first hurdle had been successfully surmounted.

The next couple of trips were spent finalising undergraduate entry to read English, philosophy and classics in translation during in my first year. Once arrangements were confirmed, I relaxed completely and savoured my final couple of voyages navigating this magnificent ship as extra chief officer. No – in the light of my impending departure the company never promoted me Mate! I was not too concerned. I remained convinced that 'swallowing the anchor' and venturing into a new career was the correct course for me to follow. The challenges of navigation and collision avoidance in particular, plus the 'comradeship' of the sea, I would truly miss, but other than that I would leave the merchant navy without regrets. It was time to move on in life and doubtless carry many diverse experiences and countless happy memories along with me. If my resolve required further stiffening, this came from the excellent news that my local education authority would pay a very generous 'mature students' allowance' for the three-year degree period, and finance a PGCE afterwards. Just how 'mature' I was during my undergraduate three years, however, is quite another story…